Life
After Death

AN ANALYSIS OF THE EVIDENCE
Robert Davis, PhD

REDFeather
MIND | BODY | SPIRIT
An Imprint of Schiffer Publishing, Ltd.

Other Schiffer Books by the Author:

The UFO Phenomenon: Should I Believe? ISBN: 978-0-7643-4764-1

Other Schiffer Books on Related Subjects:

Afterlife: What Really Happens on the Other Side: True Stories of Contact and Communication with Spirits. Barry R. Strohm. ISBN: 978-0-7643-4734-4

"Tails" of the Afterlife: True Stories of Ghost Pets. Peggy Schmidt. ISBN: 978-0-7643-3253-1

ISBN: 978-0-7643-5438-0
Printed in the United States of America

Published by Schiffer Publishing, Ltd.
4880 Lower Valley Road
Atglen, PA 19310
Phone: (610) 593-1777;
Fax: (610) 593-2002
E-mail: Info@schifferbooks.com
Web: www.schifferbooks.com

For our complete selection of fine books on this and related subjects, please visit our website at www.schifferbooks.com. You may also write for a free catalog.

Schiffer Publishing's titles are available at special discounts for bulk purchases for sales promotions or premiums. Special editions, including personalized covers, corporate imprints, and excerpts, can be created in large quantities for special needs. For more information, contact the publisher.

We are always looking for people to write books on new and related subjects. If you have an idea for a book, please contact us at proposals@schifferbooks.com.

To my wife Randy:
I am forever grateful for your love, kindness,
and selflessness.

To my children Michelle and Scott:
You provide a constant source of love, joy, and pride.

To my grandson Jack (Tinybean):
Your smile and sparkle fills our lives with
unimaginable delight.

Contents

CHAPTER ONE

INTRODUCTION

Knowing that our life will end has driven us to search for a possible way out in the form of time without end. An infinite life extension is what we all want, and maybe death is just a transitory phase as a natural continuation of life. Or maybe comedian Woody Allen answered it best by saying, "No one gets out of this world alive." The concept as to whether the essence of our being, "gets out of this world" after death of the physical body has concerned humankind from earliest times. Ever since we stopped crawling out of the primordial soup and evolved into inquisitive and inventive complex language-based bipedal primates, people have wondered if upon death we diminish into a void of nonexistence, persist in an alternate realm of existence, or revive in a cycle of reincarnation. But while on this topic, here's a cheerful thought for you: You are going to die. One day your brain will cease functioning and you will become a nonentity. Or will you? We all have questioned, at least once in our life, what happens when the hard drive crashes and the screen fades to black. Is death really the grand finale? Despite claims to the contrary, however, there is no conclusive proof of a form of existence after death. And while you may not require such proof, I do.

The question whether or not one's "consciousness"—a term to be used instead of "soul" or "spirit"—survives death, has been a concern ever since we evolved to a point capable of self-awareness, abstract thought, and intuition. The primary issue is whether or not consciousness is independent of the brain. If so, it may survive death. But science has yet to determine whether consciousness acts independent of the brain, what it is, what it does, how it functions, where it originates, or even why it has evolved. And if consciousness should persist after our last breath, it deepens the mystery as to what it is and what new form of existence awaits it after the brain ceases to function.

While many consider death the definitive end, there exists anecdotal, theoretical, and experimental evidence to suggest otherwise. But despite such evidence, the concept of life after death is a dilemma that ultimately rests with you. You may regard this obscure and unproven notion as irrelevant and not worth discussing since it may represent wishful thinking, religious, and/or cultural indoctrination, or possibly even a touch of one's "gut feeling." Or maybe your belief in life after death has been shaped by philosophical, religious, scientific, emotional, and/or intuitive reasons. Achieving a confident perspective is not an easy task, and adopting an agnostic viewpoint may even present a greater challenge when trying to decide if you "*should believe.*" That is, if you believe you will be reunited with deceased loved ones upon death, it will be difficult to accurately interpret evidence that either supports or refutes your position and may actually perceive opposing viewpoints to be weak in principle and resist revising your belief. But given our innate tendency to have confidence in information consistent with our beliefs and to reject opinions that differ with our viewpoints, one's perspective should ideally be based on an objective assessment of the evidence. Thus, if the concept of life after death is to be evaluated without bias, it is necessary to find a way of bypassing the barriers of religious preconceptions and wishful thinking before deciding if you "should believe." Yet one thing is very clear: millions of people, on faith-based belief alone, consider life after death a valid concept, which, if true, will certainly have profound implications at the individual, societal, and religious/spiritual levels. Such ramifications are a matter of speculation and awe.

Belief in life after death can be traced back to our ancestors in the Stone Age period who buried weapons and food with the deceased and built shelters for them when they returned. According to sociologist G. Vulliamy, "the ceremonial and burial rites of uncivilized man are the expression of what is, to him, the unquestionable and proven truth, that the souls of men are immortal."[1] Research of children's ideas about "past lives" even suggest that our bias toward believing in life after death is a part of human intuition that naturally emerges early in life. In fact, studies have revealed that most people who lost a partner see, hear, or sense them in some way, and about ninety percent of widows claim to experience contact with their deceased husbands. The obvious question is whether or not this experience results from wishful thinking, a psychological disorder, or an actual genuine encounter with the deceased.

Most of us have a natural fear of the unknown, and the ultimate unknown of death. When death looms it is impossible not to wonder "What's next?" Do "I" (i.e., awareness, personality, memories, preferences, etc.) enter the emptiness of non-experience where "nothing" is precisely what happens next or does "something" persist in a form of consciousness after my death? According to historian A. Toynbee, the concept of death alone is represented as an "unconscious fear of oblivion, which is more frightening than death itself."[2] Sociologist P. Ariès also described this fear by stating, "humans are afraid of death the way children are afraid of the dark, only because their imaginations have been filled with phantoms as empty as they are terrible."[3] Religion, which has attempted to replace one's fear of "phantoms" and the unknown with teachings that promise a life after death, has provided an answer in the form of "eternal life" to millions over time. And several religions, which advocate immortality and that Heaven or Hell awaits us, is an important psychological construct that influences behavior and motivation. Such beliefs may inspire you to live each moment with dignity, hope, meaning, and to deal with the inevitability of death with security and comfort knowing you will persist and eventually be reunited with deceased loved ones. It must add some degree of purposeful meaning to life. In fact, studies have indicated that those who firmly believe in life after death generally are more spiritual, loving, compassionate, empathetic, and environmentally conscious, among other positive attributes. One obvious negative aspect, however, is represented by those who advocate murder in the form of religious wars and suicide bombings, with disastrous consequences on both a personal and societal level.

Despite mainstream science's steadfast position that "dead is dead," the majority of the general population disagree. A survey of over 15,500 Americans between the ages of eighteen and sixty compiled in 2014 by The Austin Institute for the Study of Family and Culture revealed that seventy-two percent believe in life after death, though not everyone holds the same vision of post-mortem existence. Only thirty-seven percent believe in a bodily resurrection from the dead, though this figure varies considerably among religious affiliations. Fundamentalist Protestants and Mormons, for example, believe overwhelmingly in revival (eighty-six and ninety-four percent, respectively), as opposed to only thirty percent of liberal Catholics and twenty percent of Jews.[4] A 2014 CBS news poll of 1,017 adults in the United States also revealed that just over forty percent believe in Heaven or Hell.[5] But for what it may be worth, while we cannot completely ignore our instinctual aversion to the prospect of death, one may ask at its approach, why we are so attached to our personal characteristics, memories, and body? In fact, research suggests that people across many different cultures instinctively believe that some part of their consciousness lives on after-death, i.e., people find it easy to conceive of the separation of the mind and the body.[5a] In a study on the beliefs about the existence and nature of an afterlife on psychological symptoms (e.g., anxiety, anger, depression, intrusive thoughts, and yearning) among recently bereaved older spouses, for example, "maladaptive" coping behavior was reported in late-life spousal loss. This symptom was especially found to occur in those either uncertain about the existence of the afterlife or holds a "pessimistic view of what the afterlife entails."[5b]

A paradox exists between one's hope that death is not the end, on the one hand, and scientifically derived evidence that provides a definitive answer on the other. And since millions of people maintain a faith-based belief in some form of life after death, if science has something to say about it, we should listen. But since science contradicts many religious views, most people require empirical, scientific-based evidence to verify a life without end. And most scholars, who adopt the materialistic viewpoint that consciousness is an outcome of brain activity, remain highly skeptical of the anecdotal evidence and theories that suggest that consciousness may continue in some post-mortem realm of existence. This perspective is inconsistent with the spiritual notion that consciousness is not the same as the brain. In fact, many leading physicists contend that consciousness is a form of energy not bound by established concepts of space and time and is independent of the brain. If valid, then consciousness may survive death. But if mainstream science is correct, once the hard drive is shot, so goes memory and one's conscious perception of reality.

There has been a long-standing pursuit to prove the survival hypothesis—individuals are composed of both a body and a non-physical part which persists beyond death. Ever since the formal investigation of this concept was initiated by a group of Cambridge University scholars of the Society for Psychical Research in Britain in 1882, many independent scholars and organizations have attempted to test this hypothesis through research among several highly debated topic areas as follows:

1. Near-death experiences (NDE)—individuals presumed to be clinically dead for brief periods report the continuation of conscious perception;
2. Veridical out-of-body experiences (OBE)—one who reports being separated from their body and accurately perceives events beyond the reach of their senses;

3. Reincarnation—existence of a post-mortem, non-physical characteristic of one's identity, which is renewed in another physical body;
4. Trans-communication—two-way communication, which includes mediumship, apparitional experiences, after death communication (ADC)—i.e., someone is contacted directly by a family member or friend who has died without the use of psychics, mediums, or therapists—and electronic voice phenomena (EVP)—i.e., sounds on electronic recordings that are interpreted as voices from the deceased;
5. Parapsychology—investigation of paranormal and psychic phenomena, which includes telepathic communication—i.e., communication without the use of sensory systems or physical interaction—precognition—i.e., ability to obtain information about an object, person, location, or physical event through extrasensory perception (ESP);
6. Quantum theory— the mathematics believed to underlie all physical processes in nature, and the probability for any particular thing to happen consists of models on the nature and behavior of matter and energy on the atomic and subatomic level, which suggests that consciousness may not be localized to our body or the present time—i.e., consciousness is an essential component of the universe, and all matter possesses subjective characteristics of consciousness, the foundation of everything;
7. Veridical apparitions—accurate perceptions of the deceased;
8. Mediumship—the reporting of accurate and specific information of the deceased without prior knowledge, fraud, and in the absence of "normal" sensory input;
9. Cognitive and neurobiological evidence, theories, and perspectives on the nature of consciousness and its relationship to the brain.

Several assumptions applied in the study of these topic areas have served as a foundation to test the survival hypothesis. These include:

1. Consciousness is a by-product of brain activity. There are no non-spatial or non-temporal connections between individual physical brains, which allows for extrasensory perception. After we die our consciousness is eliminated along with the body. We are gone forever.
2. Consciousness is not dependent on the brain and can affect physical matter outside the body. It extends beyond normal space/time and its influence ends when the body dies.
3. Consciousness extends beyond the brain and survives death. It suggests a mechanism and explanation for NDE, OBE, ADC, mediumistic communications, reincarnation, and apparitions.

Driven by our instinctive sense of curiosity, we all like a good mystery to solve, and the concept of life after death is as mystifying as it gets. Combined with our innate attribute to do anything to prevent death, we possess a natural tendency to contemplate and likely fear our ultimate demise. So, "should I believe" consciousness exists as a separate entity apart from the brain, which persists and continues to perceive reality after death? Well, I believe strongly on the basis of an objective assessment of the collective evidence, that life after death cannot be either irrefutably ruled in or out. But don't let this viewpoint misguide your interpretation of the many perspectives, theories, and experimental evidence presented in this book. Try to maintain an unbiased viewpoint when analyzing the information associated with two fundamental interrelated questions related to the survival hypothesis:

1. Is death just a phase on the natural continuation of life?
2. Can consciousness persist in the absence of brain activity or does the brain construct reality—is consciousness our brain?

Within this context, it is hoped that regardless of your level of knowledge of the many controversial and intriguing issues on life after death, and associated preconceived beliefs, this book may help you to develop a more informed perspective to decide if you "should believe."

CHAPTER TWO

CONSCIOUSNESS

Introduction

The nature and function of consciousness must first be addressed before the concept of life after death is considered. After all, if we happen to be immortal, then it must be a non-physical form of consciousness not bound by space and time that, in some way, persists after death. Researchers have attempted to identify the brain's neural substrate responsible for consciousness, as manifested in the ability to perceive and interpret the relationship between oneself and the environment, self-awareness, intentionality, and abstract thinking, among other associated topics (e.g., NDE, OBE, reincarnation, apparitions, mediumship, parapsychology, and quantum physics, etc.), which incorporate the possibility of the continuity of consciousness after death.

The concept of consciousness has been a source of fierce controversy among scholars for centuries. Religions such as Christianity, Judaism, and Islam, for instance, generally associate consciousness with the brain, which interrelates with the human "soul." Those who ascribe to the consciousness-body dualism theory proposed by R. Descartes in 1641, believe that consciousness and the brain are separate but affect each other. In contrast, materialists believe that consciousness is associated with brain activity and can be explained in terms of matter and physical phenomena. And if consciousness is simply a by-product of brain functioning, then our ability to experience the world will, of course, cease once the brain's neuroelectric activity ends. Mainstream science, for instance, considers consciousness an outcome of the parallel processing of vast numbers of coding networks linked by the synchronized firing of nerve cells throughout the forebrain, from the cerebral cortex to other specialized centers of cognition, which give rise to sensory impressions. Alternatively, if consciousness is not dependent for its existence on a normal operating brain, then our sense of self may survive bodily death in some unknown realm of existence.

Consciousness and the Brain

Human consciousness has been a focus of study in the fields of neuroscience, biology, psychology, physics, as well as in philosophy. Scholars across these disciplines have attempted to better understand the nature and meaning of consciousness, and how our brain provides a sense of an individual "self." This objective has been approached in different ways consistent with the theoretical principles and research methods unique to each discipline. But despite these efforts, there remains no widely accepted theory of how the brain facilitates self-awareness, intention, and abstract thought. Our limited understanding of the nature of consciousness leaves open several questions fundamental to the ambiguous concept of life after death. Consequently, the need for continued research to better understand the consciousness-brain relationship has been advanced by many leading scientists, psychologists, and philosophers who contend that to prove whether or not consciousness depends on the brain may require a theory yet to be developed.[1] Philosopher D. Chalmers summarizes this perspective as follows:

> "Science is at a sort of impasse in its study of consciousness," and "radical ideas may be needed to move forward. Consciousness, the subjective experience of an inner self, could be a phenomenon forever beyond the reach of neuroscience. Even a detailed knowledge of the brain's workings and the neural correlates of consciousness may fail to explain how or why human beings have self-aware minds."[2]

A similar perspective by theoretical physicist and mathematician E. Wigner, who received half of the Nobel Prize in Physics in 1963, is that, "physics will have to be replaced by new laws, based on new concepts, if organisms with consciousness are to be described in order to deal with the phenomenon of life, the laws of physics will have to be changed, not only reinterpreted."[3] Consistent with this position, mathematical physicist R. Penrose wrote: "To understand consciousness demands a major revolution in physics. There is something very fundamental missing from current science. Our understanding at this time is not adequate and we're going to have to move to new regions of science."[4]

Since the neurological processes that govern and regulate consciousness remain elusive, it is important to be aware of the tentative nature of almost anything that can be said about how the brain facilitates the first-person experience. In fact, there is even considerable controversy in the use of the term "consciousness," which is often used in different ways. In other words, is consciousness our brain, experiences, the perception of "I" or oneself, or our waking state? In biology and medicine, for instance, consciousness is studied in terms of brain mechanisms of arousal and responsiveness (i.e., alertness through disorientation, loss of communication, and depth of coma), and on identifying brain regions that mediate sensory and motor signals that induce subjective feelings such as self-location and the first-person perspective (i.e., from where do I perceive the world?). In contrast, consciousness studies in psychology and cognitive science tend to focus on asking verbal reports of experiences and subjective states (e.g., self-awareness, subliminal messages, denial of impairment, altered states produced by drugs, and meditation). In light of such diverse theories of consciousness, it is not surprising that different research approaches have been used to study this ambiguous concept. Cognitive psychologist S. Pinker concisely reflects this spectrum of opinion by simply stating that as far as consciousness goes, "we have no scientific explanation."[5] Similarly, theoretical biologist S. Kauffman stated that "nobody has the faintest idea what consciousness is. I don't have any idea. Nor does anybody else,"[6] whereas, physics professor A. Goswami considers consciousness, not the material world, as the primary reality.[7]

A related perspective is held by neurologist Sir J. Eccles, who considers that "evolution could account for the brain but not for the mind, and that only something transcendent could explain consciousness and thought."[8] According to Nobel Prize winner physicist M. Planck, "I regard consciousness as fundamental. I regard matter as derivative from consciousness. We cannot get behind consciousness. Everything that we talk about, everything that we regard as existing, postulates consciousness."[9] Neurosurgeon E. Alexander believes that the "brain does not create consciousness" and that "no neuroscientist can explain the physical mechanism by which the brain gives rise to consciousness."[10] In contrast, neurologist S. Novella remarked that "the evidence leads to only one interpretation and that is consciousness is what the brain does. Consciousness is a neurological phenomenon."[11] Maybe psychologist M. Monti succinctly summarized the mystery of consciousness in his statement that "defining our mind as consciousness is, without having a scientific definition of this phenomenon, extremely difficult to study."[12]

Numerous concepts derived from neurobiological models have helped to advance our understanding of the mysterious concept of consciousness. But while most neuroscientists acknowledge that consciousness exists, most do not attempt to study it. They consider it a philosophical issue best left to philosophers to explain or that we should focus research on other aspects of brain function because the neurological substrate mediating consciousness is unlikely to be identified. Among those neuroscientists who do study consciousness, the predominant explanation is that consciousness is associated with neuroelectric activity in one or more regions of the brain; an extraordinarily complex and poorly understood system of synchronized activity of about 100 billion neurons with associated inter-connected neural pathways. Most patterns of ongoing neuronal activity arise from the brain itself, while other specialized neurons are elicited when external stimuli are processed by their corresponding sense organ. The resulting volley of nerve impulses flow both towards and away from the central nervous system for associated encoding/decoding, memory storage, perception, and the related interpretation of incoming stimulation. But while the act of retrieving past experiences from the brain's coded representations of such experiences is dependent on normal brain function, this widely accepted principle is disputed by those who consider that consciousness and memory may exist after death of the body. Now widely accepted as a working hypothesis, neuroscientists F. Crick, co-discoverer of the structure of DNA, and C. Koch contend that conscious perception arises from a "temporal synchronization of the oscillations of neuronal activity."[13] Consistent with this position, neuroscientist and psychiatrist G. Tononi considers consciousness to be mediated by brain cell networking. He remarked that, "As cells become more interlinked, information can be combined more readily and therefore the essence of complicated thought can be explained. The more possible links between cells, the more possible combinations there are and therefore a greater number of 'thoughts' are possible."[14]

Despite these proposed theories, there is no definitive objective evidence that shows how brain cells produce and regulate thoughts and the subjective essence of one's sense of self. Through the application of brain imaging techniques (e.g., electroencephalography (EEG), magnetoencephalography (MEG), functional magnetic resonance imaging (fMRI), and positron emission tomography (PET) scanning), however, scientists are now striving to identify specific brain regions that become metabolically active in response to a thought or feeling to determine if a purely subjective response can be measured and correlated with a neurologic signature of the concept of "self." A neurobiological model based on this concept considers consciousness an outcome of several specialized systems such as those regulating perception, attention, and language that represent a type of "global workspace."[15] Support for this model was proposed by psychologist M. Monti, who used fMRI techniques to analyze the "network properties" in the human brain during "unconsciousness" from anesthesia. He concluded that consciousness does not "live" in a specific brain region but rather "arises from the mode in which billions of neurons communicate with one another."[16] A recent fMRI study of subjects who reported the sense of knowing a word before recalling it in a memory task implicated the anterior insula region of the brain as the mediator of awareness.[17] In a recent unique study by neurologist O. Blanke, neuroimaging robotic technology was applied on subjects while exposed to induced changes in self-location to determine if the brain plays a critical role for the feeling of one's sense of awareness in space. Blanke reported that perceiving the world from this perspective is mediated in a brain region called the temporo-parietal junction (TPJ).[18] This finding, concommitent with supporting evidence from a study of patients with brain damage in the TPJ who reported out-of-body experiences, led Blanke to conclude that: "Our findings on experimentally and pathologically induced altered states of self-consciousness present a powerful new research technology and reveal that TPJ activity reflects one of the most fundamental subjective feelings of humans: the feeling that 'I' am an entity that is localized at a position in space and that 'I' perceive the world from here."[19]

Scientists have been studying the function of specific regions of the brain using electrical stimulation for many decades. Despite such effort, they have never been able to alter consciousness. Recently, however, the possible neurological components that govern this fundamental characteristic of consciousness was detected by neurologist M. Koubeissi who claimed to have turned consciousness on and off in an awake epileptic woman.[20] Electrical stimulation in the claustrum and insula brain region triggered a loss in consciousness, but when stimulation ended, she regained consciousness and could not recall the event. The involvement of this brain region, considered important for the integration of information about the state of the body for cognitive and associated conscious processes, led Koubeissi to reason that: "I would liken it to a car. A car on the road has many parts that facilitate its movement—the gas, the transmission, the engine—but there's only one spot where you turn the key and it all switches on and works together. So while consciousness is a complicated process created via many structures and networks, we may have found the key."[21]

Consciousness, Non-local Intuition, and the Quantum World

Consciousness and the brain informs us of reality and what we know and may even possibly have a physical effect on what we perceive. Scientists have explained how we experience reality using revolutionary principles in science and consciousness studies within the theoretical world of quantum physics (i.e., the behavior of atoms and subatomic particles). Many physicists who ascribe to the theoretical relationship between consciousness and the structure of matter do so since subatomic particles like photons (i.e., the smallest elemental unit of electromagnetic radiation) and electrons (i.e., the smallest particle of an atom) are composed of energy, and that since matter is energy, human consciousness must be connected to it and can alter its behavior. Quantum physics has shown that such particles are not really objects and do not exist at definite spatial locations and times. Instead, they seem to show "tendencies to exist," forming a world of potentialities.[22] In fact, models within quantum physics inform us that information must live on, no matter what. It's like energy—it can only be transformed and not destroyed. With this in mind, the case for the mechanism that enables consciousness to extend beyond the physical brain arises from quantum physics. At the quantum level all subatomic particles are entangled through quantum correlation and non-locality. This suggests a mechanism for a type of awareness that interrelates with matter and energy. Quantum physics was described by theoretical physicist Amit Goswami, as follows: "Quantum physics is a new paradigm of science based on the primacy of consciousness . . . The new paradigm resolves many paradoxes of the old paradigm and explains much anomalous data."[23]

An extension of this viewpoint is represented in the quantum mind theory of consciousness, which proposes that quantum physics may be an integral part of brain activity and the foundation to explain consciousness. Neuroscientist H. Romijn, for example, proposed that photons in brain neurons contribute to a biological quantum (i.e., the smallest discrete amount of something) connection that serves as a basis for consciousness.[24] A similar opinion conveyed by physicist E. Wigner is that consciousness represents a fundamental component of quantum measurement. He stated that, "The illusion of the classical scientific paradigm that is shattered by the quantum principle is the assumption that there is an immutable objective reality 'out there' that is totally independent of what happens in consciousness 'in here.' Quantum theory forces a new kind of logic in science that is still mathematical and disciplined."[25]

The behavior of subatomic particles, which serve as the foundation of quantum mechanical phenomena, has many strange characteristics. Experiments in quantum physics, for instance, have demonstrated the instantaneous connections remain between particles that once interacted physically but then became separated; that is, this quantum entanglement of one electron of an entangled pair somehow "knows" what measurement has been performed on the other and the associated outcome.

Strangely, this occurs despite the apparent inability to explain how such information is communicated between the particles, which at the time of measurement may be separated by distances of more than billions of light-years. This paradoxical behavior is referred to as "non-locality"—the ability of two objects to instantaneously know about each other's states even when separated. For example, particle A and particle B interact and become mysteriously bonded. Then, when particle A undergoes a change, particle B undergoes the same change, even though they are not visibly connected; that is, even though they are separated they remain linked in such a way that the quantum state of any one particle cannot be adequately described without consideration of the others.[26] An extension of such enigmatic behavior of subatomic particles may be applied to consciousness and its influence on physical systems.

Quantum theory, for instance, suggests that subatomic particles exist in an undefined state of potentialities and do not become "real" until a mind interacts with them to give them meaning. This has been demonstrated in experiments by which simply making a measurement or by through the observer's conscious intent, the outcome of an experiment can be changed. Considered by noted physicist Albert Einstein as "spooky action at a distance,"[27] the apparent interconnection of subatomic particles being observed and the observer has been demonstrated in the "double-slit experiment," whereby the behavior of electrons act differently when witnessed than when no one is watching as it passes through two slits in a barrier. For example, the particle behaves like a speeding train and goes through one slit or the other, but if a person doesn't watch the particle, it acts like a wave and passes through both slits at the same time. Accordingly, matter and energy can behave as either a wave or particle based upon one's conscious perception. This effect is also seen when a single electron passes through two different holes on a screen simultaneously. It remains a single particle on the other side but if a light is flashed on it to observe through which hole it passes, then it will pass only through one of the two holes.

Such experimental outcomes led D. Radin, Chief Scientist at the Institute of Noetic Sciences, to consider that entanglement in the subatomic quantum domain is responsible for the non-local events we experience. He wrote, "Observation not only disturbs what has to be measured, they produce it. We compel the electron to assume a definite position. We ourselves produce the results of the measurement."[28] Physician J. Schwartz and physicist H. Stapp also contend that the answer to how mental states can influence physical states lies in the discoveries of quantum physics[29] and "consciousness," which serves as the most "perplexing subject in science." A similar perspective was advanced by Niels Bohr, one of the foremost scientists of modern physics, who concluded that "everything we call real is made of things that cannot be regarded as real," and that "there is no local cause for an event, and when an event occurs, it instantaneously alters the universe."[30] Other noted scientists such as physicists E. Wigner and B. Josephson and mathematician J. von Neumann argue that this non-local effect may form the basis of consciousness. These perspectives, combined with the associated implications of the inexplicable behavior of subatomic particles of how consciousness creates reality, have generated more questions than answers within mainstream science.

One significant question is that if separated subatomic particles can be entangled, is it then possible for consciousness to also be entangled at a distance and, if so, how? In other words, is the consciousness of the observer vital to the existence of physical events being observed? According to physicists P. Davies and J. Gribbin, the observer plays an "essential role in fixing the nature of reality at the quantum level."[31] Accordingly, to better understand reality and its role in the physical universe we must consider the nature and effect of consciousness. But do we dare extrapolate the characteristics of this subatomic-like phenomenon to the concept of consciousness and the mind-brain relationship? After all, since we are composed of subatomic particles, do we then have the potential ability to interact with other forms of consciousness on a similar invisible pathway? That is, if something is non-local, it is not localized to specific points in space, such as our body, or to specific points in time, such as the present. Thus, they are infinite in time and present at all moments—past, present, and future. Consequently, they are eternal. This difficult-to-grasp concept may best be illustrated by documented non-local experiences. One such compelling example is represented in a highly credible account by metaphysicist B. Mango, who sensed the details of an unsolved murder that was later reported to validate every aspect of her experience, as follows:

My husband and I were driving down River Road in New Milford, CT, which abuts Bridgewater, CT. We passed a small beach appearing through a gap in the woods—one of the few "beaches" alongside the Housatonic River. I became highly agitated as we approached this area and begged my husband to stop the car. My agitation turned into sheer panic. My heart was beating impossibly fast. I felt as if a 500-pound weight was crushing my chest, and it was nearly impossible for me to catch my breath. I was dizzy, light-headed, and extremely nauseous. Immediately, I knew exactly what had transpired here. This was the spot where M. Measels had been murdered. I visualized the murder while simultaneously experiencing every emotion that was energetically embedded there. In between gasps of breath and extreme nausea, I described the murder to my husband as follows: I pointed to a tree and said: "Oh my God, this is where she was raped. Then she was dragged across the street to the beach area . . . I'm going to be sick . . . She may have been raped again on the beach. Oh my God, I feel like I'm going to die. I see Maryann on the beach half-conscious and being dragged into the water by at least two men. Her head is being held under the water and she is drowning. She's being drowned to death. Oh my God, get me out of here; I'm going to be sick, and I'm having a panic attack." I began sobbing hysterically. It took well over an hour for my body to recover. Emotionally, I remained exhausted, sad, and depressed for a few days. Approximately eighteen months later, my husband was reading our local newspaper. He suddenly shouted, "Oh my God, Barbara; everything you said came true." Three of the eight co-conspirators had confessed to the murder location, the murder itself, and events leading up to it. This was a breakthrough moment for the New Milford Police Department. It was also the first time any details of the crime had been made public, in any capacity. Every single detail I had experienced correlated exactly with the newspaper account of the crime.[32]

Validated experiences such as this provide indirect evidence to help justify how consciousness and our physical material world may interact. And such anecdotal evidence should serve as a foundation for studies that may advance our understanding of the mind-brain relationship, the theoretical non-local aspects of consciousness, and even life after death.

For lack of a precise explanation of the principles that may govern and regulate such enigmatic concerns, several scholars adopt the century-old theory of panpsychism—that is, consciousness is a universal feature of all things. Subsequently, the idea has been advanced that consciousness exists in molecules and atoms, perhaps as some kind of quantum mechanical effect. In fact, physicist M. Tegmark proposed that there is a state of matter, like solid, liquid, and gas whereby atoms are somehow capable of processing information that gives "rise to subjectivity."[33] This concept, referred to as the perceptronium theory, was inspired in part by neuroscientist G. Tononi whose integrated information theory has become a popular notion in the science of consciousness. This theory predicts that, "devices as simple as a thermostat or a photoelectric diode might have glimmers of consciousness; a subjective self."[34] Tononi even developed a unit called "phi," which is alleged to measure how "conscious an entity is." Taking these considerations a step further, physicist R. Lanza contends that life and consciousness are fundamental to the universe, and that humans are "eternal" and created the "concept of life and death through their own consciousness."[35] Lanza believes that consciousness exists outside of the constraints of time and space and can exist in or outside of the body. In other words, it is non-local in the same sense that quantum objects are non-local. Parapsychologist J. Utts and Nobel laureate and theoretical physicist B. Josephson state that science needs to adapt to accommodate such evidence. They wrote: "What are the implications for science of the fact that psychic functioning appears to be a real effect? These phenomena seem mysterious, but no more mysterious perhaps than strange phenomena of the past which science has now happily incorporated within its scope."[36]

Combining both a scientific and philosophical-based theory of consciousness, physicist R. Jahn concluded that if consciousness can exchange information with the physical environment, then it can have the same "molecular binding potential" as physical objects since it follows the principles of quantum mechanics.[37] That is, consciousness follows the principles of quantum mechanics. Physicist D. Bohm, a student of Albert Einstein, also agreed that it makes no sense to separate physical effects from spiritual effects. He proposed that, "the results of modern natural sciences only make sense if we assume an inner, uniform, transcendent reality that is based on all external data and facts. The very depth of human consciousness is one of them."[38] Nuclear physicist J. Hayward shared a similar perspective:

> Many scientists who are still part of the scientific mainstream are no longer afraid to openly state that consciousness/awareness could, in addition to space, time, matter, and energy, be a fundamental element of the world—perhaps

even more fundamental than space and time. It may be a mistake to ban the spirit from nature. It is even questioned as to whether matter should be considered a fundamental element of the universe."[39]

Several researchers in the field of parapsychological studies share this similar viewpoint; that is, consciousness is not limited to the brain. This position is based on experimental evidence of non-locality, which suggests that humans can exchange information without the use of our sensory systems (i.e., transcend space and time) and intentionally effect change in other people and physical systems at a distance. This perspective is consistent with that held by physicist N. Herbert who considers consciousness a "process lying outside the laws that govern the material world—it is just this immunity from the quantum rules that allows the mind to turn possibility into actuality."[40] Similarly, H. Stapp, who worked with some of the founding fathers of quantum physics, stated, "a scientist physically affects quantum systems by choosing which properties to study. Similarly, an observer can hold in place a chosen brain activity that would otherwise be fleeting. This shows that the mind and brain may not be one and the same."[41] This concept was summarized by neuropsychologist P. Fenwick who stated, "the experiments and current understanding of non-locality in nature is sufficient to postulate that non-locality is the antecedent attribute of energy and matter, which permits perception and is the root of the consciousness which manifests in the evolved organisms existing in three dimensional reality."[42]

Certain aspects of such theoretical concepts may be represented in both physiological and psychological (e.g., consciousness and intuition)-based experiments, which suggest that one can respond to external stimulation before consciousness processes the event; that is, *non-local intuition*, may represent non-local characteristics of particles at the subatomic scale (e.g., observer effect, quantum entanglement). For example, although physicists initially believed quantum entanglement was of little significance, fMRI and EEG studies now suggest that its effects may be associated with brain activity. Researchers have measured EEG correlations between the brains of spatially separated people to determine if an objective measure of a subjective sense of connection is reflected in brain activity. Interestingly, this cause-effect relationship was supported in studies whereby the stimulation of one individual's brain was reported to have been transmitted and instantaneously measured in a distant individual's brain using such objective measurement techniques.[43] If valid, the notion of "linked minds" may be possible. Justification for this concept was reinforced by psychologist C. Alvarado in an EEG-based study of social interaction at a distance in paired participants who were not "connected by any traditional channels of communication."[44] When one of the pair received a one-second stimulation from a light signal, a weak but robust statistically significant response was also detected in the Alpha range EEG activity of the other member of the pair. If replicated by independent investigators, this outcome would provide more definitive neurophysiological evidence of a connection between individuals at distance. Although distant individuals may somehow be coupled in this manner, there is no conclusive evidence that "human entanglement" is related to "quantum entanglement."

In fact, many physicists maintain that non-local connections between entangled particles cannot transfer information.[45]

In a comprehensive review of the literature, D. Radin reported that approximately fifteen percent of pairs of people show "non-chance EEG correlations."[46] This evidence suggests that intuitively perceived information may be non-local; that is, it is time independent and does not obey the inverse square law for space/time energy propagation. But understanding the mechanics of non-locality does not exist in traditional scientific models. Some physicists explain non-local intuition on the basis of super-luminal speed of propagation (i.e., instantaneous communication) or the zero point field as a dimension that is resonant with all parts of the universe simultaneously.

In a related experiment to test the validity of non-local intuition, Radin asked subjects to imagine that they could perceive and alter a low-intensity laser beam in a distant interferometer. The results, which indicated that one's intuition modified the photons' quantum wave functions and the pattern of light produced by this device, led Radin to conclude that, "conventional explanations" for these results were "implausible." One's intuition is capable of "gaining knowledge about the world and with the predicted effects of observation on a quantum system. Intuitive knowledge arises from perceptions that are not mediated through the ordinary senses."[47]

Radin and his colleagues also attempted to find experimental evidence of consciousness influencing quantum effects using an extension of the double-slit experiment.[48] Their study involved asking meditators to imagine that they could see which of the two slits the photon passed. Briefly, the results from 137 subjects of both experienced meditators and non-meditators, who took part in 250 sessions consisting of alternate sets of thirty seconds of observation with thirty seconds of rest, indicated a significant effect size with the meditators. This positive outcome led them to conduct an Internet-based experiment that comprised over 5,000 sessions completed by human subjects and over 7,000 performed by a "Linux" robot as a control. The subsequent outcomes, which also demonstrated a significant effect,[49] requires further research by independent investigators to determine if such non-local effects can be replicated to help validate non-local intuition.

In a related study to test the perception of information of a distant or future event, neuroscientist Benjamin Libert analyzed EEG recordings to determine precisely when subjects made a decision to act prior to simple behavioral tasks (e.g., moving fingers). Interestingly, Libert found that the brain responded a few milliseconds before the decision to act, which he termed the "readiness potential."[50] A similar conclusion was made by Radin who observed that skin-conductance activity reacted appropriately consistent a few seconds prior to randomly presented emotionally calming or upsetting computer pictures.[51] Similarly, experiments using electrocardiogram measures of heart rate variability detected a significant pre-stimulus cardiac change starting about eighteen seconds before participants knew the future outcome of an event.[52] Collectively, the evidence from these studies suggest that the brain's regulatory mechanism may be activated just before conscious will to allow a brief period for consciousness to override a decision. Despite objective evidence of correlations between non-local intuition and associated physiological measures, further justification is required to validate this cause-effect relationship. This is a necessary step to help explain the possible force that may govern and regulate the means for such information transmission.

The possibility that human intention can affect physical systems has also been studied in a variety of group settings (e.g., meditations, ceremonies, and important global events[53] and in individuals.[54]) This theory was tested as part of the Global Consciousness Project (GCP) led by psychologist R. Nelson, the Director of the Princeton Engineering Anomalies Research Lab (PEAR). In this unique study, the output of a worldwide network of one hundred computer random event generators (REG) that continuously emitted ones and zeros in a random pattern, was analyzed by a supercomputer at Princeton University to identify any statistically significant deviation from randomness that may be influenced by major world events. Interestingly, such deviations were reported when major events elicited the attention of millions of people to a single point in time. This outcome led the researchers to conclude that such changes in the REGs were caused by a field of consciousness strong enough to affect artificial intelligence, which proves "we are all one."[55] More specifically, the researchers found a significant level of coherence between the REGs, indicating a hyper-dimensional "forewarning" of a large impending event facilitated by the collective attention focusing on the event. The period immediately surrounding the event showed a "huge spike in coherence" as humanity's collective mind was focused consciously on events as they unfolded. This result suggests that consciousness may be more fundamental than any form of energy/matter in space-time (i.e., that it is "sub-quantum"). What is especially both interesting and difficult to understand is that this anomaly was mostly predictive, often happening hours before the original event occurred. For example, researchers found one such significant irregularity several hours before the terrorist attacks on September 11, 2001. The mathematical analysis of the data showed that the New York computer broke the 1 to 0 ratio of 50:50 to 1:35. Similar results occurred before attacks by Al Qaeda in Madrid in 2004, and London in 2005, the tsunami that devastated Southeast Asia, and the election of President Obama. Despite existing controversies associated with the PEAR study, the replication of their research outcomes by independent investigators would reinforce the proposed existence of a "global consciousness" that knows of a major event before our individual consciousness does. What is most interesting, however, is that this same type of intuitive foreknowledge was reported in the electrocardiogram and EEG studies by Libert and Radin noted previously. The collective study results, therefore, suggest that one's consciousness may have the potential to react to a strong emotional event before it is actually experienced.

Concurrent with the GCP, the same researchers conducted thousands of experiments with hundreds of subjects to further evaluate if our minds may affect the normal functioning of electronic devices. Curiously, subjects instructed to use their intention to influence the REG towards a one or zero were able to produce a significant change in the direction of their will.[56] The researchers determined that the probability of this result happening by chance rather than by an influence of the human mind was less than 1 to 1 billion. Though the influence was small, the significant consistency of the results led them to conclude that our brains are capable of communicating on "invisible pathways," i.e., non-locality.[57] The change in the random behavior of the REG was even more pronounced when the collective consciousness of millions of people were focused on a single event as part of the GCP. Similarly, R. Nelson reported that REGs in group situations behaved non-randomly in situations that evoked both intense subjective experiences and as an outcome of meditation involving a large number of people worldwide at the same time.[58] For example, millions of people watching the television broadcasts of the O. J. Simpson murder trial altered the output of nearby REGs during periods of high emotional content[59]; that is, participant intentionality created a non-random effect to bias the skewed distribution of the REGs from randomness toward more order. Despite the compelling evidence generated by PEAR, however, alternative explanations of their research results include experimenter and methodological biases, statistical, REG malfunction, and electromagnetic interference.[60] In spite of such potential confounding variables, one theoretical explanation for the reported PEAR results was summarized by physicist C. Clarke who remarked:

> On one hand, Mind is inherently non-local. On the other, the world is governed by a quantum physics that is inherently non-local. This is no accident, but a precise correspondence. Mind and the world are aspects of the same thing. The way ahead, I believe, has to place mind first as the key aspect of the universe. We have to start exploring how we can talk about mind in terms of a quantum picture. Only then will we be able to make a genuine bridge between physics and physiology.[61]

Other attempts to demonstrate the validity of Clarke's contention that "mind and the world are aspects of the same thing" have been performed using one's healing intention on biological functions in remote individuals and on nonhuman processes. Several studies suggestive of non-local effects, for instance, have been reported by the benefits of healing prayer[62], distant healing in cardiopulmonary and AIDS patients[63], and in mice infected with mammary adenocarcinoma. Directed intention has also been associated with significantly faster healing in injured mice and higher germination and faster growth rates in shocked plants.[64] Employing more objective measures to assess the influence of human intention, physiologist L. Hendricks reported the existence of interpersonal EEG coupling between healer and subject pairs by which the healer produced a "connection between the healer and the subject."[65] Another interesting experiment employed experienced meditators to determine if their intention can affect change in the pH of water within an electrical device.[66] Briefly, once imprinted through meditation, the device was then sent overnight to a laboratory 2,000 miles away where it was turned on. According to the researchers, the results showed a very large "unambiguous change in the water's pH state" simply through its being in the vicinity of the electrical device that had been imprinted with that intent. Another example of communication on "invisible pathways" was provided in a study by physicist R. Dobrin who reported that subjects were able to increase the energy field output of biophotons (i.e., very weak emissions of light radiated from the cells of all living things) by up to sixty-seven percent through conscious intention.[67]

Experiments demonstrating that rats learning a new maze benefited non-locally from the experience of others who had previously learned the maze, led parapsychologist R. Sheldrake to conclude that humans can also react to non-local information. He remarked that humans can "perceive, cognize, and give meaning to non-local information across a range of complexity, from inanimate objects, simple organisms, animals, and other humans."[68] This perspective was reinforced by professor of materials science and engineering W. Tiller who demonstrated that one's intention can increase the conductivity (i.e., the ability to transmit energy) between a molecule and vacuum level. This finding led him to conclude that consciousness can affect or interact with a "power greater than anything conventional instruments have been able to measure thus far."[69] In fact, several noted scientists have suggested that a person's mind or body could be affected by the thoughts of another person far away through the following mechanisms:

1. Maxwell's original equations;
2. Magnetic currents traveling in a particular region of space-time which includes the quantum vacuum;
3. Laboratory measurements of humans radiating high electrostatic charge at will as "indicative of the possibility of such a broadcasting telepathic mechanism."[70]

While evidence to support non-local intuition is an important step towards understanding the potential capabilities of consciousness, it is another thing entirely to explain the nature that governs and regulates this phenomenon. Within this context, Tiller discovered that the vacuum space considered as empty, contains immensely powerful substances that cannot be seen, which can be affected by human intention. An in-between substance made of particles he called "deltrons" are activated, which affect the substances we see. Interestingly, he contends that the energy in the vacuum space of a single hydrogen atom is as "great as all the electromagnetic energy found in everything within fifteen billion light-years of our space-time cosmos." What is especially interesting is that he believes that human intention can act on this powerful realm that mainstream science views as empty space. According to Tiller, this allows one to observe and measure the impact of human intention on this otherwise undetected substance.[71] Based on this principle, an instrument he developed, called an "Intention Host Device," provided the means by which good intentions broadcasted by the device significantly helped to:

1. Enhance the skill sets and integration of thirty-four autistic children, and relieved the depression and anxiety of their parents, and

2. Reduce depression and anxiety in hundreds of people located over 1,000 miles away.[72]

It should be noted, however, that his experimental methodology and evidence is considered highly controversial and "full of holes" by several physicists.

Despite existing anecdotal and experimental evidence suggestive of non-locality, concepts proposed by the Quantum Holographic Principle, the Synchronized Universe Model, or the Quantum Bayesianism theory (i.e., quantum information is a function of our own minds)[73], which theoretical physicist N. Mermin considers to be the "most powerful abstraction we have ever found[74]," may provide the foundation to validate and explain the nature and potential of consciousness. Clearly, however, evidence to support non-locality must be reproduced by independent researchers and must await new developments in science to definitively explain this phenomenon. Additionally, the difficulty controlling numerous confounding variables in clinical tests of non-locality diminish the validity of the resulting outcomes and associated conclusions.

Mainstream science considers that neurons and their chemical synapses are the fundamental units of information in the brain, and that conscious experience arises when a certain level of neurological complexity occurs in the brain. In fitting the brain to a computational view, such explanations omit incompatible neurophysiological details and the absence of testable hypotheses of how consciousness involves awareness of what we are sensing and the control of voluntary actions. A related, perhaps more ambitious and challenging perspective, argues that the fundamental nature of all reality is consciousness itself, and that, rather than consciousness being seen as an emergent epiphenomenon of physicality (including the brain) it is physicality that is an emergent epiphenomenon of consciousness. This concept represents the complete opposite of materialism (i.e., the philosophical view of idealism).

As quantum physics evolved from its early 20th century roots, it has become increasingly difficult to keep consciousness out of our scientific understanding of the nature of physical reality and how we experience it. This led psychologist J. Klimo to develop a theoretical model that integrates quantum physics and the study of consciousness into a new field called "Quantum Idealism."[74a] In current mainstream scientific thinking, and in cognitive science and consciousness studies in particular, there is something called the "hard problem." This problem is how to explain what we know intimately and experientially as our own self-aware consciousness and all its "qualia" only in terms of its completely physical origins of bioelectrical and chemical matter and energy interactions at the neuronal level in the brain. Nobody has yet been able to successfully solve this "hard problem." If, however, the picture is inverted, then the new hard problem to be faced by any idealist viewpoint would be trying to explain how all things spatiotemporal and completely matter-and-energy physical in nature can be derived solely from an all-constituting underlying reality that is pure consciousness. Klimo's approach might eventually turn out to be a more fruitful root.

Discussion

Scientific principles within the domain of quantum physics may hold the key to unlock the mystery of how consciousness relates to the brain during life, as well as during brain death. This potential outcome is supported, in part, by experimental results of subatomic quantum entanglement, which should serve to stimulate active research of this phenomena in humans. But before a possible all-encompassing theory is developed and confirmed, a required prerequisite is to devise appropriate techniques to identify, if at all possible, the underlying neurological correlates of consciousness, the mind-brain connection, and non-local intuition. After all, if a field of consciousness strong enough to affect physical systems, human physiology, and artificial intelligence is confirmed, such evidence may suggest that a form of energy exists apart from the body. Consequently, this finding may provide supporting rationale for the persistence of consciousness following the death of the body. After all, neuroscientists have been unable to adequately explain how the brain facilitates one's concept of self, beliefs and reasoning, and decision-making processing. And until we attain a better understanding of these elusive concepts, the controversies surrounding consciousness and its possible continuation after death will continue to serve as a source of debate, controversy, and above all, hope.

CHAPTER THREE

THE NEAR-DEATH EXPERIENCE

Introduction

Advancements in life-sustaining medical resuscitation techniques are helping people survive trauma after being pronounced clinically dead (i.e., absence of cardiac, respiratory, and cerebral activity). Interestingly, many people who survive a threat to their life also describe an overwhelming experience in which they report to be conscious and apart from their body. This distinctive state of consciousness is termed a *near-death experience* (NDE). NDEs are not rare in occurrence. Survey studies indicate that the incidence may be approximately four percent of the general population[1] and ten to twenty percent of those who survive cardiac arrest report such experiences.[2] According to psychiatrist and leading researcher in the field of near-death studies, Bruce Greyson, NDEs are a "profound psychological event including transcendental and mystical elements, typically occurring to individuals close to death or in situations of intense physical or emotional danger."[3] An NDE has also been reported during states of meditation[4], severe psychological events[5], and even in healthy individuals present during a relative's death.[6] The incidence of an NDE falls in the ten to fifteen percent range[7] with an estimated 200,000 people per year in the United States and millions worldwide having reported an NDE.[8]

The NDE, one of the most intriguing research topics in the physical and social sciences, has served as a primary source of evidence to support the possibility of life after death. This phenomenon was stimulated by psychologist and physician Raymond Moody, who documented anecdotal accounts of NDEs in those who survived a life-threatening situation or were clinically dead and brought back to life in his book *Life after Life* in 1975.[9] Since then, numerous books and research results have been published that address the possible nature and validity of this real and unexplained subjective experience. While mainstream science regards the NDE as a neurological-induced hallucination, several NDE researchers consider it as possible evidence for life after death, existence of the soul, and/or that our consciousness is independent of the brain.[10] But if you think an NDE is due to a blood-deprived chaotic functioning brain, then a purely physiological explanation is the answer.

Components of the Near-Death Experience

Components of the NDE, which seem inconsistent with physiological and psychological principles, challenge the scientific model that neurological activity in the brain facilitates consciousness.[11] In fact, to an experiencer, an NDE is so vivid and real that it is believed to represent the separation of one's consciousness from the brain. In a comprehensive literature review, psychologist C. Agrillo identified the most commonly reported characteristics of the NDE:

1. Awareness of being dead;
2. Improved mood (e.g., intense feelings of pure love, euphoria, happiness, and well-being);
3. Out-of-body experience (OBE);
4. Entering a tunnel-like realm;
5. Sensation of movement;
6. Perception of heavenly or hellish landscape;
7. Encounter with deceased relatives, religious figures, or beings of light; and
8. Experience of a life review.[12]

A detailed description of the general form of an NDE was initially introduced by Moody as follows:

> A man is dying and, as he reaches the point of greatest physical distress, he hears himself pronounced dead by his doctor. He begins to hear an uncomfortable noise, a loud ringing or buzzing, and at the same time feels himself moving very rapidly through a long dark tunnel. After this, he suddenly finds himself outside of his own physical body, but still in the immediate physical environment, and he sees his own body from a distance, as though he is a spectator. He watches the resuscitation attempt from this unusual vantage point and is in a state of emotional upheaval. He notices that he still has a "body" but one of a very different nature and with very different powers from the physical body he has left behind. Others come to meet and to help him. He glimpses the spirits of relatives and friends who have already died, and a loving, warm spirit of a kind he has never encountered before, "a being of light," appears before him. This being asks him a question non-verbally, to make him evaluate his life, and helps him along by showing him a panoramic, instantaneous playback of the major events of his life. At some point he finds himself approaching some sort of barrier or border, apparently representing the limit between earthly life and the next life. Yet, he finds that he must go back to the earth, that the time for his death has not yet come. At this point he resists, for by now he is taken up with his experiences in the afterlife and does not want to return. He is overwhelmed by intense feelings of joy, love, and peace. Despite his attitude, though, he somehow reunites with his physical body and lives. Later he tries to tell others, but he has trouble doing so. In the first place, he can find no words adequate to describe these unearthly episodes. He also finds that others scoff, so he stops telling other people. Still, the experience affects his life profoundly, especially his views about death and its relationship to life.[13]

Existing in another realm, often described as a beautiful pastoral landscape of vivid colors and music, where one typically has encounters with friendly spirit beings and/or deceased friends or relatives[14], has been reported in about twenty-five percent of NDE cases. Psychologist K. Ring also reported this feature in about forty percent of his study sample.[15] Many NDEers report to encounter a boundary, where it is understood that if crossed, a return to their body would be impossible.[16] Communication often focuses on whether the individual is to die or return to the physical body, which often includes the impression that it was their choice, but sometimes the "being" orders the return to their body, which occurs with reluctance.[17]

Researchers have reported that the feeling of peace is a predominant feature of the NDE, ranging from fifty-five to ninety-nine percent among various sample populations.[18] The transition from darkness to the reported alternate realm is also sometimes accompanied by the appearance of a brilliant golden light that has been reported to range widely in occurrence from twenty-three to seventy percent.[19] While in this realm, it is not uncommon to receive information about an intrinsic knowledge of reality that consciousness is immortal and that love is the primary essence of life. Typically, NDEers also perceive deceased individuals with whom they were emotionally close, but in about thirty percent of the cases, the deceased person was either not a close friend or someone never met, such as a relative who died before the experiencer's birth.[20] Cardiologist Pim van Lommel, for example, reported an NDEer who saw his deceased grandmother and an unknown man. Later shown a picture of his biological father, whom he had never known and who had died years before, he immediately recognized him as the person seen in his NDE.[21] Skeptics, however, generally consider that the deceased relatives and/or divine beings are likely induced by the socio-cultural context.[22]

A common feature of an NDE is the OBE. NDEers report that while out of the body they became aware of events beyond the reach of their senses and have normal perceptions of their environment and physical body.[23] An OBE, reported to occur in about sixty percent of NDEers, is often very vivid and resembles everyday waking experiences rather than dreams. In many cases, the NDEer reports having a second body referred to as an astral body and feels that their consciousness is contained within this body in a manner similar to that when awake.[24] And when their astral body travels away from their physical body, they may report that:

1. Their consciousness goes with it;
2. They don't believe they left their body; and
3. That their consciousness linked to this second body will persist after death.

Many who report this experience do not sense leaving their body, but recognize this only when they observe their body and realize that it is "me down there." Several studies have determined the incidence of this highly variable NDE component to be in the range of twenty-four to ninety-nine percent.[25]

Surprisingly, one study estimated that about ten percent of the general population have had an OBE.[26] And while the OBE may occur spontaneously, some people report the ability to voluntarily induce an OBE using different techniques. The vast majority of induced OBEs, commonly termed "astral travelers" report to be "still embodied" but in a body whose "shape, external characteristics, and spatial location are easily altered at will." Although rare in occurrence, some also describe a "silver cord" connecting their new astral body to the old one.[27] A much smaller percentage of those who have spontaneous OBEs mention being embodied, although some report being disembodied. Many NDEers attempt to interact with the environment during the OBE phase of the event to indicate they are alright but are not successful.

A panoramic life review consisting of vibrant visual images of the person's life may appear sequentially from childhood or all at once during the NDE. A significant aspect of this review involves seeing, understanding, and emotionally experiencing the impact of their actions on others during their life. This process may also incorporate fantasies about the future, and the visualization and reactions by others of their death.[28] Proponents of the NDE interpret this account as the realization of where life improvement is needed and in the decision of whether to return to the body.

What is most curious about the reported NDE "life review" are the common perceptions that: 1) time and space do not exist, 2) telepathic communication ensues, and 3) immediately they are where they want to be (non-locality). A representative personal account of this experience is as follows: "Not only did I perceive everything from my own viewpoint, but I also knew the thoughts of everyone involved in the event, as if I had their thoughts within me. This meant that I perceived not only what I had done or thought, but even in what way it had influenced others, as if I saw things with all-seeing eyes. Time and distance seemed not to exist. I was in all places at the same time, and sometimes my attention was drawn to something, and then I would be present there."[16a]

One may experience a positive or negative NDE. The positive NDE often incorporates a beautiful scenic environment while the rare (less than five percent) negative NDE may include a "hellish" one (e.g., a dark cave or fire), described to be inhabited with so-called "demons." In the positive NDE, one feels loved by the "presence" of a being and all of their life experiences seem acceptable, whereas, the negative experience may incorporate voices claiming that the NDEer's life never really existed, the perception that their life is about to end, and/or being judged for past actions.

The NDE is often described as perceived as "real" or even "realer than real"[29] and by a sense of "certainty" of the experience, typical of perception during life.[30] Studies to evaluate characteristics of real and imagined event memories in NDEers who survived a coma concluded that NDEs are not imagined events.[31] In fact, NDE memories have more features than any kind of memory of real and imagined events or memories related to an unconscious state such as a coma. In contrast, one study demonstrated that physiological mechanisms triggered during an NDE are responsible for the reported more vivid perception of real and imagined events in their lives.[32] Furthermore, an analysis of a large collection of NDE cases in the University of Virginia archive revealed that eighty percent of the NDEers reported the clarity of thinking to have been unimpaired during their NDEs (forty-five percent "clearer than usual" and thirty-five percent "as clear as usual"); seventy-four percent reported the speed of their thinking to have been unimpaired (thirty-seven percent "faster than usual" and thirty-seven percent "at the usual speed"); sixty-five percent reported their logic to have been unimpaired (twenty-nine percent "more logical than usual" and thirty-six percent "as logical as usual"); and fifty-five percent reported no decline in control over their thoughts (nineteen percent "more control than usual" and thirty-six percent "as much as usual").[33] This evidence contradicts what would be expected if consciousness is dependent on normal brain function, especially since during an NDE the brain is severely compromised. Consequently, if we assume that an aspect of consciousness behaves independently of the brain during an NDE/OBE, the question emerges as to whether the brain inhibits cognitive function rather than facilitating it by normal embodiment.

In a study of NDE cases with "objective perceptions," forty-eight of seventy (sixty-nine percent) subjects reported an OBE, and twenty-three of the forty-eight OBE cases reported "precise perceptions corresponding to verified details in the environment and/or to scenes that took place just as described, thus giving a precise idea of when the actual experience occurred."[34] Anecdotal accounts of four NDEers who reported having explored their surroundings are presented as follows:[35]

1. "My displacements were subject to my will with instantaneous effect. Instant zooming of my vision, without any displacement on my part. When I was on the outside in the park at tree level, I remember experiencing this zoom effect very clearly since I could see inside a tree without having moved."
2. "I see everywhere at once, except when I target an object towards which I am 'hurled' at great speed, as if I was zooming onto it. It is like a rapid zoom to be there where I am looking. Like a very fast zoom, I cannot recall if it really is a displacement, or simply a zoom, but I was where I was aiming at, so there is a displacement. It is very pleasant and fun."
3. "My consciousness, like a beam of light, can move around very fast, nearly instantly. This gaze, just like thought, can in addition move about very rapidly from points that are distant to one another."
4. "Moving around is done as if time does not exist anymore (or nearly). We 'think' about where we wish to be and we make a volitional effort and we get there instantaneously (or nearly, since there is a sensation of movement, but very fast)."

If consciousness is a by-product of the brain, then if the brain is injured, consciousness should also be adversely affected in some way. However, brain research suggests that when one is close to death, consciousness may be unaffected. Consequently, consciousness and the brain may function independently. Support for this concept was provided by psychologist A. Batthyany, who reviewed thousands of written NDE narratives from online repositories of experiences from the Near-Death Experience Research Foundation (NDERF) website to examine the quality of vision and cognition during NDEs. Part of this objective was to replicate earlier similar studies, such as that by radiation oncologist and founder of the NDERF J. Long, who found that about seventy-four percent of more than 1,200 NDEers reported "more consciousness and alertness" during their NDE.[36] Similarly, Batthyany found that forty-seven percent of his large population database reported enhanced vision, forty-one percent had unchanged vision, and about thirty-five percent said they had increased awareness and mentation, which he considered "quite remarkable, given that these patients were in a severe medical crisis and often unconscious." Consequently, this result led him to conclude that "the more severe the physiological crisis, the more likely NDEers are to report having experienced clear and complex cognitive and sensory functioning."[37] If valid, the question arises as to whether this evidence indicates that consciousness may be both independent of the brain and immortal. According to Greyson:

> No one physiological or psychological model by itself explains all the common features of NDE. The paradoxical occurrence of heightened, lucid awareness and logical thought processes during a period of impaired cerebral perfusion raises particular perplexing questions for our current understanding of consciousness and its relation to brain function. A clear sensorium and complex perceptual processes during a period of apparent clinical death challenge the concept that consciousness is localized exclusively in the brain.[38]

Both the empirical and anecdotal evidence are reinforced by the similarity of content among large population samples and the credibility of individual NDEer testimony. Collectively, while this evidence signifies the NDE as a valid phenomenon, numerous hypotheses remain to be tested to better understand what governs and regulates the phenomenon.

Evidence of Life after Death?

It remains a daunting, if not impossible task, to determine the nature and validity of reported remote sensory observations in NDEs. To do so, researchers must somehow reliably determine if an NDE represents either:

1. One's consciousness leaving the body; or
2. A deceptive, illusory process facilitated by neurological changes associated with a severely compromised dying brain.

Although controversial, many NDE researchers consider the testimonies alone of those who have had an NDE and/or OBE to constitute strong evidence of a possible form of life after death.

Researchers have primarily employed survey- and interview-based phenomenological methods in NDEers to evaluate the phenomenon. Based on a comprehensive survey study in more than 1,200 NDEers who reported an imminent, life-threatening event at the time of their NDE, J. Long concluded that NDEers provide "evidence of life after death."[39] Several study outcomes by the NDERF addressed in his book *Evidence of the Afterlife* include the following:

1. The level of alertness during NDEs is usually greater than that experienced during everyday life and is generally realistic and often verified later by the NDEer or others as real;

2. Normal vision occurs in NDEs among those with significant impaired vision and who were blind from birth;
3. NDEs occur under general anesthesia when conscious experiences should be impossible;
4. Life reviews in NDEs include real events in one's life even if the events were forgotten;
5. Beings encountered are usually deceased relatives;
6. The NDEs of very young children are similar to those of older children and adults;
7. The NDE is extremely consistent worldwide; and
8. Life changing aftereffects following NDEs are often significant, enduring, and follow a consistent pattern.[40]

An abbreviated sample of several independent NDE study results, which corroborate these conclusions, is as follows:

1. B. Greyson reported that eighty percent of 520 NDEers described their thinking during the NDE as "clearer than usual" or "as clear as usual."[41]
2. An interview study revealed that eighty percent of thirty-one blind subjects (fourteen were blind from birth), of whom twenty-one had an NDE and ten an OBE, claimed to be able to see during their NDE or OBE. Of those blind from birth, five reported they were sighted during the experience.
3. In a study by physician E. Kelly, ninety-five percent of seventy-four NDEers who had encounters during their NDE were deceased relatives.[42]
4. Pediatricians M. Morse and P. Perry indicated that eight of twelve children reported the experience of leaving their bodies and traveling to other realms during their NDE—a feature of adult NDEs.[43] Similarly, physician C. Sutherland, who reviewed scholarly literature of NDEs in very young children, concluded that, "the age of children at the time of their NDE does not in any way determine its complexity. Even prelinguistic children have later reported quite complex experiences. Age does not seem in any way to affect the content of the NDE."[44]
5. An analysis of more than 400 NDEers conducted by M. Morse revealed that those who had NDEs as children had less death anxiety and increased psychic abilities and intelligence than non-NDE subjects.[45]
6. Professor of counseling J. Holden documented that ninety percent of NDE reports of perceptual experiences during cardiac arrest, prolonged respiratory arrest, or sensory isolation contained "no errors."[46] About thirty-five percent of these reports were independently corroborated by intensive care nurse P. Sartori.[47]

A remarkable NDE account featured in news worldwide is that of internationally recognized brain neurosurgeon E. Alexander. Although he did not believe in the afterlife or a non-physical spirit and considered such stories as hallucinations and products of imagination, during a week-long coma due to a severe case of bacterial meningitis, he had an NDE that facilitated a profound impact on his life and belief in the afterlife. The NDE motivated him to write the best-selling book *Proof of Heaven* where he confirmed that our life on Earth is just a "test" that helps our "souls evolve and grow," and to succeed in doing so one must live life with "love and compassion."[48] A few revealing statements from his book are as follows:

1. His NDE was "so real that the experience as a human on Earth is just an artificial dream in comparison";
2. "The fabric of the afterlife was love. If you wish to understand the Universe, you should know love";
3. "You are more precious and loved than you can possibly imagine. You are always safe and never alone. The unconditional and perfect love of God affects everyone"; and
4. "All communication was telepathic. There was no need of words."[49]

Two other personal accounts which typify an NDE are below:[50]

Peggy: "At one point my consciousness must have pulled away from my body because I suddenly observed it from a short distance as it sobbed. As I watched, I saw some shiny, clear object lift away from my body. It was obvious to me it was my ego. The moment my ego started lifting, my consciousness went back into my body and I felt distress thinking, 'It's my ego, it's my ego,' not wanting it to leave me. I felt like I had to have it or I wouldn't be alive. It pulled away from me anyway, and in it I saw all the things that I had done wrong in my life. I was stunned because I thought all that was part of me and simply couldn't be separated from me. I can't tell you how happy I was when it dawned on me that that was never me."

Steve: "As I floated above the water, I knew that my physical body was eight feet below the surface of the water, but it didn't bother me. Now separated from my physical body, I found that I could survive without all the pain and suffering of physical existence. I had never thought of it as pain and suffering when I was in my physical body, but now, after experiencing such total bliss and harmony, it seemed like everything prior to this was like being in some sort of cage."

A few contrasting viewpoints on the nature of the mind-body relation as it pertains to the NDE evidence include the following:

According to philosopher D. Rousseau, the collective NDE evidence supports the concept of dualism. He stated that, "Not only does NDE evidence indicate favor of some kind of mind-body substance dualism, but it is rich in information about the nature of this distinctly existing mind and its relationship to the body. During an NDE the mind appears to be in working order as a thing in itself while the interaction with the body is completely or nearly completely suspended."[51] Physician L. Dossey shared a similar perspective: "If the mind is non-local, it must in some sense be independent of the strictly local brain and body. And if the mind is non-local, unconfined to brains and bodies and thus not entirely dependent on the physical organism, the possibility of survival of bodily death is opened."[52] Psychiatrist C. Freeman proposed a counter argument to Rousseau and Dossey in his statement that, "We know that memories are extremely fallible. We are quite good at knowing that something happened, but we are very poor at knowing when it happened. It is quite possible that these experiences happened during the recovery, or just before the cardiac arrest. To say that they happened when the brain was shut down, I think there is little evidence for that at all."[53]

Veridical Perception

A difficult challenge to materialistic models of NDEs comes from those who report that, while out of the body during an NDE, they became aware of events beyond the reach of their ordinary senses even if they had been normally conscious. "Veridical perception," a term used to denote accurate perceptions of events from a vantage point outside the physical body during an NDE, are rare in occurrence. An NDE scale, developed by B. Greyson to identify a non-illusory veridical perception, incorporates the appearance of three simultaneous occurring NDE components.[54] The objective of this scale was to employ essential criteria to test the validity that consciousness may function independently of the body and possibly persist following death of the body. This includes:

1. "Normal or enhanced mentation when the physical body is ostensibly unconscious;
2. Seeing the physical body from a different position in space; and
3. Perceiving events beyond the normal range of the physical senses."[55]

The primary objective for NDE researchers has been to document an irrefutable veridical perception during an NDE. If valid, either there are levels of consciousness and associated neural activity beyond our ability to measure, or that some aspect of our consciousness is independent from the body. A major criticism of perceptions of events at a distance from the body, however, is that they often depend on the person's testimony alone. Although controversial, a method to document a valid veridical perception during an NDE has been employed in several studies with limited, if any, success.

To help accomplish this goal, a research project called the Awareness in Resuscitation study was conducted to evaluate veridical perception during a reported NDE in cardiac arrest patients in several hospitals. This involved placing a picture or symbol visible only to one looking down from the ceiling on shelves in rooms where the patients were resuscitated.[56] Of the 2,060 subjects interviewed, research director and critical-care physician Sam Parnia, reported that about two percent of the subject's recounted "verified detail during periods of clinical death." He also indicated that forty percent of those who had been resuscitated reliably reported some form of consciousness after they had been declared clinically dead; that is, despite the absence of brain activity, these individuals reported a sense of awareness which should have been impossible. According to Parnia:

> The evidence thus far suggests that in the first few minutes after death, consciousness is not annihilated. We know the brain can't function when the heart has stopped beating. But in this case conscious awareness appears to have continued for up to three minutes into the period when the heart wasn't beating, even though the brain typically shuts down within 20-30 seconds after the heart has stopped.[57]

Neurologist Kevin Nelson, however, contradicted Parnia's conclusion by noting that, "These are not return-from-death experiences. To him, near-death and out-of-body experiences are the result not of dying but of hypoxia—a loss of consciousness, not of life itself."[57a]

While controversial, several studies have documented more than twenty cases in which accurate perceptions of unexpected or unlikely details occurred during an OBE.[58] Psychiatrist E. Cook and psychologist E. Kelly[59] identified numerous cases of accurate OBE perceptions of unlikely events with some cases corroborated by independent witnesses.[60] In one intriguing veridical perception experiment, a subject who claimed to be able to leave her body was asked to identify a five-figure random number placed high on a shelf invisible to anyone on the bed where she slept. Despite odds against getting a five-figure random number correct by a guess is 100,000 to one against, the individual successfully recalled the number.[61] Another subject who claims to have OBEs at will was reported to successfully identify objects placed on a platform so high from the ground that they could only be seen from the ceiling. The odds against these results being due to chance were calculated at 40,000 to one.[62]

An interview study to document a veridical perception during an NDE was conducted by cardiologist M. Sabom in patients who had an NDE while undergoing cardiac resuscitation and "seasoned cardiac patients" who did not have an NDE during their arrest.[63] In response to the question to describe a cardiac resuscitation procedure, as if they were watching from a third-person perspective, eighty percent of the non-NDE patients made at least one major error in their descriptions. Surprisingly, none of the NDE patients made an error. Nineteen percent of the NDEers also related accurate details of specific unexpected events during their resuscitation.[64] P. Sartori replicated Sabom's study and found similar results in hospitalized patients.[65] She concluded that those who had an OBE described their resuscitations accurately, whereas every cardiac arrest survivor who had no OBE provided inaccurate information.[66] Additional supportive evidence of verifiable out-of-body perceptions during NDEs was provided by J. Holden.[67] Upon review of ninety-three case reports, forty-three percent were corroborated during an interview with an independent informant. Holden also reported that ninety percent of NDE reports of perceptual experiences under physically challenging conditions such as cardiac arrest, prolonged respiratory arrest, or sensory isolation contained no errors; around thirty-five percent of these reports were independently corroborated.[68]

Similarly, in another study, independent corroboration of a veridical perception was reported in thirty-two percent of 288 OBE cases of perceptual events which "could not have been experienced using one's ordinary senses."[69] In fact, the experience was even reported to someone else prior to being verified. Based on the collective evidence, the majority of NDE researchers believe that consciousness, memory, and perception can function when the body is "clinically dead."[70]

Veridical perception study results appear inconsistent with the notion that purported OBE perceptions are hallucinatory in nature. Addressing the frequent belief that such NDEs are illusory, B. Greyson noted that if NDEs are hallucinations, then "how come they are incredibly accurate and bring up verifiable information?"[71] Added support for veridical perception during an NDE was provided in a case documented by P. Lommel of a person in a coma on artificial respiration in the intensive care unit for more than a week.[72] Upon regaining consciousness he was able to describe accurate details in the emergency room and the procedure, including the "cart in which the nurse had put his dentures." In fact, the nurse corroborated his account. B. Greyson also documented a compelling case of a person who described events while reportedly out of the body during an NDE that was verified by others.[73] This incident involved a patient who described watching his surgeon "flapping his arms as if trying to fly."[74] Interestingly, the surgeon verified his report by explaining that he always flattens his hands against his chest while rapidly giving instructions by pointing with his elbows to avoid contaminating his hands before surgery.

Those reportedly met during an NDE are identified by their appearance and communicated with telepathically. Some NDEers also contend to have encountered others whose death was impossible to have known. An example of such an event was provided by P. Lommel of an individual who stated the following:

> During my cardiac arrest I had an extensive experience and later I saw, apart from my deceased grandmother, a man who had looked at me lovingly, but whom I did not know. More than 10 years later at my mother's deathbed, she confessed to me that I had been born out of an extramarital relationship. My father being a Jewish man who had been deported and killed during the Second World War, and my mother showed me his picture. The unknown man that I had seen more than 10 years before during my NDE turned out to be my biological father.[75]

One of the most compelling cases of veridical evidence in NDE research was reported by M. Sabom in one who reported an out-of-body perception while pronounced clinically dead for an hour. While connected to a machine to stop heartbeat and brain activity during a procedure to remove a life-threatening brain aneurysm, the patient reported remarkably detailed veridical perceptions that were later verified to be accurate.[76] According to Sabom, "This case is considered to be one of the strongest cases of veridical evidence in NDE research because of Pam's ability to describe in detail the unique surgical instruments used while she was dead, what the nurses said to the doctors while operating, and the procedures used. Pam had this spectacular ability to describe in detail these events while she was clinically brain dead."[77]

Compelling evidence of veridical perception come from individuals blind from birth who reportedly describe accurate visual perceptions during their NDEs. In a two-year study of NDEs in the blind, K. Ring and S. Cooper published their findings in a book entitled *Mindsight*, this being a term used to describe visual-like images that are similar between the blind and sighted.[78] This study documented twenty-one blind individuals who reported visually accurate information obtained during an NDE. Of these subjects, nine lost their sight after age five, two were severely visually impaired, and ten never experienced sight. In-depth interviews established that of the ten individuals blind from birth, five reported they were sighted during the experience. The other five had no sight or were unsure whether they had sight or not. Of the eleven adventitiously blind or severely visually impaired, all except one reported having normal vision during the NDE. Ten individuals of the total population also claimed to have seen their bodies after leaving them during their NDEs. Based on the collective results, the researchers concluded that the experiences of those who reported to have sight during the NDE were the same as normal sighted NDEers. This included feelings of separation from the physical body, journeys through a tunnel or dark space, feelings of peace and well-being, encounters with a bright light, and a life review.[79] Moreover, one blind woman whose optic nerve was destroyed at birth reported to have been able to see during her NDE in precisely the same way as sighted persons. Two individuals blind from birth also reported clear visions of both earthly and "paradise" environments during the NDE.[80] Based on these results, K. Ring concluded:

> Even if we cannot assert that the blind see in these experiences in any straightforward way, we still have to reckon with the fact that they nevertheless do have access to a kind of expanded supersensory awareness that may itself not be explicable by normal means.[81] In answer to our earlier question as to what these individuals experience, if not seeing, we submit that it is transcendental awareness, a distinctive state of consciousness and mode of knowing in its own right, which is operative in blind and sighted persons alike during their experiences and which now stands in need of explanation."[82]

Testimony of an NDE occurring in one subject with legal blindness is as follows: "Everything was very bright and sharp. I am legally blind without my glasses, but the nurse took my glasses off before they took me to the delivery room, but I could see clearly what the doctor was doing."[83]

A rare type of NDE which R. Moody termed the "shared death experience" (SDE) occurs when an NDE is shared by someone who is not dying, but is emotionally connected or in close proximity to someone who is concurrently in the "life/death transition."[84] Typically, the SDE occurs in one who is providing assistance to a confused individual who is dying through sudden and unexpected means. P. Sartori, for example, documented several cases where people present at the bedside of their dying loved one reported taking part in a "transcendent experience of a partial journey into death."[85] She also verified incidents where people miles away from their dying loved one became emotionally overwhelmed at the same time of their death.[86] According to leading NDE researcher P. M. H. Atwater: "What makes these so spectacular and challenging is that all or most of the experiencers see each other actually leave their bodies as it happens, then dialogue with each other and share messages and observations while still experiencing the near-death state. Their separate reports afterward either match or nearly so."[87]

While a SDE does not provide conclusive proof of the distinction between the brain and consciousness, it does provide compelling anecdotal evidence of a veridical perception, especially if more than two people are involved, and where there is significant distance between the individuals.[88] The acquisition of external, verifiable information about the physical surroundings, which defies logical explanation, requires corroboration from several independent large-scale research studies to assess the validity of veridical perception during an NDE.

Another type of NDE is evidenced by accounts of end-of-life dreams and visions (ELDVs). This experience, documented in a study of sixty-three hospice patients receiving end-of-life care, is manifested often by at least one vision per day (primarily through dreams) of a dying person's deceased friends and relatives before their death.[88a] The ELDVs were considered "distinct from hallucinations" by the researchers who concluded that, "the impact of pre-death experiences on dying individuals and their loved ones can be profoundly meaningful. . . . These visions can occur months, weeks, days, or hours before death and typically lessen fear of dying, making transition from life to death easier for those experiencing them." The researchers also noted that such dreams and visions, described by patients as "clear and vivid," facilitated "great comfort and reassurance" to the patient as opposed to the acutely disturbed state of mind often symptomatic of the dying process. The researchers reported that the content of the ELDVs was consistent in the following ways:

1. 46% featured deceased friends or relatives; 17% had living friends or relatives and 10% had other people; and
2. 35% had a variety of other content which included deceased pets or animals, living pets or animals, religious figures, past meaningful experiences, among other content.

Interestingly, the content of ELDVs may have a psycho-cultural component as evidenced by visions of deceased relatives in Americans and of religious figures in those from India.

Such experiences likely contribute to the fact that the vast majority of NDEers no longer fear death. They apparently come to a realization that, in some way, their consciousness and associated perceptions endure despite death. One such account is as follows: "It is outside my domain to discuss something that can only be proven by death. For me, however, the experience was decisive in convincing me that consciousness lives on beyond the grave. Death was not death, but another form of life."[72a]

Life-Changing Transformations

Anecdotal evidence of NDE-based life-changing behavioral and/or spiritual transformations represent a unique and paradoxical aspect of the NDE. These outcomes include an increase in the appreciation of life with a strong desire to live life to the fullest, self-worth, compassion towards others, and belief in life after death. Other positive outcomes reported by some NDEers is that they come back with healing ability, a better understanding of "universal order and purpose," and "paranormal gifts."[89] A decrease in materialism, competitiveness, and fear of death have also been noted.[90]

Nearly all people who have experienced an NDE lose their fear of death due to the realization that there is a continuation of consciousness after death. Decreases in death anxiety following an NDE, for example, have been reported in several studies (e.g., from sixty-three to zero percent, and from forty-five to zero percent).[91] One NDEer stated that, "It is outside my domain to discuss something that can only be proven by death. For me, however, the experience was decisive in convincing me that consciousness lives on beyond the grave. Death was not death, but another form of life."[92]

P. Lommel concluded in a study of the behavioral transformations in NDEers that, "patients with an NDE did not show any fear of death, they strongly believed in an afterlife, and their insight in what is important in life had changed: love and compassion for oneself, for others, and for nature."[93] In a longitudinal interview study of NDE survivors two and eight years following their cardiac arrest, and a matched control group of survivors of cardiac arrest who did not report an NDE, the NDEers "did not show any fear of death, strongly believed in an afterlife, and their insight in what is important in life had changed: love and compassion for oneself, for others, and for nature." According to the researchers, the NDE facilitated an understanding of "the cosmic law that everything one does to others will ultimately be returned to oneself: hatred and violence as well as love and compassion. Remarkably, there was often evidence of increased intuitive feelings. Furthermore, the long-lasting transformational effects of an experience that lasts only a few minutes was a surprising and unexpected finding."[93a] This conclusion was supported in one survey study that revealed that eighty-four percent of fifty-one NDEers who reported a fear of death before their NDE declined to only two percent after their experience.[94] Based on these results, it is not surprising that several studies have documented a dramatic increase in the belief in life after death resulting from an NDE (e.g., thirty-eight to one hundred percent, twenty-five to ninety-six percent, and twenty-two to ninety-two percent).[95] These findings were confirmed by cardiologist Michael Sabom, who reported that seventy-seven percent of sixty-one NDEers said their NDE increased their belief in life after death.[96] A similar estimate was also reported by K. Ring, (e.g., eighty-six percent of seventy-four NDEers developed an increase in their belief of life after death).[97]

In addition to the many reported positive outcomes resulting from an NDE, most people also report an "enhanced intuitive sensibility, like clairvoyance and clairaudience, or prognostic dreams, in which they dream about future events."[98] P. M. H. Atwater, who interviewed more than 3,000 NDEers, also concluded that more than fifty percent reported to have developed "healing hands" following their experience.[99] Similarly, K. Ring found that forty-two percent of more than 600 NDE subjects reported an increase in healing abilities.[100] These reported abilities, however, require confirmation by the scientific and medical community.

Despite the reported positive outcomes in NDEers, a pronounced adverse effect on family relationships has been curiously noted. B. Greyson, who reviewed the literature over the past thirty years on the behavioral effects of NDEs, concluded that NDEs typically produce "positive changes in attitudes, beliefs, and values, but may also lead to interpersonal and intrapsychic problems."[101] Family members, for example, have reported difficulty in accepting the NDEers expressions of love towards others, the perception of social connections in behavior as "silly," and the new interest in the paranormal. This is evidenced by a dramatic increase in the divorce rate, which range between seventy to ninety percent.[102]

The quantitative life-changing transformative evidence is further reinforced by the documented qualitative personal revelations resulting from an NDE as follows:[103]

a) "In this place, wherever it is, I did not have the limited consciousness I have on Earth. It felt like I had 125 senses to our normal five. You could do, think, comprehend, and so on, you name it, with no effort at all. It's as if the facts are right before you in plain sight with no risk of misinterpretation because the truth just is."

b) "I look at is as a psychological healing process. I feel that my NDE was the best thing that ever happened to me. Without my NDE I would not be happy today."

c) "After the NDE, value changes came. I felt that the materialism and external stuff that was a big focus before just didn't matter anymore. My priorities in life took a complete turnaround. I felt there was a purpose for my life."

d) "I'm trying very hard here on Earth, but I know where my true home is and how it feels. I remember it like it was today. I went directly to the Most Beautiful Golden Light. Real true love. So much peace, protection, calmness."

e) "The most prominent thing I felt after the NDE was a need to correct and change all of the things I did not like about myself. This memory of the life review sickened me. I continually saw myself and hated what I saw. It was the life review that sparked my desire for change and also allowed this change."

f) "This experience changed my life in many ways. For one, I am no longer the least bit afraid to die. I know that I would not want to suffer, but I know that the actual dying process is nothing like what I thought it would be, and that it was probably the most beautiful and peaceful experience I have ever had. I realize now that our time here is relatively short, and it makes me want to live my life to the fullest. The only things left after one leaves his or her body are energy, love, personality, and knowledge."

g) The founder of a one-year online education program (CreateU) became very motivated to develop this company after an NDE.[104] She commented that "something happened to me in that hospital room that I can't explain. Who I was before and who I am now are different. The things that used to matter now don't." Within two weeks after her NDE, she realized the need to help people achieve their career goals by developing CreateU.

Such NDE-based personal accounts about the meaning of life was supported in the NDERF study conducted by J. Long and colleagues.[105] In this study, fifty-eight percent of the approximate 400 people who had an NDE answered "yes" to the question: "During your experience, did you encounter any specific information/awareness regarding love?" According to Long, transformative experiences of a unique love—"a love that is total, unconditional, and enormous speak not just to what happens after we die, but to what matters while we live."[106] He noted the unique consistency of responses that "could not be explained by preexisting cultural or religious beliefs" in the following anecdotal statements:[107]

"No human can ever love with the love I felt in that light. It is all-consuming, all-forgiving. Nothing matches it. It is like the day you looked into the eyes of your child for the first time magnified a million times. It's indescribable."

"I felt the presence of pure love. This is very hard to describe. Everything made sense: God exists, God is love, we are love, and love creates all that is. . . . I was surrounded by pure love. First I was cold and in pain, but then I was warm and comforted."

"I know that love is all there is and that God loves all of His children deeply and equally. There are no stepchildren in the family of God. We are all divine."

"I came to realize that God is more loving and caring than I could ever imagine."

In a related study by K. Ring, similar behavioral transformations were found to have been facilitated in separate groups of subjects who reported to have had either an NDE or contact experience(s) with a so-called "unidentified flying object" (UFO).[107a] Quite surprisingly, both groups manifested an increase in social concern, spirituality, appreciation of life, self-worth, compassion towards others, telepathy, and belief in life after death. Interestingly, in a comprehensive quantitative and qualitative study conducted by the Dr. Edgar Mitchell Foundation for Research into Extraterrestrial and Extraordinary Encounters (FREE) on 3,234 individuals who reported to have had UFO related contact experiences with non-human intelligence (NHI), similar behavioral transformations to those documented in Ring's UFO-NDE study were also observed.[107b] More specifically, based on a diverse range of physical, psychological, perceptual, and anomalous aspects of both reported conscious and non-conscious based recall of their UFO-NHI contact experience(s), approximately three-quarters of this large sample population claimed to have incurred positive behavioral outcomes as a direct result of their inexplicable encounter (e.g., increase in self-acceptance, self-worth, compassion, ability to love others in an impersonal way, and/or sensitivity to the suffering of others, and belief in life after death, among others). Further, during their UFO experience, sixty percent reported that their "thoughts were sped up" (i.e., "faster than usual" or "incredibly fast"); eighty percent claimed that their senses were either "more vivid than usual" or "incredibly vivid"; fifty-eight percent claimed to have felt "separated from their body"; seventy-seven percent reported feelings of either "peace" or "pleasantness"; forty-one percent reported seeing a "light clearly of mystical or other worldly origin"; twenty-five percent saw a "deceased or religious spirit"; seventy-six percent maintained to have entered "some other, unearthly world"; seventy-seven percent stated that "time stopped or did not exist"; fifty-nine percent "felt one or united with the world"; and forty-one percent suddenly seemed to "understand everything about the universe."

Collectively, the similarity of reported psychological outcomes facilitated by an NDE/OBE and UFO encounter in the K. Ring study, and in UFO-NHI experiencers in the FREE study, obviously challenge theories in conventional physics and psychology. Clearly, many more questions than answers are generated by such study results. More specifically, can aspects of psycho-cultural influences, psychological aberrations (e.g., psychosis, dissociative experience, post-traumatic stress disorder, absorption and magical ideation, illusions, and an openness to unusual concepts), or something else that we cannot conceptualize nor explain using known scientific principles, facilitate the behavioral transformative attributes reported by contact experiencers? Consequently, it is important for there to be independent replication of such studies within the physical, behavioral, and social sciences to help determine the validity of the reported contact experience and associated behavioral outcomes facilitated by each different contact experience. The difficulty for researchers, however, is that one can't control for when such behavioral transformative experiences specifically occur. This makes studying them directly almost impossible since it is very difficult to conduct research (e.g., psychological and physiological) at a time when symptoms spontaneously emerge.

One explanation for the reported transformations is that the impact of the experience was due to its occurrence in a life-threatening situation rather than from the nature of the NDE itself. This perspective is supported by a study on the attitudes to life, death, and suicide in a group of people who had been in a life-threatening situation and had an NDE, and a control group of non-NDEers who did not have a life-threatening experience. The researchers concluded that the NDEers and nonNDEers actually changed in the same respects.[108] Alternatively, studies have shown that life-changing transformations are not as apparent in those close to death without having an NDE; that is, the NDE alone may be responsible for these reported effects.[108a] Consequently, the NDE, whether it is either a pure physiologic event or the separation of consciousness from the physical body, appears to have an intense positive and enduring impact on one's attitudes and values. Regardless of the underlying cause, however, the fact that many individuals exhibit such similar positive behavioral changes is a blessing to those transformed by their experience.

Theories

Explanations to account for the components of an NDE include physiological-, psychological-, consciousness-, and quantum physics-based theories.[109] The question whether the similar characteristics of NDEs are mediated by either one or more forms of cerebral dysfunction, or reflect the persistence of consciousness after the body's death, challenges mainstream science to identify the neural correlates that facilitate this cognitive event during severely compromised physiological states. Researchers also contend that OBEs can be induced by NDEs, sensory deprivation, dissociative states, psychedelic drugs, dehydration, and electrical stimulation of the brain, among others. Unfortunately, established scientific principles and associated experimental protocol are not ideally suited to objectively test theories pertaining to the nature of this phenomenon. Consequently, researchers must rely primarily on anecdotal accounts and indirect physiological measurement techniques to understand the foundation of the NDE. Despite the limitations associated with the reliability and validity of such techniques, most NDE-based research has attempted to test two overarching theories:

1. The survivalist theory—memories, self-identity, cognition, and emotions continue to function independently from the body.[110]
2. The naturalistic theory—the NDE represents hallucinations and depersonalization induced by changes in the neuroelectric and biochemical state of a dying brain.[111]

Not surprisingly, there exists a variety of explanations for the NDE. Support for the survivalist theory is found in several large-scale NDE studies, which have led researchers to conclude that medical explanations such as the chaotic activity of the dying brain or hallucinations related to medications or disturbances in bodily chemistry do not give rise to the NDE; that is, the NDE is meaningful and unlike the bizarre hallucinatory symptoms induced by drugs or psychosis.[112] In contrast, many interpret the commonly reported NDE features such as calmness, the sense of floating, looking down at one's body, and traveling in a tunnel, as symptoms of a coping mechanism facilitated by increased levels of endorphins due to oxygen deprivation in the brain (i.e., naturalist theory). This position is reinforced by those who experience a sense of detachment and a lack of emotional response during traumatic events who also undergo a similar effect.

A common skeptical perspective is that even when patients accurately report events that occur while their brain and heart are not functioning, there may not be a true separation of their consciousness from their body. Instead, the perceptual content is related to prior knowledge, false memories, and hallucinations generated by an abnormal functioning brain concomitant with the mind's attempt to "fill in the gap" after a period of cortical inactivity. A counter argument proposed by B. Greyson is that, "unless we have some reason to suspect that NDEers are highly suggestible and have some strong motivation to imagine having had their NDEs, it seems irrational to assume that all NDEs are false memories."[113] Support for Greyson's position is provided by anecdotal evidence represented by most NDEers who report their OBE to be realistic in the same way as perceptual experiences while awake and by some who consider it more real and vivid than waking consciousness.[114] Not surprisingly, many NDE researchers interpret this experience as evidence that consciousness survives bodily death.

The perplexing NDE accounts that include visits to Heaven and/or seeing angels and God may incorporate a combination of several contributing factors such as abnormal sensory input, oxygen deprivation, and endorphin-induced euphoria that may continue to create a surreal, yet realistic experience. Consequently, when the person recalls the NDE, the strange experiences may be interpreted as spirit beings, alternate realms of existence, and conversations with God and deceased relatives. The OBE in those who report the ability to see and hear events that their body shouldn't be able to perceive are more difficult to explain (i.e., veridical perception). However, even when pronounced "clinically dead," it may be possible for one to still experience sensory input and recall prior knowledge, which are incorporated into their NDE.[115] That is, they may not really be "dead."

The possibility that existing medical criteria for "death" may not accurately define "death" presents a confounding variable in NDE research and medical practice in general. This controversy, which serves as the primary argument against the validity of an NDE, implies that there may be no justification for declaring one clinically dead if the person subsequently can be resuscitated. After all, if one is resuscitated and has an NDE, some degree of neurologic activity must have been present despite being declared clinically dead. Accordingly, the NDEer may still be alive at the time of their experience. Many scientists, for instance, contend that despite the medically accepted clinical sign of death following a cardiac arrest (i.e., a flat-line EEG within ten to twenty seconds of the arrest), active brain function may still exist but is undetectable by EEG technology.[116] Consequently, one may still be conscious during an NDE despite being pronounced "clinically dead." Another explanation is that the NDE arises during the rapid transition from consciousness to unconsciousness and/or in the reverse process from unconsciousness to consciousness and not specifically during the period of clinical death. This argument, however, is countered by Lommel who contends that "experiences which occur during the recovery of consciousness are confusional" while NDEs are not.[117]

The controversy over the clinical criteria to define "death" is one reason why those in the medical and scientific community reject NDEs as compelling evidence to support the concept of life after death. In fact, B. Greyson emphasized that, "no one feature or type of NDE can decisively support the survival hypothesis since those reporting NDEs are alive and their bodies were still functioning sufficiently to be revived."[118] M. Sabom concurred that, "loss of biologic life, including death of the brain, is a process and does not occur at a single, definite moment."[119] Based on an analysis of several studies, which have indicated the persistence of brain or related physiological activity up to a week following the diagnosis of brain death, Sabom concluded that, "even when a person is deemed 'brain dead' by strict clinical criteria, brain activity can often still be demonstrated days later, raising the question of when, if at all, death had actually occurred."[120] These perspectives raise important questions about both the definition of death and the associated NDE. In other words, what does "near death" really mean if the definition of "death" itself is a topic of debate within the medical and scientific community?

The clinical death debate may be compounded by a rare resurrection called the Lazarus Phenomenon, represented by patients who appear to be clinically dead but sometimes spontaneously return to life.[121] Geriatrician V. Adhiyaman, who identified thirty-eight cases of this phenomenon in the medical literature reported that on average about a third of these patients recovered after being declared clinically dead. Reviews of the medical literature, however, have found only about seventy cases of this phenomenon since 1982.[122] Interestingly, a related genetic study on the organs of mice and zebrafish immediately after death led researchers to conclude that hundreds of genes with different functions (e.g., fetal development, cancer, etc.) "woke up" immediately after death and peaked about twenty-four hours later.[123] An important question, which emerges as an extension of this result, is that if human genes are also proven to be active up to one to two days after death then is the person technically still alive at that point? The many existing controversies surrounding "clinical death" may best be summarized by geneticist P. Noble who stated, "clearly, studying death will provide new information on the biology of life." Apparently, the definition of clinical death, an important variable in medical practice and associated NDE research, remains tenuous for several reasons.

Several proposed physiological and psychological theories and associated commentary and/or evidence to explain the NDE are as follows:

1. Temporal Lobe Paroxsym: Abnormal neural discharges in the temporal lobe or limbic system. Although a seizure or electrical stimulation of the temporal lobe may induce a memory and/or an OBE, it is still very different from the reported autobiographical "life review" associated with the NDE. Seizures and electrocortical stimulation of this brain region also do not elicit memories of communicating with deceased relatives and/or existing in a different environment reported by NDEers.

2. Cerebral Anoxia: A reduction in oxygen and increase in carbon dioxide in the brain. Anoxia, which can induce hallucinatory experiences and an impression of being located outside the body, has been suggested as a physiological basis to explain the NDE.[124] However, the reported bizarre imagery induced by anoxia is uncharacteristic of the NDE. This theory is also countered by an NDE study in cardiac patients in which higher oxygen levels were reported in those during an NDE than in a non-NDE control group.[125]

3. Neurochemical Release: Researchers have speculated that the NDE occurs from a sudden release of specific brain neurochemicals (e.g., endorphins or endopsychosins) that act on the limbic system and the temporal lobe, which cause an analgesic effect and sense of well-being. Since endorphins are not potent hallucinogens, however, it is difficult to understand how it may be

responsible for causing the unique complex perceptual content of NDEs. Other chemicals (serotonin, adrenaline, vasopressin, and glutamate) have also been implicated for the NDE, but their effects have not been demonstrated and are not supported by empirical evidence.[126]

4. Cortical Disinhibition: The reduction of normal control by the central nervous system serves to destroy the identification of the self within the physical body during life-threatening situations; that is, one's consciousness attempts to make sense of this extraordinary event. It is difficult to rationalize, however, why the "disinhibited brain" activates memories of deceased relatives and not those of living relatives, among other perceptual experiences associated with the NDE.

5. Ketamine: A neuroprotective agent that induces hallucinogenic and dissociative symptoms during stress, has been reported to be responsible for all the features of the NDE.[127] Ketamine, however, typically induce illusions that evoke fear, whereas most NDEers report their experience as pleasant and "realer than real." Accordingly, ketamine probably does not facilitate the NDE.

6. Depersonalization/Dissociation: A psychological detachment from one's body and/or confusion over the identity and reality of one's self. This psychological aberration has been considered more common among NDEers than in those close to death without NDEs in response to a perceived threat of death.[128] Researchers have also concluded that the pattern of dissociative symptoms reported by NDEers is consistent with a response to stress and not with a psychiatric disorder. Dissociation is likely not a cause though since individuals typically report that during their NDE their sense of self was strong and more real than in the normal waking state. Moreover, depersonalization differs from NDEs in its age and gender distribution, "unpleasant and dreamlike quality," and separation of the "observing self from the functioning self."[129]

7. Sleep Disorder: Sleep paralysis, which affects up to forty percent of people at some point in their lives, is characterized by sleep terrors, dissociative disorder, and sleepwalking, among others. It occurs when an individual is in rapid eye movement (REM) sleep but their brain awakens partially and paralyzes the body to prevent it from acting out dreams. Several researchers consider that sleep paralysis and hypnopompic (i.e., conscious state that precedes complete awakening from sleep) and hypnagogic (i.e., transitional state from wakefulness to sleep) dream states may pre-dispose one to have an NDE.[130]

An OBE has been implicated as a symptom of sleep paralysis since it occurs during the dissociated REM sleep state. One study reported seventeen such OBE cases associated with sleep paralysis in which the individuals viewed themselves lying in bed, generally from a location above the bed.[131] Another study, which concluded that an NDE arises from such sleep patterns due to abnormal temporal lobe activity, considers REM sleep-induced hallucinatory experiences to be similar to many features of an NDE.[132] In fact, REM intrusion patterns resulting from different arousal systems controlling the sleep-wake states were more often found in NDEers than in non-NDEers.[133] Consequently, OBEs represent an expression in both the NDE and sleep paralysis state, and that persons with NDEs appear to have an "arousal system predisposed to both REM intrusion and OBEs."[134] One study, for example, concluded that ninety-six percent of the NDE subjects having sleep paralysis also had an OBE either during sleep transition or near death.[135]

The possibility that the OBE is a symptom of sleep paralysis led researchers to measure the brain's blood flow using positron emission tomography scanning during REM sleep. The researchers reported a significant positive correlation between cerebral blood flow and REM sleep in structures in the limbic system that facilitate memory and the recollection of images.[136] Subsequently, the researchers concluded that the OBE may represent a disinhibition of the limbic system due to a loss of oxygen rather than the separation of consciousness from the body.[137]

8. Neurophysiological Model: Based on existing NDE theories, a neurophysiological sequence of events to explain the NDE may be represented as follows: sensory isolation causes one to feel detached from the body; endorphins are then released which evoke a sense of well-being; then as oxygen levels decrease in the brain, the compromised visual system somehow creates the illusion of a tunnel and lights, and temporal lobe seizures promote a life review. Scientists also attribute the tunnel effect, a common element in NDEs, to the neurological inactivity of the parts of the brain responsible for visual peripheral perception. This may result in the reported bright light surrounded by darkness, which generates the impression that one is traveling through a tunnel during an NDE.

    Another physiological explanation for the OBE involves an abnormality located where the temporal and parietal lobes meet in the brain (i.e., temporoparietal junction).[138] This region is thought to regulate self-perception as one component of consciousness. Based on a functional neuroimaging study to identify areas activated during an OBE, researchers concluded that this experience is due to the simultaneous activation of several structures in this brain region.[139] Interestingly, during an OBE self-perception is altered but global self-consciousness is retained. In contrast, during depersonalization both global self-consciousness and self-perception are retained but the person feels dissociated from their surroundings.[140] Consequently, the question as to whether an NDE or OBE is the result of increased activity in this and/or other brain regions or whether consciousness separates from the body under traumatic circumstances, remains unresolved.

9. Psycho-Cultural: The role of psychological factors in influencing one's susceptibility to NDEs has been the focus of much research. A questionnaire survey, for example, found that while NDEers were not more fantasy-prone than control subjects, they experienced greater sensitivity to non-ordinary realities as children, a higher incidence of child abuse and trauma, and scored higher on a measure of psychological dissociation. Some researchers have also considered that the reported observation of deceased relatives and a beautiful landscape during an NDE represent an illusion produced by expectations of

what will happen at death.[141] For example, in a cross-cultural study in NDEers from two different cultures, researchers who compared the deathbed experiences of 442 persons living in the USA with those of 435 individuals living in India found them to be significantly different.[142] This finding may explain why individuals seen during the reported NDE differ considerably among those with different socio-cultural backgrounds.

The NDE may represent memories of events that never happened or altered memories of real events.[143] Leading NDE researcher and parapsychologist S. Blackmore, for instance, considers NDEs to be imagined memories facilitated by both a physiological and psychological mechanism.[144] That is, the NDE itself is biologically determined as a symptom of the dying process, but the interpretation and details can be influenced by the experiencer's prior knowledge and beliefs, particularly in situations of physical or psychological threat. Blackmore also attributes the life review to a psychological defense mechanism during a life-threatening event that involves a "retreat into a timeless moment of pleasant, prior memories."[145] Alternative explanations such as wish-fulfillment and death-denial have also been advanced to explain the NDE. Other psycho-cultural-based NDE studies have also shown[146]:

1. No relationship between prior knowledge and the incidence of an NDE;
2. No evidence of psychopathology (e.g., psychoticism, hysterical tendencies, danger seeking, and general adaptation) in those who report an NDE; and
3. The absence of religious affiliation and religiosity influences on the probability or features of an NDE.

10. Psychotic Experiences: According to a 2015 World Health Organization (WHO) mental health survey from 31,261 adults who were asked about lifetime and twelve-month prevalence and frequency of six types of psychotic experiences (PE), i.e., two hallucinatory and four delusional; about one in twenty people in the general population has experienced at least one PE in their lifetime not associated with drugs, alcohol, or dreaming.[147] Thus, it is not atypical for one to exhibit either normal dissociative, imaginative states to more severe psychotic and schizophrenic mental states. About sixty-four percent of individuals with PEs also reported only one to five lifetime occurrences with hallucinatory experiences being more common than delusional experiences (5.2 percent vs. 1.3 percent).[148] The obvious question that emerges from these incidence statistics is the extent of influence and degree of PEs in those who report anomalous perceptual experiences such as an OBE/NDE. Thus, do individuals who appear sane fall higher on the schizotypy dimension, and are more likely to exhibit anomalous perceptual experiences (e.g., apparitions, mediumship, past-life recall, etc.)? Although the lifetime prevalence of PEs is rare (e.g., 5.8 percent), with nearly one-third of individuals who have PEs report only one event in their life, researchers must still control for this potential confounding variable in anomalous perceptual studies.

11. Gamma Brain Wave Activity: An interesting result from a recent physiologic study has been proposed to explain the nature of the reported realism of the NDE. Researchers, for instance, identified a brief increase of brain wave activity (i.e., gamma oscillations) that occurred within the first thirty seconds after cardiac arrest in anesthetized rats. The observation of this heightened cortical activity in the near-death state, which exceeded levels found during the conscious waking state, led study director and neuroscientist J. Borjigin to conclude that, "the reduction of oxygen or both oxygen and glucose during cardiac arrest can stimulate brain activity that is characteristic of conscious processing. It also provides the first scientific framework for the NDEs reported by many cardiac arrest survivors."[149] If valid, then increased brain activity might explain why people who say they had an NDE report that what they experienced seemed more real than the physical world.

The many physiological, psychological, and/or sociocultural theories proposed to explain the NDE remain unproven and require additional research to better understand their potential role in facilitating an NDE. Theories and associated evidence for NDEs are also highly controversial since doubt is raised about the NDEer's ability to think, reason, and recall actual experiences in their unconscious state. This controversy is further compounded by the unique problem attempting to conduct research to explain the foundation for the NDE. It is almost impossible, for example, to obtain empirical evidence since patients are unconscious during an NDE. Another key research question to resolve is that if the NDE is physiologically induced, then why is an NDE not reported by all who have been near death? The answer as to why some people have NDEs, while others do not, may provide the needed evidence to help explain the nature of the NDE.

Prospective studies on patients who have had a complete loss of brain function apparently report NDEs, despite the elimination of suspected physiological brain events and situations (e.g., induced by pharmacological agents, sleep disorder, neurochemical release, cortical disinhibition, epileptic discharges, and direct brain stimulation, etc.), which may contribute to the common features reported in an NDE. Even patients whose EEG have flat-lined report life-changing experiences. Moreover, studies on blind individuals who perceived visual images during NDEs support the notion of perception without a physiological substrate.[150] Neurophysiological processes, however, must have some role in NDEs since certain features of NDE-like experiences can be artificially induced in several ways. The most significant criticism of all psychophysiological theories to explain the features of the NDE is that it occurs during conditions of significantly altered brain function when one's consciousness is dramatically compromised. The NDE enigma is further compounded by the controversy pertaining to the definition of "clinical death," an important confounding variable in NDE research. Consequently, the many conflicting viewpoints and research evidence to explain and validate the NDE suggest that it is premature to assert that any proposed NDE theory either enhances or diminishes the possibility that the NDE provides compelling evidence of life after death.

Consciousness, Quantum Physics, and the Near-Death Experience

An obvious paradox associated with the nature of the NDE pertains to the reported sense of one's existence from outside one's body during a period of clinical death. After all, the accepted, although unconfirmed concept within mainstream science is that consciousness and memories are mediated by the brain which should not exist during clinical death. Despite this contradiction, during an NDE individuals allege to:

1. Possess knowledge of existence in another dimension without a body;
2. Perceive time as if the past, present, and future exist simultaneously and instantaneously (i.e., non-locality);
3. Be linked with the memories and consciousness of oneself and others, including deceased relatives (i.e., universal interconnectedness); and
4. Experience a loss of "universal wisdom and love" they had experienced during their NDE upon return to their body and wakeful consciousness.

Attempting to explain such incomprehensible experiences that are undeniably inconsistent with medical and scientific principles presents a unique and insurmountable challenge to say the least. Theories within quantum physics, however, have been advanced to possibly provide insight on the NDE and the means by which consciousness and memories interact with both the living and presumed dead during clinical death.

Quantum physics, which explains the nature and behavior of matter and energy on the subatomic level, tells us that there exists a wave aspect to our immortal consciousness in phase-space with non-local interconnectedness. This intangible concept, which has been extended to the indefinable concept of life after death, implies that one's consciousness is somehow converted from an aspect of particles to an eternal aspect of waves upon death. While the underlying scientific principles are both highly theoretical and complex, it does nevertheless attempt to explain the consciousness-brain relation and associated reported aspects of an NDE during clinical death. It remains a daunting task for NDE researchers, however, to adequately apply evidence to test such theories since those with an NDE are not dead, but are very close to death.

Several theories based on principles in both quantum physics and consciousness have been advanced to explain the NDE. These include the "Theory of Essence"[151], "Nonlocality Theory of Consciousness," "Quantum Theory of Consciousness"[152], and the "Holographic Theory of Consciousness"[153], among others. While the assumptions of these theories vary, they all agree that consciousness is the ground of all being, is non-local, and may function independently of the brain. If proven valid, then consciousness is not limited by spatial and temporal parameters, and may be capable of experiencing other realms of existence from a perspective independent of the brain. Accordingly, if consciousness is not confined to the brain nor a product of it, it may persist after bodily death.

Quantum physics supports elements found in NDEs. Similarities may be found between components of the NDE and quantum field concepts of non-locality, universal interconnectedness, and an alternate dimension beyond our time-space; that is, all events are related and influence each other instantaneously and in reciprocity, and only subjectivity remains. P. Lommel simplified this concept by stating, "as soon as the function of the brain has been lost, as in clinical death, memories and consciousness do still exist, but the receptivity is lost, the connection is interrupted."[154]

The quantum hologram theory (QHT) may provide the essential underlying principle to explain this quantum-consciousness concept. C. Hogan, a physicist and director of the Fermilab Center for Particle Astrophysics, generated interest in this theory when he discovered proof of a holographic universe in the data of a gravitational wave detector.[155] The QHT, which has potential important implications for explaining the NDE, addresses how at the quantum level, everything such as atoms, cells, plants, animals, and people are connected within a network of information. In other words, electrons in an atom in the human brain, which are connected to the subatomic particles in every other human brain and even with every star in the universe, may provide the foundation to explain how reality appears to be perceived not only as spatial but as a whole space-time during an NDE. Similarly, in a holographic universe the past, present, and future all exist simultaneously; a phenomenon documented in NDE research from the life review and the notions of a spatio-temporal time perspective. According to physician J. P. Jourdan, this concept may be supported by his proposed "hyperdimensional model" of the NDE experience, as represented in the following testimonies by eight NDEers[156]:

1. "Feeling that time no longer existed";
2. "In fact, there was no time, it was like a moment of eternity";
3. "Time did not exist. Now it's a real knowledge for me, time does not exist";
4. "On the other side, time does not exist. One truly realizes it. Time is a completely mental concept. A thousand years may be instantaneous";
5. "I had a horrible feeling of eternity. I had an experience where time no longer unfolded. Furthermore, no past, no future, just an eternal present. I had the feeling that all that was real, the feeling of 'living' in eternity";
6. "Past, present, future are merged in a single concept, that's what I experienced";
7. "The notion of time has nothing to do with ordinary life, that's for sure. Physical, material time does not exist. Time does not flow. To say that there is another 'time system,' I do not know,"; and
8. "Time is no longer linear. Your own life is in 3D and the fourth dimension is fully integrated. At that time, if I had watched a man, I could have known everything about him. His age, height, blood type, his siblings, the amount of all his taxes, his diseases. All in a single concept."

The unique similarity of such anecdotal reports suggest that consciousness could be the result of interactions between 4D and 5D phenomena and/or universes; a theory supported by many neuroscientists[157], cosmologists[158], and philosophers[159]. This paradox may best be explained by assuming that if we try to take apart something constructed holographically, we will only get smaller wholes instead of the pieces of which it is made. This "whole in every part" nature of a holographic universe may represent the mystical features reported in the NDE. According to physicist F. A. Wolf, for instance, NDEs can be explained using a holographic model where death represents a "shift" in consciousness from one dimension of the hologram to another[160] (i.e., atoms and subatomic particles can exist in two or more locations simultaneously). This abstract concept may be represented in the NDEers descriptions of "no time," "eternal present," and "being out of time," which indicate a form of time spatialization. Such an enigma may be further characterized by C. Ebert who described her husband's final words as follows:

> That week before Roger passed away, I would see him and he would talk about having visited this other place. I thought he was hallucinating. But the day before he passed away, he wrote me a note: "This is all an elaborate hoax." I asked him, "What's a hoax?" And he was talking about this world, this place. He said it was all an illusion. He wasn't visiting heaven, not the way we think of heaven. He described it as a vastness that you can't even imagine. It was a place where the past, present, and future were happening all at once.[161]

Additional anecdotal evidence to support the "holographic universe" concept may also be represented by a change in normal visual perception (i.e., single vantage point) reported by many NDEers who claim to:

a) be "everywhere at once";
b) have an "enlarged vision"; and
c) experience perception by transparency.

Seven individual accounts consistent with this type of perception are as follows[162]:

1. "I visited various places I managed to identify afterwards. I remember a window in a village, a building with very white plaster, sand-carved windows. My curiosity was attracted to details. This is quite important, since we cannot do this normally, like seeing inside and outside at the same time, an impression of a quasi-holographic vision. Not a panoramic view, but seeing in front, behind, all details simultaneously which is completely different from ordinary sight. It is very rich."
2. "I had a 360° spherical-like vision. I saw everything and had different points of observation: above, sideways, from the front, underneath, it was really extraordinary to see and be all of it at the same time. When I saw the sofa, the furniture, and the room in which I was, I was simultaneously above, sideways, from profile, facing forwards . . . it was very clear."

3. "Here you see this, then elsewhere you see something else, you know everything, from one place to another from the spot where you are. For example, if I want to go to the window, I have to move. But there you don't move, you're everywhere. Unbelievable, but it's great!"
4. "I could see everything at once, and if I focused on one thing, I could see this thing through any obstacle and in every detail, from its surface to how its atoms were organized, truly a global and detailed vision."
5. "I could see in front and behind oneself simultaneously, through objects, a holographic view."
6. "I felt like a soap bubble with eyes strolling about above at ceiling level, in a space which seemed a little 'closer' than real space. Behind a wall was a woman dying in the resuscitation room. I saw the instruments, the doctors' gestures and their conversation, I could see through the curtains which hung in front of the glass partition."
7. "I could see up close and also transparently. I remember seeing a stick of lipstick in one of the nurses' pockets. If I wanted to see inside the lamp which illuminated the room, I'd manage, and all of this instantly, as soon as I wanted to."

The possible connection between quantum physics and brain function was proposed by researchers who suggested that consciousness and quantum processing reside in the microtubules (i.e., fibrous, hollow rods that support and shape cells) of brain cell neurons.[163] Mathematical physicist R. Penrose explained the theoretical model of microtubule consciousness as follows:

Let's just say the heart stops beating and the blood stops flowing [during a NDE]. The quantum information within the microtubules is not destroyed, it can't be destroyed. It just distributes and dissipates to the universe at large. If the patient is resuscitated, revived, this quantum information can go back in the microtubules and the patient says, "I had a NDE…" If they're not revived, and the patient dies, it's possible this quantum information can exist outside the body, perhaps indefinitely as a soul. This account of consciousness explains things like near-death experiences and out-of-body experiences.[164]

Another quantum-based explanation for the NDE and OBE pertains to the possible existence of an infinite number of universes that comprises all reality. The "many-worlds interpretation" proposed by physicist Hugh Everett III is one of several hypotheses that ascribe to the concept that observations correspond to a different universe within a "multiverse."[165] This principle supports the theory of quantum immortality—an interpretation of quantum mechanics that theoretically allows one to have a continuous "infinity of minds in parallel universes where death doesn't exist."[166] The multiverse theory views reality as a branched tree in which every possible outcome of every event defines or exists in its own universe. This theory lends support to the common feature reported by NDEers of visions of possible futures should he/she decide to remain in the other realm or return to life. One representative example is provided in the NDE testimony of K. Schaeffer as follows:

In a fit of fear and panic I began crying. No, I couldn't be dead. What would happen to my son? In an embrace of love, they calmed me by showing me that my son, my entire family would be okay after my death. My mother could lean on my grandmother. It would take time, but she would heal. My husband, hurt, sad, and lonely would also heal and eventually find love once again. I was shown my funeral. But wait, my son. I couldn't leave my son. I was told others would be a mother for me. First grandparents, and then they showed me Jake's life. I saw a new mom for Jake when he was about 7 or 8. I couldn't let go of my human life. Finally, my hysteria was calmed by a higher spirit who seemed to envelop me in love. My guides were instructed to allow me to return."[167]

Other similar perspectives advanced to help support the validity of the NDE-based quantum-consciousness connection are as follows: According to neurosurgeon E. Alexander:

"the reductive materialist (physicalist) model, on which conventional science is based, is fundamentally flawed. At its core, it intentionally ignores what I believe is the foundation of all existence—the nature of consciousness. From their [Albert Einstein, Neils Bohr, and Erwin Schrodinger] experiments one could infer that consciousness has a definite role in creating reality. I believe that the core of that mystery is that consciousness itself is deeply rooted in quantum processes.[168]

The similarity of NDE study results and associated conclusions led P. Lommel to postulate that, "There are good reasons to assume that our consciousness, with the continuous experience of self, does not always coincide with the functioning of our brain: enhanced or non-local consciousness, with unaltered self-identity, apparently can be experienced independently from the lifeless body. People are convinced that the self they experienced during their NDE is a reality and not an illusion."[169]

A fundamental, yet seemingly elusive question, is whether quantum theory validates the independent distinction of consciousness and the brain, non-local consciousness, and the concept of a universal consciousness that is free of time and space. Such underlying quantum principles may in fact provide the conceptual framework for understanding the NDE/OBE and life after death. Despite the reported characteristics of the NDE, which seem analogous to these principles, the over-arching issue is to explain how consciousness may be experienced independently of the body during the loss of all brain activity. That is, is our consciousness itself a non-local phenomenon? Unfortunately, the answers will likely remain tenuous at best since explaining the NDE and associated concept of life after death in terms of quantum physics appears incomprehensible using an objective, testable framework. This major limitation is further compounded by the fact that mainstream science, which equates consciousness with the brain, does not regard the NDE as evidence of life after death.

Discussion

It is a daunting scientific challenge to explain the often-reported interconnectedness with the consciousness of other persons and of deceased relatives, and the profound transformative changes in one's core beliefs as facilitated by the NDE. This mystical experience, which certainly contradicts established scientific principles, seems conceptually implausible. Yet, scientists continue to debate the meaning of anecdotal NDE testimony. The majority of NDE researchers, for instance, contend that consciousness, memory, and perception can still function despite one being declared clinically dead. But considering that during an NDE the brain is not "dead" since their brain functions normally afterwards, it must have been functioning in some minimal undetectable capacity during the experience. Despite this reasonable assumption, however, many researchers are convinced that the NDE represents duality between the physical brain and consciousness itself.

The NDE's inconsistency with accepted scientific principles, and the absence of irrefutable proof that it signifies the dissociation between consciousness and the brain, may lead one to dismiss it as strong evidence to justify life after death. And given that science does not even have a widely accepted theory to explain consciousness, most scholars are reluctant to even accept, let alone investigate the phenomenon. Nevertheless, the NDE phenomenon, which has challenged current scientific theories of the brain, consciousness, and associated psychological considerations, has stimulated research to better understand how consciousness, memory, and perception occur under conditions in which current physiological models deem it improbable. And if out-of-body perceptions are in fact veridical representations of external reality beyond sensory involvement, such evidence may contribute significantly towards understanding consciousness and its relation to the brain, and the possibility of even life after death.

Despite the controversial NDE research evidence, the reported persistence of complex cognitive processes in those with severely compromised brain function implies that consciousness might not be dependent on the brain; a required condition to support the survival hypothesis. And although many researchers have speculated about possible physiological and psychological mechanisms responsible for the NDE, no evidence exists to conclusively explain what governs and regulates this phenomenon. It is not even clearly understood what physiological conditions are minimally required for cognitive functioning, sensory perception, and memory, let alone how the brain facilitates consciousness and associated attributes of one's sense of self, intuition, and abstract thought.[170]

Despite the anecdotal descriptions provided by NDEers of a strangely profound occurrence that defies logical explanation, the NDE evidence, considered by many researchers as support for the possibility of life after death, provides no conclusive justification for the continuation of consciousness after the death of the body. And regrettably, scientific methodology to better understand the NDE is limited since many aspects of the incident cannot be appropriately tested; more specifically, no analysis can be performed to determine if someone actually visited Heaven or met deceased relatives while at the brink of death. Despite this research obstacle, among others noted prior, it is essential that researchers focus on both the psychological and physiological aspects of the NDE as a fundamental component of any endeavor to better understand this phenomenon. Clearly, appropriate experimental protocols must be further developed and applied to those who experience an NDE to determine the possible nature which governs and regulates this intriguing phenomenon. The associated outcomes may eventually have potential significant implications on both an individual and societal level.

CHAPTER FOUR

APPARITIONS

Introduction

A sensory experience of a person who is not physically present, who has died, and who is reportedly able to physically materialize is termed an "apparition." An apparitional figure is generally considered to be a form of energy referred to as a ghost, spirit, soul, or consciousness of someone who either does not realize one's death, or is strongly emotionally connected to their prior earthly existence.[1] Apparitions, which have been represented in stories from the Bible to present day as ghosts, angels, and even the Virgin Mary, have been advanced as evidence to support the possibility of the continuity of consciousness after death. This notion is supported by anecdotal apparitional experiences and by mediums who claim to be able to communicate with the deceased "trapped" in our dimension to persuade them to accept their death and move "toward the light" to enter an alternate realm.

Many people believe in ghosts because of either a personal experience, for a sense of comfort that our deceased loved ones exist, and/or for religious/cultural reasons. Collectively, these factors contribute to the high incidence in the belief of ghosts among the general population. A 2005 Gallup poll, for example, found that thirty-seven percent of Americans believe in haunted houses[2], and according to a 2013 HuffPost/YouGov poll, forty-five percent believe in ghosts[3]. Several surveys during the past century in Great Britain[4] and the United States[5] have also reported that between ten to twenty-seven percent of the general population believe they have had a sensory perception of an apparition, and about fifty percent of those who lost a spouse report a form of contact with him/her.[6]

The Phenomenology of Apparitions

Collectively, survey- and interview-based studies have contributed to a better understanding of the phenomenology of apparitions. This includes the following commonly reported characteristics and observed experiences:

- The apparition appears real, solid, may cast a shadow, occlude objects, and be perceived in a mirror.[7]
- It is unusual for an apparition to communicate with the observer, and any communication usually contains just a few words.[8]
- The vast majority (about eighty percent) of experiences are visual.[9a] Less frequently, other sensations and/or a "felt presence" are reported.[9]
- The apparitional experience is of very short duration, typically lasting less than a few minutes.[10]
- An apparitional experience is relatively common. The incidence of the observation of an apparition ranges from about ten to thirty percent.[11]
- Approximately twenty-five percent of apparitional experiences are witnessed by more than one person at the same time.[12]

- In group experiences, all members may not perceive the apparition. About sixty percent of cases are not collectively experienced.[13]
- The apparition's appearance changes as one observes it from different angles.[14]
- The apparition's head may turn to follow one's movements.[15]
- The apparition has been reported to leave through a door and make appropriate noises (e.g., clothing, walking).[16]
- The apparition often materializes and dematerializes instantly, and no physical evidence is manifested other than photographs.[17]
- About seventy percent of apparitions are those the experiencer knew to be dead and about ten percent have reported an apparition of a living person.[18]
- A study of 337 experiencers who reported encounters with the dead found that twenty-eight percent of the apparitions were of people who died violently, twenty-nine percent occurred suddenly but naturally, and about two-thirds were male.[19]
- Recurrent apparitions who perform the same activities in the same location on each occasion tend to have a friend or relative as the experiencer.[20]

Psychologist A. Gauld studied the characteristics of 172 apparition cases to determine if there was a higher frequency of features indicating intelligence and intention than cases without apparitions. The apparition cases were characterized by a higher number of phenomena and by better-quality scores on scales of detail and testimony. A higher frequency in the apparition group of reports of doors or windows opening or shutting, and hands seen or felt were also noted. These results led Gauld to conclude that hauntings may be modified by their apparitional content.[21]

Theories

Theories to explain the nature of this phenomena vary widely. Some of the phenomenological characteristics of apparitions suggest they are physical, although other features indicate a possible subjective or psychic explanation. Apparitions may be considered physical since they are reported to hide objects, form shadows, make noise, produce a reflection, and are sometimes experienced by more than one person. A psychological and/or psychic rationale, on the other hand, is supported by testimony that objects perceived to move do not, there is no remaining physical evidence, and that during a group experience only some may perceive them. Alternative explanations proposed for the "sensed presence" and apparitional experiences include atmospheric or geomagnetic activity, and altered perceptions and states of consciousness induced by neurological changes in the brain caused by stress, and/or oxygen deprivation. One commonly held apparitional theory is represented by psychologist J. Assante who stated that, "Ghosts are not all there, literally speaking. A ghost is only a portion of the core self. It is an electromagnetic imprint created by a human and is perceptible (to some) under certain atmospheric and emotional conditions."[22]

Theories proposed to explain the nature of various types of apparitional experiences include the following:

- *Super-Psi*: The Super-Psi theory considers that all supposed contact with the deceased is explained in terms of telepathy or clairvoyance from living people. In other words, projections of telepathically acquired information enables the experiencer to acquire extrasensory information and to then induce the apparitional experience in others.[23] Physicist R. Johnson explained this theory as a "psychic aether" that acts as a link between consciousness and matter. A medium is also alleged to use this ability to obtain information and present it as evidence of the appropriate deceased person to others. Consequently, the survival hypothesis is contradicted by proponents of this theory.[24]

Evidence to support this theory was generated from an extrasensory perception (ESP)-based experimental study that analyzed psychics' perception of apparitional activity in alleged haunted homes.[25] The researchers prepared a documented list of what "ghosts" were doing in specific locations where observed. Psychics were then invited to the homes and asked to identify "correct" actions and locations from a list that contained both true and false randomly listed items. The researchers found that some psychics were able to accurately identify, to a "highly significant degree," the "ghosts" location and activity, whereas, a control group of skeptics scored uniformly at chance on this task. This result suggests that the psychics may have succeeded by using ESP.[26] The question remains, however, as to whether this outcome confirms the "ghosts" existence as a valid form of measurable energy.

- *Psychokinesis*: One theory that has gained some support among parapsychologists is that poltergeist activity (i.e., physical disturbances) results from psychokinesis (PK), an alleged psychic ability that has an effect on a physical system without physical interaction. Despite the lack of empirical support, one common explanation for PK is that emitted electromagnetic energy in the brain may somehow interact with electromagnetic energy in the environment leading to spontaneous poltergeist events.[27] However, while energy from a living person may explain the poltergeist phenomenon, it does not account for the many phenomenological features of the apparitional experience.[28]

- *Neurological*: A physiologic-based theory to explain the apparitional experience is that it represents a symptom induced by neurological alteration in the brain caused by complex geomagnetic activity. This concept evolved from experiments that demonstrated that the "sensed presence" of a "being" can be reliably evoked by weak magnetic fields applied across the temporoparietal region of the brain's two hemispheres.[29] This outcome, combined with the finding of existing strong magnetic fields in reported haunted environments[30], have led researchers to conclude that neurological factors, and not the subjects' beliefs or suggestibility, are responsible for facilitating this experience.[31]

The neurological theory has gained support from evidence demonstrating that a person can be induced into sensing a "presence." This outcome was achieved in an experiment that allowed the subject's finger to control a robot's mechanical arm that was positioned behind them to enable it to touch their backs.[32] Mysteriously, when back-touching and finger movements occurred a half-second apart, the subjects actually reported seeing several "ghosts" positioned around them and even believed they were touching their backs. This behavioral effect suggests that a "sensed presence" can be artificially induced using a technique that alters one's perception. However, attempts to reproduce the apparitional experience using various experimental protocol have been criticized for their inability to faithfully duplicate the actual perceived apparitional experience. Consequently, it would seem necessary to include experiencers as experimental subjects to evaluate the similarities and differences between the evoked "sensed presence" and the nature of their "real" apparitional experience. This analysis may help to better understand the relationship between each phenomenon and their associated implications.

Another neurological based explanation for an induced "sensed presence" is associated with acoustic energy. This theory is based on the detection of infrasound (i.e., sound with a frequency below 20 Hertz) in environments where presences were reported.[33] However, since this perception was more often described as feelings rather than visual sightings, infrasound may explain only a small percentage of apparitional experiences. An apparitional experience has also been theorized as an illusion created by the mind.[34] Support for this concept is based on studies that concluded that experiences of "supernatural" phenomena are most likely to occur in threatening or ambiguous environments.[35] For example, a sensed presence, possibly facilitated by stress as a coping mechanism to help one manage a hazardous situation, has been reported by explorers who felt as if someone was following them on their expeditions.[36] Interestingly, evolutionary psychologists have proposed that such experiences may be triggered by a type of innate detection mechanism developed to protect us from predators.

- *Consciousness*: A consciousness-based theory for apparitions has been proposed from reported observations of "ghosts" of living persons.[37] Sociologist H. Hart, for example, analyzed the reported characteristics of apparitions in the literature and concluded that apparitions of the living are identical to those of the dead.[38] Interestingly, in eighty-two percent of cases of apparitions of the living, these living people either reported having an out-of-body experience or had been focusing their attention on the experiencer, often with the idea of "going to him or her."[39] Since apparitions of the living are phenomenologically similar to apparitions of the dead, and in some instances show evidence of intention, Hart attributed the influence of consciousness by the surviving personality in at least some apparitions of the dead. He also advanced the concept of "persona," which represents a combination of activity of the surviving person (i.e., the agent) and the living person's memories of the agent when alive. That is, if apparitions of the living represent a form of conscious-like energy that may be projected from that individual to the experiencer, then by default, some apparitions of the dead may also consist of this same energy.

- *Psychological*: The skeptical interpretation of apparitional experiences is that the image is not physical and its perception is not associated with ESP from the living. Rather, it reflects one of many psychological-based possibilities, such as the experiencer's suggestibility, untruthfulness, misinterpretation of their perception, exaggeration of incidents that have a rational explanation, psychotic induced hallucinations,[40] or hallucinations that occur at the transition from wakefulness to sleep (i.e., hypnagogic imagery)[41]. Our innate tendency to recognize patterns in random perceptions (i.e., pareidolia) may also cause people to misinterpret visual and auditory input to believe they have "seen ghosts."[42] In other words, apparitional encounters are simply subjective methods of interpreting information that do not actually have a basis in physical reality.

A possible psycho-cultural explanation has been supported in a study that revealed that religious apparitions were greater among individuals from India than the United States; that is, Christians saw Jesus or angels, and Hindus saw their god of death or his messengers. According to psychologist C. Brandon: "When the dying are passing, they are visited by those who will comfort them during their travel to the other side. For a dying Christian, that might mean Jesus; a Buddhist may see Buddha. For others, an angel, a beautiful woman, or Druid priest would bring more comfort."[43]

A few studies have evaluated the psychological profile of experiencers to determine the potential influence of behavior as a predisposing factor for sensing an apparition with conflicting outcomes. One study, for example, concluded that apparitional experiencers did not differ significantly from the general population on measures of psychoticism, neuroticism, and extraversion.[44] In a study of adults grieving over a recent death, however, those who reported an apparitional experience of the deceased were found to be more "neurotic and extraverted" than non-experiencers.[45] Additionally, several studies demonstrated that apparitional experiencers were highly inclined to manifest fantasy-proneness—a personality trait characterized by difficulty differentiating between fantasy and reality.[46] Interestingly, the most important characteristic of those who have apparitional experiences is a prior belief in ghosts and hope they are present. Psychological factors, however, do not account for the same apparition to be experienced simultaneously by more than one person nor by characteristics associated with apparitional phenomenology.

- *Alternative Perspectives*: The phenomenology of apparitional experiences has been described and investigated for their reliability by the Society for Psychical Research (SPR).[47] This included cases where the apparition communicated information of which: 1) the experiencer was unaware, 2) occurred with an unexpected event involving the experiencer, and 3) the apparition was interested in fulfilling some goal that had consumed them in life.[48] Such cases, however, have led some SPR investigators to debate their validity. Paranormal researcher F. Myers, for example, who concluded that apparitions represent the "manifestation of persistent personal energy," was criticized by SPR's skeptic F. Podmore who believed that most post-mortem apparitional accounts were either fraudulent or created by the experiencer's mind, possibly in response to the reception of psychic information.[49]

One commonly held perspective pertaining to the validity of apparitions was expressed by senior research fellow of the Committee for Skeptical Inquiry J. Nickell, who wrote, "There was no credible scientific evidence that any location was inhabited by spirits of the dead. Limitations of human perception and ordinary physical explanations can account for ghost sightings; for example, air pressure changes in a home causing doors to slam, or lights from a passing car reflected through a window at night."[50] Based on interviews with experiencers, Fellow of the British Psychology Society D. Fontanna countered Nickell's viewpoint by stating that, "They claim not to be subject to hallucinations, deny they had any 'emotional need' to see the apparition at the time, and regard the idea that they were projecting outward memories received telepathically from him or her while they were alive as impossibly far-fetched."[51]

An explanation based on the psychological status of the deceased was advanced by psychologist I. Stevenson. He considered the high incidence of apparitional experiences in those whose deaths were "sudden" as being due to the fact that the "suddenness of death increases motivation on the part of the agents to communicate the desperate situation in which they find themselves to persons they think likely to be interested."[52]

In the final analysis, although there remains a lack of convincing apparitional-based evidence to support the survival hypothesis, it is still premature to firmly accept or reject any theory to explain this phenomenon. Nevertheless, there may be an element of truth in one or more of the many theories advanced to account for apparition and poltergeist type events.

Apparitional Experiences

Research approaches designed to document the validity of an apparitional experience include case collections, surveys, and the application of instrumentation techniques (e.g., Geiger counters, electromagnetic field and ion detectors, infrared cameras, and audio recording devices). If apparitions exist as physical energy one would expect objective, tangible evidence to support their presence, but no such unequivocal evidence exists to do so. Consequently, numerous anecdotal and experimental studies on the nature and validity of apparitional experiences have served as a source of considerable controversy.

Apparitions have been traditionally categorized by the nature and type of sighting experienced. These include collective, crisis, postmortem, reciprocal, and poltergeist cases as follows:

- *Collective Sightings*: Cases where more than one person reports the same apparition simultaneously are not uncommon. One study reported identifying more than 120 cases in the literature in which apparitions were perceived by two or more people.[53] Although skeptics generally attribute such accounts to mass hallucinations, the simultaneous experience by multiple witnesses of the deceased lend some validity to the phenomenon. One such shared encounter by a women named Lois is as follows:

  Two days after the death of her husband, Ray, Lois just happened to pass by her bedroom where she saw her son, Jesse, sitting on the side of her bed. He was eight at the time and was unable to deal with his father's death. Right next to him was Ray, who had his arm around his son and was talking to him in a calm voice. Ray looked up and smiled at his wife, then gestured for her to go away. She moved off to give them privacy, and after a fifteen-minute wait, Jesse came out to tell her what his father had said: "Daddy told me that he has gone and won't be coming back and not to worry about him. Everything will be all right." This event marked the boy's turning point for healing.[54]

One study of collective sightings found that among "46 cases in which more than one person was in a position to be a percipient, 26 (56 percent) were reported as collective."[55] A similar result was noted by researchers who reported that when two or more persons are present at the time an apparition is perceived, two or more persons perceive it in two-thirds of such cases.[56]

- *Crisis Sightings*: This type of sighting is represented by one who reports a life-like apparition of a friend or relative at a time the person was dying or in a serious accident. During this incident, which tends to occur less than twelve hours before or after the crisis, the person experiencing the apparition is unaware of this event. What is especially intriguing is that at the time of the sighting, the experiencer often is not thinking of the dying person, and the apparition is perceived as a real person.[57] An example of a documented crisis sighting investigated by the SPR of a women who was unaware that her brother was killed during World War II is represented as follows:

  On the day of the incident, she had a strong feeling to turn around; on doing so she was amazed to see her brother. Assuming that he had been visiting, she placed her child in bed, and then went to greet her brother only to find him not there. When no trace of her brother was found, she suspected he was dead. Surprisingly, the loss of her brother in combat on the same day she saw his apparition was confirmed weeks later.[58]

- *Postmortem*: The postmortem sighting involves an apparition of a person who has been dead for at least twelve hours. Several studies have revealed that about two-thirds of recognized apparitions are deceased and that a common feature of such cases involves the attempt by the apparition to communicate specific information that is unknown to the experiencer.[59] One popularized postmortem incident is the "Chaffin will" case as follows:

> In 1905, J. Chaffin made a will leaving his estate to his third son, Marshall, of which his family disapproved. In 1919, he modified the will to divide the estate equally among his four sons, with the condition they care for their mother. The new will, of which the family was unaware, was placed in a Bible, and a memo identifying the will's location was sewn inside his coat. When Chaffin died a few years later, Marshall obtained probate of the original will. Several years after his death another son, James Chaffin, experienced an apparition of his father wearing the coat in a dream who said, "You will find my will in my overcoat pocket." Intrigued by this experience, James searched for the coat and learned that it had been given to his brother, John. Upon finding the coat, James found the message revealing the will's location and the Bible containing the will. This will, which was submitted to probate, was claimed to be in J. Chaffin's handwriting by ten witnesses.[60]

Beyond the possibility of fraud, the most plausible explanation for the "Chaffin will" case is that the second son, James, had somehow learned from his father about the second will and that he had forgotten about it until the memory was recovered in a dream. Another possible explanation is that James Chaffin learned of the existence and location of the will by "reading" what was written on the paper in the overcoat pocket, a task requiring ESP. For unknown reasons, he may have considered the information as though it was coming from his late father. Certainly, an alternative explanation is that J. Chaffin actually communicated with James from another realm of existence.

A postmortem case from a woman whose word according to psychologist H. Irwin, "I have no reason to doubt" is as follows:

> When I was a teenager, one of my friends, a young girl, was diagnosed with cancer. She lost her arm, but the operation did not stop the spread of the disease, and she died shortly afterwards. In life, she had always been particularly close to my brother, and one day when I entered his room shortly after her death, I saw her sitting there in the chair she always occupied when she came to see him. She and I talked together for some time—just about ordinary things, very matter-of-fact.[61]

Another example from an individual considered to be "very objective and clear-headed" by Irwin is presented as follows:

> I was on a residential yoga retreat with a group of other members of our yoga group, and one day when we were taking a walk in single file and in silence through the woods, Brian, one of the founder members of our group who had

recently died, was suddenly walking next to me. He was as tall as in life, a big smile on his face, but not quite solid. I would describe him as semi-transparent. He placed his left hand on my shoulder and we walked together through the woods. I was struck by the fact that he still had the two deformed fingers on his hand that were a birth defect, and I said to him, "Oh, Brian, I thought we were mended when we get to heaven." We walked together for about a minute and then he disappeared just before I left the woods. Later I realized that he materialized with the two deformed fingers as clear proof of identity.[62]

One documented postmortem case, considered as genuine by the SPR, is that of S. Bull who died in a cottage with eight other family members.[63] Several months following his death, many children became nervous, believing someone was outside. Eventually, a reported solid apparition of Bull walked into his widow's bedroom, stood by the bed, and placed his hand on her forehead, which she reported as feeling firm but cold.

In this next example, G. Jonas, a caretaker of the Yorkshire Museum in York, UK, reported that he and his wife both heard footsteps above their basement kitchen. Upon going up to investigate, he saw an elderly man leaving the museum director's office. Jonas, who assumed him to be an eccentric professor, asked him if he was looking for the director. According to Jonas:

He did not answer but just shuffled past me and began to go down the stairs towards the library. Being only a few feet from him, I saw his face clearly. He looked agitated, had a frown on his face, and kept muttering, "I must find it, I must find it." He looked just as real as you or me. He was standing between two tall book racks. He seemed anxious to find something. I stretched out my right hand to touch him on the shoulder. But as my hand drew near his coat he vanished.[64]

A highly credible witness, Dr. James of the German Max-Planck Society, reported the following postmortem sighting in his college dormitory room:

I awoke one night, and in the twilight was able to see a young man with curly black hair. I was terrified and told the alleged neighbor that he had the wrong room. He simply cried and looked at me with great sadness in his eyes. When I turned on the light, the apparition had disappeared. Since I was one hundred percent sure it had not been a dream, I told the housemaster about the strange encounter the next morning. I gave her a detailed description of the young man. She suddenly paled. She looked through the archives and showed me a photo. I immediately recognized the young man who had visited me in my room the evening before. When I asked her who he was, she replied with a quivering voice that it was the previous renter. She then added that my room had become available because he had taken his life shortly before.[65]

In some postmortem cases apparitions warn loved ones of danger. In one such incident, E. Worrell saw a man in her building hallway who led her downstairs into the apartment of a widow she did not know. She found the person unconscious on a bed after a suicide attempt. After she recovered, the woman showed her a photograph of her late husband who she recognized as the man who led her downstairs into the apartment.[66]

Postmortem apparition cases have also been reported to involve a person who has recently died appearing to loved ones to announce his or her death. In many such cases, the death was unexpected and later confirmed to have occurred immediately before the apparitional experience. One of several confirmed cases is that of L. Poynter who was killed in combat. On the day of his death he appeared to his sister who reported that he walked into her bedroom, bent over and kissed her, and then smiling happily, suddenly vanished. It was not until two weeks later that the family was informed of his death on the same date prior to his sister's experience of his presence.[67] A similar case is that of G. Watson who was awakened by someone calling her name. Upon wakening, she saw her paternal grandfather who told her, "Don't be frightened. It's only me. I've just died." When she told her husband, he telephoned the family and learned that he died unexpectedly just before his wife's experience.[68]

An intriguing anecdotal account of one of many encounters with apparitions was depicted by psychologist J. Assante:

> Many entities are indescribably beautiful; others, not much more than a speck of light. It crossed my bedroom one night when I was half asleep; a stocky golden entity carved out of pure, solid love, a love so powerful, certain, and condensed, so compacted, there was no room for the more vulnerable aspects of human love, like compassion. An entity of this caliber is so far beyond human capacity that we cannot really form a conception of it, let alone describe it.[69]

- *Reciprocal*: One curious type of sighting is termed "reciprocal apparition." In this case, during an OBE or dream of being in another location, a person at that location sees an apparition of that person; that is, the apparition is a living person who afterwards recalls seeing the experiencer in the location where the event occurred. Interestingly, in reciprocal cases, the agent often has a strong desire to "go to" the percipient at the time of the apparition. Numerous reciprocal apparition cases have been documented[70], one of which was provided by physician L. Dossey:

> A nurse became friends with a quadriplegic man who required several hospitalizations for pneumonia and other complications. During one of these hospitalizations, the nurse, feeling guilty that she had not recently visited this patient, had a dream in which she seemed to go to him in the hospital, stood at the end of his bed, and told him to keep fighting. Shortly afterward, the patient's sister told this nurse that he had reported seeing her standing at the foot of his bed, telling him to keep fighting.[71]

- *Poltergeist*: An alleged type of entity responsible for physical disturbances is termed a poltergeist. One well-documented poltergeist case consisted of reports by thirty individuals of more than 2,000 mysterious incidents that included throwing household items, chairs being smashed, and unexplained fires.[72] Another authenticated case verified by the police occurred at the home of B. Wilson who reported consistent poltergeist activity. Curiously, the police witnessed a kitchen cabinet floating in the air without any means of support.[73] Further, paranormal investigator R. Sprague provided an account of one of the many poltergeist experiences by workers at the Belasco Theatre in New York City. He wrote:

> It was my first night working in this particular theater, and I'd heard many stories concerning strange noises, smells, sights, and feelings. But nothing quite like this. The usher would go on to tell me that every night, this usher would be the "closer." She'd make sure the entire theater was empty of patrons and employees, she'd shut off all the lights, and she'd lock up all the doors. Upon leaving, she would always say goodnight to the original owner of the theater, Mr. David Belasco. Though one night would prove unusual as she completely forgot to do so. She locked the last remaining door and turned to leave. Suddenly, every single door of the front lobby forcefully swung open. The usher stared in disbelief as she knew full-well she'd locked them all. There simply was no apparent reasoning for the doors to have done what they did. Completely in shock, the usher reported what had happened to the police, and asked for a theater transfer the following morning, never to return.[74]

The "collective" and "postmortem" apparition case sightings, which lend some support to the survival hypothesis, tend to occur less frequently than the "reciprocal" and "crisis" sightings that are suggestive of telepathy between living persons. According to I. Stevenson:

> These exceptional cases are sufficiently numerous and some of them are sufficiently well authenticated so that the proponent of the telepathic hypothesis of apparitions is obliged either to ignore them altogether or to account for them by what appear to me to be improbable secondary explanations. Some apparitional experiences seem to be exclusively the work of percipients, whereas others may arise, at least partly, from the activity of deceased or dying persons who may be regarded as in some sense "present" where they are seen.[75]

The few apparitional cases presented, combined with the many thousand documented cases in the literature, indicate that apparitions are an authentic experience that cannot be explained solely on the basis of imagination, psychological disorders, or deceit in each reported incident. Several features of the "postmortem" apparitional experiences are especially noteworthy since they are often reported to:

1. Be physically real as in life;
2. Behave normally (e.g., walking, smiling);
3. Be seen whether or not the observer knew that the person concerned was dead; and

4. Have exchanged communication in some cases.

Collectively, the validity of the evidence to support the theory that an apparition represents one's existence that survives bodily death is, however, tenuous since it is almost always anecdotal in nature involving only one person.

Instrumental Transcommunication

Over the past few decades apparitional researchers have utilized Instrumental Transcommunication (ITC), a technique used in the analysis of alleged communication from discarnate individuals to attempt to obtain verifiable evidence to support the survival hypothesis.[76] The audio form is called electronic voice phenomena (EVP). The validity of ITC/EVP evidence, which has served as a source of considerable controversy, is considered by skeptics as either misinterpreted sounds, radio frequencies, people whispering, and/or interference (e.g., magnetic or digital).[77] An alternate "non-being"-related interpretation is that EVP represents a form of auditory pareidolia (i.e., interpreting random sounds as being familiar communication) and apophenia (i.e., perceiving patterns in random information).[78] The brain, in other words, has a tendency to translate abstract patterns into meaningful information, which increases one's expectation that a voice will be heard in the recordings. According to psychologist J. Alcock, EVP recordings represent expectation and wishful thinking of communication from the deceased which "wither away under the light of scientific scrutiny."[79] Proponents of EVP, on the other hand, contend that noise energy in recording and other electronic devices is somehow converted into intelligent communication by the deceased. Support for this position was provided by M. Macy, Convener of the American Continuing Life Research Foundation, who wrote:

> The research laboratories in Europe are reporting extended, two-way communication with spirit colleagues almost daily, receiving wide-ranging information through telephone answering machines, radios, and computer printouts. The evidence collected by this now extensive group of reliable witnesses—including reputable scientists, physicists, engineers, electronic technicians, doctors, professors, administrators, clergymen, successful businessmen—is undeniably convincing to those who systematically investigate the EVP and ITC. The consistency of the evidence from different parts of the world is overwhelming.[80]

Experimental studies conducted on ITC/EVP have revealed conflicting results. Evidence to support communication with the deceased, for instance, was provided in a study by psychologist S. Darnell from thirty individuals whose identity remained blind, and who each recorded questions of their own choice to alleged discarnate beings by ITC.[81] Tape recordings made over several weeks were played several times to allow sufficient time for potential "beings" to answer the questions. The results, which revealed that a number of the questions received audible tape-recorded answers, were interpreted as evidence to support a paranormal explanation rather than PK from the living (i.e., Super-ESP hypothesis). This conclusion was based, in part, on the fact that for PK to have been responsible for this outcome, the researcher would have had to use clairvoyance to identify the random moments when the recorders were on, identify the questions asked, respond with appropriate answers, and to then use PK to somehow impress this information on the recording tape. Added support for a paranormal explanation was also provided by investigator A. MacRae who conducted EVP sessions to determine if different individuals would interpret the recordings the same way. Based on the results from seven people who were asked to compare some selections to a list of five phrases he developed, and to choose the best match, he concluded that the similarity of results indicated that EVPs were of "paranormal origin."[82] In contrast, the results from ITC experiments conducted by scientists at the Institute of Parapsychology at the University of Freiberg led them to conclude that voice recordings represented evidence of PK and not communication with the deceased.[83] One common perspective to support a non-discarnate model for ITC was provided by professor of history B. Regal who remarked that the "majority of EVPs have alternative, nonspiritual sources; anomalous ones have no clear proof they are of spiritual origin."[84] Additionally, evidence for a non-discarnate explanation was provided by psychologist I. Baruss, who conducted several EVP experiments using a radio tuned to an empty frequency under controlled conditions. The inability to demonstrate a paranormal basis for the recordings led the researcher to conclude that, "While we did replicate EVP in the weak sense of finding voices on audio tapes, none of the phenomena found in our study was clearly anomalous, let alone attributable to discarnate beings. Hence we have failed to replicate EVP in the strong sense."[85]

The conflicting ITC/EVP experimental evidence should serve as a foundation for researchers to attempt to develop more reliable methods to obtain possible objective, verifiable forms of evidence to evaluate the validity of this phenomenon.

After-Death Communication

An After-Death Communication (ADC) is a reported experience that occurs when one is contacted directly by someone who has died. A form of ADC is the deathbed vision (DBV), represented by cases in which a sick individual reports the bedside appearance of a dead relative, friend, or a being of light to guide one through the dying process. During this encounter they are informed of their impending death even though their condition may not be life-threatening. In some cases, correct details of the exact date and hour of their death were provided, and in numerous cases, testimonies from more than one witness have been verified.[86]

Spontaneous ADC experiences have been reported to positively impact the grieving process and the DBV can provide for a spiritually transforming experience on dying individuals and their family.[87] Physician M. Morse, who reported DBV cases where dying children described beautiful realms of post-mortem existence and deceased relatives unknown to them, led him to conclude that DBVs are, "a forgotten aspect of life's mysterious process, and can have a wonderfully comforting and healing effect on both the dying patient and the family."[88] Similar effects have also been noted after assisted ADCs; the experience of hearing from deceased loved ones during readings with mediums. In a study of the dreams and visions experienced by fifty-nine hospice patients nearing the end of life, psychologist C. Kerr and colleagues concluded that, "End of life death visions are a common experience during the dying process, characterized by a consistent sense of realism and marked emotional significance. These dreams/visions may be a profound source of potential meaning and comfort for the dying, and therefore warrant clinical attention and further research."[89]

It is not uncommon for family members and hospital personnel to claim that a dying person, suddenly revived, reports to see or hear the deceased or other beings. In fact, the results from the extensive Afterlife Encounter Survey (AES)[90] revealed that seventy-two percent of 596 respondents believed they had either felt the presence of the dead or communicated with them, and approximately ninety-six percent reported that their encounters brought them the highest degree of comfort; that is, they felt a "profound or ineffable joy, as if they had truly connected with another dimension" and were certain that their loved ones were "very much alive in spirit."[91]

Researchers claim that ADC experiences are a natural part of the grieving process[92] and are not based on one's type of death or to timing after death.[93] Such experiences are often characterized by sensing the presence of the deceased in a variety of ways, which include visual, smell, tactile, and auditory phenomena; powerful dreams; and communication through ITC equipment.[94] Communication often takes place between the dying individual and known dead family members, who are most commonly seen, followed by religious beings. Results from the AES indicated that about twenty percent of those who had a spontaneous ADC were with deceased relatives of the experiencer; grandparents arrived more frequently than siblings, and siblings more often than parents.[95] Feelings of peace and comfort are also reported by the majority of individuals experiencing ADCs, which can occur over a period of hours to months before death. Mysteriously, compelling anecdotal accounts include experiences in which the deceased provides information not known by the living, which is eventually proven to be true.[96] Many such ADC experiences also incorporate the arrival of the deceased at the exact time of death but before the recipient is aware of that death by other means.

In a comprehensive study, founders of the After-Death Communication Project, Bill Guggenheim and Judy Guggenheim analyzed ADC evidence obtained from more than 3,300 firsthand accounts from 2,000 interviewees who reported contact with a deceased relative or friend. More than 300 short stories, in the experiencer's own words of their ADC, were provided in their book *Hello from Heaven*.[97] One of the most convincing accounts of an identical ADC, experienced simultaneously by a husband and wife a few days following the death of Benjamin's mother, is represented in an abbreviated excerpt from this book as follows:

Mollie's version:

The night of his mother's funeral, my husband Ben and I went to her house and visited with his family. As we got back to the car, I looked at the front door and saw his mother standing in the doorway waving good-bye to us! She looked like she normally did. It was definitely her! She looked very peaceful, very healthy, and younger. In times past, when we would visit her she always stood by that door and waved good-bye. So this was just like she had done many times before.[98]

Benjamin's version:

The day of my mother's funeral, my wife, Mollie, and I visited my cousin and her husband at Mother's house. We stayed well into the night, and then Mollie and I got into the car. I put the key in the ignition, and as I did I looked up. About ten yards away, I saw my mother standing in the doorway. She would always stand in the doorway out of kindness and courtesy to make sure we had gotten safely to the car. She appeared to be in good health and was very solid. She was waving good-bye. I got the definite impression that this was a "don't worry" type of message. Instantly, I had a tremendous physical feeling, almost like being pinned to the ground. It was like a wave came over me and went completely through me from head to toe. I tried to speak but I couldn't. At the same time Mollie said, "Ben, I just saw your mother in the doorway!" I bowed my head and said, "So did I," and I began to cry. And I felt a sense of relief, like "good-bye for now."[99]

The many shared ADCs in their study led the Guggenheims to conclude that ADCs are "objective experiences." They also considered that testimony of an ADC perceived simultaneously by two or more people together at the same time and place, "provides the most convincing evidence yet that ADCs are genuine contacts by deceased loved ones, exactly as the 2,000 men, women, and children who participated in our research assert."[100] Researcher of psychic phenomenon E. Bozzano, who also reported numerous DBV testimonies from more than one witness, concluded that ADCs presented via the auditory or visual system "provide accurate information of the death of the person concerned before the percipient knows it occurred."[101]

Studies conducted by professor of physics and ADC researcher W. Barrett led him to conclude that those very close to death may see a friend or relative at their bedside whom they thought was still living and that in all cases, the person they saw who died before them without their knowledge was verified.[102] Support for this position was provided in a study of approximately 50,000 terminally ill patients who reported that the most common type of vision was of people who had previously died.[103] This experience, which typically lasted for a few minutes, was often interpreted by the experiencer as a visit for the purpose of taking them away. Research findings obtained in collected reports from more than 1,000 doctors and nurses on the deaths of more than 100,000 people are also consistent with results from several DBV studies. Based on information provided by medical personnel, for example, about ten percent of people are conscious just prior to death and of this group, fifty to sixty-five percent report apparitional visits of loved ones, and/ or awareness of another realm of existence.[104] Additionally, a survey study by physician J. Lerma revealed that about ninety percent of 500 patients reported seeing angels of different colors with feathered wings and that up to forty angels could be in the room as death approached.[105] Parapsychologist K. Osis also concluded that the average interval between the first apparition and death was about four weeks, and in such cases, eighty-three percent saw deceased relatives of whom ninety percent were from the immediate family.[106] According to J. Assante, it is not unusual to hear the dying state, "Yes, dear, I'm coming," or, "I'm coming; just give me a few seconds," and then die immediately afterwards.[107] Intriguingly, hospice worker and ADC researcher D. Aracangel stated that she has "never sat with a dying patient who was not in the presence of an apparition."[108] Researchers have also reported patients smiling out in space, waving, reaching out with their arms, or attempting to leave their bed just before dying.

A qualitative analysis of dreams and visions in sixty-three hospice patients, performed to examine the content and subjective significance of ADCs, revealed several major characteristics which included:

1. A comforting presence;
2. Preparing to go;
3. Watching or engaging with the deceased;
4. Loved ones waiting;
5. Distressing experiences; and
6. Unfinished business.[109]

A related study, which served to determine if precognitive dreams and visions were more dependable than others in predicting death and other events, identified several features that reliable visions have in common.[110] Based on the study outcomes, M. Morse concluded that dreams and/or visions composed of at least two of the following elements are likely to be followed by real events:

a. The dream or vision has a real or hyper-real quality about it. It somehow conveys a sense of ultimate reality.
b. Sights and sounds are superimposed over ordinary reality. Mists may form, voices may be heard, angels and spirits may be seen in a real room or in the midst of a crowd of real people.
c. The dream or vision is extremely intense, often unlike anything ever experienced before. They are so vivid that they cannot be forgotten.
d. The dream or vision is coherent and contains information that has meaning for other people as well as for the one experiencing the vision. The dream or vision in question can be clearly described and understood by others.

e. A mystical white light or a spiritual being of light is involved in the dream or vision.[111]

Curiously, persons dying while conscious who experience visions of previously deceased family members or friends have also been reported in those who have had an NDE.[112] One study, for example, found that about twenty-one percent of seventy-four NDE accounts included reports of encounters with deceased persons, and that eighty-one percent of 129 reports of meetings with "spirits" were from a prior generation.[113] A similar result by parapsychologist E. Kelly revealed that only sixteen percent were from the same generation as the NDEer (e.g., siblings or spouses).[114] The researcher concluded that while such experiences may be facilitated by expectations of one's imminent death, the survival hypothesis seems more plausible since the visions include deceased persons other than the one(s) the experiencer would wish to see, and/or visions of unidentified deceased persons.[115]

Based on the collective ADC/DBV evidence and the associated personal accounts noted, it is reasonable for one to conclude that the appearance of the deceased as death approached reflects wishful thinking or a defensive hallucinatory brain response to aid one during the dying process. But can we completely dismiss the remote possibility that the deceased are in fact attempting to provide comfort during the transition from life to death? In light of the limited research on the ADC/DBV phenomena, concommitent with the acknowledgment by medical personnel that such experiences are common, there exists a need to determine the possible contributions of certain illnesses, and drug and/or brain related hallucinations associated with the dying process, to help justify and explain the nature of these real and perplexing experiences.

Discussion

Collectively, the controversial anecdotal and experimental apparitional evidence fails to conclusively support the survival hypothesis. Proponents who consider the evidence as support for this hypothesis do so for the following primary reasons:

1. Unknown information is reportedly obtained from the deceased that is difficult to account for by telepathy from the living;
2. Cases where the observer of the apparition is unaware that his or her death has taken place and receives information about notification of the figure's death; and
3. The high incidence and similarity of ADC/DBV experiences.

The apparition and sensed presence phenomena, which may represent the existence of the deceased beyond our conception of space and time, should be regarded as a real, mystifying perceptual experience. Nevertheless, the question as to whether the apparitional evidence provides conclusive support for life after death must be regarded as tenuous since an apparition has never been captured and analyzed; there is no scientific evidence of an alternate realm for consciousness to exist after death; and there is no scientific evidence that "energy" remains or can be contained in a human-looking entity after physical death. Phenomenological research of the experience from the person's point of view may eventually provide sufficient evidence to prove it to be either a misinterpretation of natural events, a psychological disorder, hypnagogic imagery, a fictitious story, telepathically acquired information, a neurophysiological-induced experience, and/or a form of energy that survives physical death. And if an apparition is in fact a living "being" from another realm of existence, verifiable evidence must be obtained through well controlled scientific experiments before accepting this "being" as proof of life after death.

CHAPTER
FIVE

REINCARNATION

Introduction

Are examples of déjà vu, Mozart's ability to compose a symphony at the age four, and anecdotal testimony of past-life recall sufficient evidence to support the continuous existence of a post-mortem, non-physical characteristic of one's identity that is renewed in another physical body? Or can they be dismissed as illusions of memory, inherited attributes, and/or unexplained aspects of cognitive function?

Reincarnation evidence is represented from children who claim to have conscious recall of their supposed previous incarnations, statements by mediums of supposed past incarnations of their clients, and induced recall of past lives through hypnotic regression techniques. This evidence is largely represented in the work of psychiatrist I. Stevenson, former Professor of Psychiatry and Director of the Division of Perceptual Studies at the University of Virginia, who documented and analyzed more than 2,500 cases of young children who had involuntary conscious memory of a previous life and the concomitant behaviors, emotional states, and physical traits consistent with that life.[1] The analysis of such reports led him to conclude that the ability to recall specific details of their claimed past life with sufficient precision, does not "prove" reincarnation, but is instead, "suggestive" of reincarnation[2]—a concept he considered as one's "mind" that may "persist and later become associated with another physical body."[3]

The Phenomenology of Reincarnation Experiences

The phenomenology of reincarnation experiences is generally based on Stevenson's extensive research database of cases he considered that "no other possible explanations" could account for the child's "conscious recall" of past-life knowledge. This database contained details of persons, places, residences, and manner and time of death associated with their past life, which he and other researchers believed to be "inconceivable for a child."[4] Information sources included testimony from children and their families, hospital and autopsy records, birth and death certificates, and photographs, among others, to determine the characteristics and validity of one's claimed past life. According to Stevenson, "in many cases the child's statements have been shown to correspond accurately to facts in the life and death of a deceased person; in many of these cases the families concerned have had no contact before the case developed."[5]

A typical example suggestive of how a reincarnation case develops is paraphrased from Stevenson as follows: It may begin when a "dying person expresses a wish to be reborn to a couple." Shortly after birth, the parents notice a "major birthmark," and between the age of two and four years old the child speaks about a previous life until about five to eight years of age. Most discuss the previous life with strong emotion, and do not "distinguish past from present" in their language expressions.

Their statements almost always "include information of their death and family in the previous life." This is especially true if the "death was violent, but occurs also—less frequently—when it was natural." Beyond that, "the child usually speaks about the family of the previous life."[6]

Stevenson identified several behaviors that occur in childhood for which reincarnation "provides a better interpretation of the observed facts than other alternative hypotheses."[7] This includes:

1. "Strong fears or phobias" not attributed to earlier trauma, nor shared by other family members;
2. "Strong interests" in activities or areas of knowledge, as well as unexpected appetites and unusual desires not consistent with one's family upbringing;
3. "Proficiency in skills not taught through instruction or learned through imitation;" and
4. The location of "unusual birthmarks and congenital deformities."[8]

Stevenson considered that since children seem to present behaviors, habits, skills, and phobias of the referenced person in their claimed previous life, one's past experiences contribute to one's attributes in their present life.[9] This evidence-based perspective, concomitant with the reported verified factual statements of deceased persons, family members, and details of their alleged previous life, represent the most compelling reincarnation evidence to support the survival hypothesis.[10] Some children even identify strongly with their past life. They often express sadness for their loved ones' and lifestyle lost from their previous life, insist on being called by their previous name, and prefer to spend more time with their prior family.[11] Parents have also reportedly heard statements from their young children, such as "When I died . . . " or "When I was big . . . "[12]

Above all, Stevenson believed that the child's manner of behavior, which strongly resembled the person claimed to be recalled from a past life, represented the most compelling evidence to "suggest" but not "prove" reincarnation. Psychologist A. Gauld, who studied many such cases, also believed that a three- to five-year-old child could not "accurately impersonate" them in this way.[13] Consequently, Stevenson considered that we are not born with a so-called "clean slate" (i.e., one's knowledge, nature, and personality are only shaped by experience) but are instead, influenced by past-life experiences. The validity of this evidence is enhanced not only by the sheer quantity and consistency of detail the children provided, but especially by Stevenson's contention that it was verifiable. Names, for instance, often proved to be accurate and in most cases were of strangers who died just prior to the child's birth. In fact, the short time lapse between one life and the next of only one to four years enabled past-life identities to be verified in about seventy-five percent of his cases.[14] Independent investigators also reported that in fifty-one percent of the ninety-nine cases considered "solved," the person the child claimed to be was unknown to the child's family.[15]

And more often than not, he was able to identify a person who once lived based solely on the statements given by the child. While some cases were stronger than others, many are extremely difficult to explain by non-paranormal means due to his meticulous efforts to discount this line of reasoning by "exposing as fully as possible all observations that weaken one's preferred interpretation of the data."[15a]

Additional evidence considered by Stevenson as "suggestive" of reincarnation included 225 documented cases of birth defects and birthmarks that he thought represented the nature of their death.[16] The correspondence, which in some instances were considered "extremely close," were verified by medical records or autopsy reports regarding the previous personality. In fact, in eighty-eight percent of such cases, birthmarks were within four inches of the wound that had killed them and nearly twenty percent had birthmarks or physical abnormalities consistent with injuries the referenced past-life individual incurred at or near the time of death.[17] Surprisingly, several cases included children who had two birthmarks corresponding to both the entrance and exit wounds of gunshot victims.[18] Similarly, a few cases included the appearance of malformed fingers of one hand of a child whose referenced person had lost fingers of one hand in an accident, and a deformed side of the face of another child whose referenced person sustained a severe head wound.

Although the majority of reincarnation evidence has been accumulated by just Stevenson and his colleagues, the reliability of their evidence is enhanced by the consistency of findings by independent investigators.[19] Psychologist E. Haraldsson, for example, reported that in eighty percent of 123 cases, details of the deceased person identified were remarkably similar with some or all of the child's conscious recall of that referenced person.[20] In fact, studies have reported that children discussed people and places they have never seen with accuracy of about ninety percent.[21] The name of the prior deceased individual was also accurately identified in about thirty percent of American cases and seventy-five percent of Indian cases,[22] and may have been related and/or to have lived close to the person who recalled the past-life experience (within seventy-five miles).[23] These findings may account for why in the majority of cases studied both the experiencer and recalled past-life individual are of the same culture, religion, gender, and speak the same language.[24]

In the most significant cases studied by Stevenson, death was usually premature and violent in nature. Interestingly, about sixty percent of subjects remembered lives that ended violently[25], and in about thirty-five percent of his cases the subject showed a fear associated with the manner of death; in other words, a fear of water if drowned, guns if shot, certain foods if poisoned. Consistent with this result were the findings by other investigators who reported that a high incident of violent deaths characterized the past-life identities of both Indian (fifty-six percent) and American children samples (eighty percent) "which far exceeds the incidence of violent deaths in the general population of India (7.2 percent) and the United States (eight percent)."[26]

Physician E. Brody, who praised Stevenson's work as "meticulous," however, still questioned the evidence used to support his position on reincarnation by stating that, "his body of knowledge and theory must be abandoned or radically modified in order to accept it."[27] In light of this commonly expressed concern, it is still difficult to reconcile how Stevenson's results could have been replicated by others if his research methods and evidence were not reliable.[28] In fact, anthropologist A. Mills concluded that, "some aspects of these cases cannot be explained by normal means. I found no evidence that the cases I studied are the result of fraud."[29]

In fact, physicist Doris Kuhlmann-Wilsdorf, whose groundbreaking theories on surface physics earned her the prestigious Heyn Medal from the German Society for Material Sciences, considered Stevenson's research findings difficult to question. She stated that the "statistical probability that reincarnation does in fact occur is so overwhelming . . . . that cumulatively the evidence is not inferior to that for most if not all branches of science."[29a] Despite the understandable controversy of Stevenson's research findings, it is certainly difficult to dispute her position.

Past-Life Experiences

While controversial in nature, anecdotal testimony verified to be consistent with one's claimed previous life provides intriguing evidence for reincarnation. Five such past-life recall cases corroborated by Stevenson are as follows:

1. Considered one of the most interesting and frequently cited cases is that of a young child named James Leininger who presented many details recalled from dreams of dying in a plane crash. He claimed to be a World War II fighter pilot named James Huston who flew from the aircraft carrier, the Natoma Bay. He also recalled the name of his best friend on the carrier and his death in the Battle of Iwo Jima. After one nightmare, his mother stated, "He was lying there on his back, kicking and clawing on the covers, like he was trapped in a plane." James was crying out: "Airplane crash! Plane on fire! Little man can't get out!" When asked who the little man in the plane was, James replied he was the "little man." When his father asked him who shot his plane down, he replied that it was the Japanese. When asked how he knew it was the Japanese, he said "The big red sun." James' father learned that only one pilot died during the Battle of Iwo Jima—Lt. James Huston from the Natoma Bay.[30]
2. Shanti Devi, who at the age of four in 1930 in Delhi, India, provided at least twenty-four statements consistent with confirmed facts in a prior life, a few of which include the following: She identified herself as Lugdi who lived in Muttra, accurately identified landmarks in Muttra, spoke the dialect of that area without having learned it, claimed to have given birth to a son who died several days later, and correctly identified Lugdi's former parents.[31] A committee of prominent individuals formed to investigate this case concluded that this information, which she could "not have obtained by dishonest means," provided "conclusive proof" of reincarnation.[32]
3. Two-year-old Marta Lorenz cited information of a prior life as her mother's

best friend, Maria de Olivero. Many of these details were not known to the child's mother but were later confirmed by several different people. She recalled more than one hundred accurate details of her previous life, which included facts of what Maria had told her best friend (Marta's mother) just prior to her death, and that she would try to be reborn as her best friend's daughter and share details of her prior life.[33]

4. Before the age of three, Pramod Sharme began to tell his mother not to cook because he had a wife in Morababad, India, who could cook, and that he owned a soda and biscuit shop there, which he asked to visit. He also claimed to be one of the "Mohan Brothers" and owned a hotel and cinema in Saharanpur where his mother still lived. According to Stevenson, his parents never heard of the "Mohan Brothers" and that when he interviewed the father and others from his claimed family in Moradabad, he was able to correctly document much of his information.[34]

5. Even though thirty-two-year-old Uttara Huddar had no memories of a past life as a child in India and had never been to Bengal, she began to exhibit memories and knowledge of foods, customs, and places in Bengal from a life 150 years before. She claimed to be "Sharada Chattopadhaya," who spontaneously emerged for only a few years as an adult. Stevenson considered that Sharada was a "previous incarnation of the person now identified as Uttara," and that "Sharada memories are a part of Uttara," which was hidden until her thirties.[35]

Psychiatrist J. Tucker, who continued reincarnation research initiated by his predecessor, I. Stevenson, documented the case of a child in Sri Lanka who told her mother the name and details of the town where she accidentally drowned and of the family and house she lived in during her prior life. Despite the fact that the child, her family, or anyone she knew had any prior connection to this town or the dead child, he established that twenty-sevey out of thirty details were in fact true. This evidence led Tucker to conclude that:

> There can be something that survives after the death of the brain and the death of the body that is somehow connected to a new child. I have become convinced that there is more to the world than the physical universe. There's the mind piece, which is its own entity.[36]

Xenoglossy, Child Prodigies, and Déjà vu

*   *Xenoglossy*: Compelling evidence suggestive of reincarnation pertains to the rare phenomenon called xenoglossy. This is represented by a person who is able to speak or write a language that could not have been obtained by natural means. In some reported cases, the person may even speak in a version of a foreign language not used for centuries. If justified, such ability would tend to rule out fraud or a case of cryptomnesia (i.e., forgotten memories).

The most detailed studies of instances of responsive xenoglossy are those by I. Stevenson. For example, one case was that of the language spoken by Jensen and the details she gave of her life, which were consistent with a previous existence in seventeenth century Sweden. While hypnotized, despite never having been exposed to the language in her present life, she claimed to be J. Jacoby of Sweden born in the seventeenth century. Curiously, she could not understand the language when she came out of the hypnotic state. She also provided accurate details of the place and time in which Jacoby lived. Three Swedish speakers who conversed with Jacoby, and four who have subsequently listened to the tape recordings, agreed that he conversed sensibly, grammatically, and with good pronunciation in Swedish. An analysis of four tape-recorded sessions showed that, if doubtful words, and words which sound alike in Swedish and in English were excluded, Jensen introduced into one conversation at least sixty Swedish words not previously used in her presence by her interviewers. Stevenson considered that with no prior training or exposure to the language, this woman could only have known Swedish if she remembered it from a previous existence. In fact, linguists and psychologists who examined this evidence were unable to determine an explanation other than reincarnation in this case.[37]

Another intriguing example involved an eleven-year-old boy who was recorded speaking Chinese.[38] The language, analyzed by a professor in the Department of Oriental Studies at the University of California, identified the dialogue from ancient China.[39] Similarly, a foreign language spoken by twins and analyzed by a professor of ancient Semitic languages at the Department of Foreign Language at Columbia University, concluded that the children were speaking a language common in ancient Syro-Palestine.[40]

In search of an over-arching explanation for xenoglossy, several researchers have come to agree with Stevenson's belief that such verified cases "suggest" reincarnation.[41] An alternate explanation is that when one is hypnotized, the personality from a previous incarnation comes through, which enables the person to exhibit knowledge that could not possibly have been acquired in this life. Some scientists have even proposed that xenoglossy may be explained by "genetic memory" (i.e., inherited complex ability and knowledge) or telepathy (i.e., obtained ability from foreign speakers). However, while xenoglossy evidence is interesting to contemplate, it remains unconfirmed and too limited in occurrence to justify reincarnation.

- *Child Prodigies*: Some researchers consider that a past life manifestation is represented by "child prodigies"—a person under the age of ten with extremely advanced expertise.[42] Wolfgang Amadeus Mozart, for example, believed his past life as a musician enabled him to exhibit such remarkable skills at a very young age. Could such extraordinary abilities without formal training represent the influence of genetic memory, the "collective unconscious" (i.e., an aspect of the mind which manifests inherited universal themes of life), exceptional learning skills, or even life after death? Stevenson, however, did not find reincarnation evidence for child prodigies.[43] He remarked, "to the best of my knowledge, no Western child prodigy has ever claimed to remember a previous life. I am not saying that the study of cases of the reincarnation type will never explain child prodigies and the varying social situations of human beings at birth. I am only asserting that presently available data cannot help us do so."[44]

Although the "child prodigy" has been advanced as evidence of reincarnation, recent studies have considered biologic/cognitive attributes as possible contributing factors to explain this phenomenon.[45] One study, for instance, identified several key components common to such cases (e.g., an average or higher IQ, extraordinary working memory, and a heightened attention to detail).[46] Interestingly, standardized tests applied to assess the cognitive profiles of eighteen child prodigies in art, music, and math, indicated that while all of the child prodigies had "exceptional memories," the music and math prodigies scored significantly higher on "working memory" than the art prodigies, and the math prodigies displayed the highest levels of "general intelligence" and "visual spatial skills."[47] Using brain imaging techniques on several math prodigies, neuroscientist L. Vandervert also considered that, "the transition from visual-spatial working memory to other forms of thought (language, art, mathematics) is accelerated by the unique emotional disposition of the prodigy and the cognitive functions of the cerebellum."[48] Clearly, a definitive explanation for this phenomenon remains tenuous at best.

• *Déjà vu:* The common experience of one's overwhelming sense of familiarity with an event or experience that should not be familiar (i.e., déjà vu) has been proposed as evidence to support reincarnation. In fact, up to seventy percent of Americans report having déjà vu. Many psychologists, however, ascribe this phenomenon to the brain's error in mistaking the present for the past. Psychologist J. Matlock, for example, considered spontaneous adult past-life experiences, which "resemble unusually strong déjà vu experiences," to be facilitated by "memory cues."[49] An alternative explanation is that déjà vu results from a "disturbance of mnemonic systems of the medial temporal lobe."[50] This conclusion was based on the facilitation of *déjà vu* by stimulation of this brain region in epileptic patients. Many parapsychologists, on the other hand, attribute this "sense" to a past-life experience, as represented in a compelling case of déjà vu reported by hypnotist B. Goldberg. That is, in different sessions years apart, two clients unknown to each other reported identical events from the opposing viewpoints of their past-life personalities.[51]

Theories

Several theories proposed to explain the behavioral and psychological manifestations displayed by the past-life experiencer must be considered before firmly concluding that the phenomenological evidence provides any degree of support for reincarnation.

The over-arching concern remains as to whether past-life recall represents one's incarnation from a prior existence or may be explained by one or more of the following theories:

1. Psychocultural;
2. Paramnesia and Cryptomnesia;
3. Genetic Inheritance;
4. Extrasensory Perception;
5. The Psychology of Past Life Experiencers; and
6. Quantum Physics.

1. *Psychocultural*: The psychocultural theory represents a principle objection to the concept of reincarnation. This theory considers past-life recall experiences by children as fantasies and memory aberrations induced by the parent's interpretation of the referred family and their cultural/religious beliefs. This concept is supported by the fact that spontaneous conscious past-life recall is reported most often in countries and cultures whose religious beliefs support the idea of reincarnation (e.g., Hindus, Buddhists, among others). Thus, cultural/ religious indoctrination may explain, in part, why reincarnation experiences are reported most frequently by those from cultures that incorporate this concept;[52] that is, while fundamental to Hinduism and Buddhism beliefs, only approximately twenty percent of Americans and Europeans believe in reincarnation.[53] Such cases, however, also occur in countries (e.g., United States, Israel) and cultures whose religions (e.g., Judaism, Christianity) do not advocate such a belief.[54] Despite this tendency, Stevenson did not firmly believe that the past-life memories in children are the result of cultural influences but did acknowledge that falsified cases have occurred in societies where a motive exists. For example, higher status is granted to those considered to possess the soul of one in a prior life.[55] According to Stevenson, "The case of the various cultures reflect, to some extent, the variations in the beliefs about reincarnation. We cannot yet explain these correlations. Two interpretations are obvious: First, the beliefs may influence the development of the cases; second, if reincarnation occurs, the beliefs may influence what actually happens from one life to another. But there may be other explanations also."[56]

Stevenson's assumption, based in part on his study that countered the psychocultural theory, indicated that of seventy-nine American children who reported having lived a previous life, only sixteen percent of families reported a belief in reincarnation, and sixty-four percent had "little or no knowledge" of reincarnation. This outcome led him to conclude that, "the children's statements often conflicted seriously with the beliefs of their parents and other members of their families."[57] Another study also noted differences between cultures in the type of deceased person to whom the children's statement referred could be named and specifically identified. In the American cases, ninety-four percent of sixteen "solved" cases were a member of the child's family, such as an older sibling or a grandparent who had died before the subject's birth.[58] In contrast, the subjects of cases in India tend to recall the life of a non-relative and more often a stranger the family never met.[59] Additionally, recalled prior lives as a member of the opposite sex are much more frequently claimed in some cultures than in others. They are unheard of among the "Tlingits, Druses, and Alevis," occur in thirteen percent of Thai cases, twenty-eight percent of Burmese cases, and up to fifty percent of cases among the Kutchin of Canada. Such cases occur most frequently in cultures that believe them possible, and most "rarely in cultures where such change is thought impossible."[60]

Despite the fact that past-life recall cases usually occur in cultures with strong reincarnation beliefs, the psychocultural hypothesis does not sufficiently account for past-life experiences in cultures that do not advocate such beliefs, nor in families that do not believe in reincarnation.[61] It also does not apply to all since there are several well-documented examples in which the two families lived far apart and were unknown to each other before the child spoke about the prior life. Above all, however, past-life memory cases are very similar regardless of the cultures from which they are reported.

2. *Paramnesia* and *Cryptomnesia*: This theory considers past-life memories as imagined or assumed experiences that are thought to be real; one's failure to differentiate fact from fantasy (paramnesia*)* and experiences that people believe to be original but are based on forgotten memories (i.e., cryptomnesia).[62] Cryptomnesia, which represents the most popular non-reincarnationist explanation, proposes that memories not ordinarily accessible to the waking consciousness, and which the subject does not recollect having acquired from another source, as being his/her own. They may emerge through automatic writing, dreams or drug states, and by past-life recall retrieved and embellished through hypnosis. Considered as "false memories" facilitated by the hypnotherapist,[63] it is well established that hypnotic memory fills in gaps of missing information with "confabulations" or made-up thoughts of what might or should have occurred.[64] A psychological-based study, for instance, revealed that children with past-life recall can be influenced in several ways to report details of events that did not occur.[65] Contrasting evidence, however, was provided by psychologist R. Kampman who conducted experiments with children he hypnotically regressed into assumed past lives.[66] By taking the children under hypnosis to the occasion on which they obtained the information, which their past life memories were based, he claimed to have traced such memories back to their sources in printed material.

In many of Stevenson's cases the possibility of cryptomnesia seems likely since the two families concerned lived near each other or the parents of the present personality possibly knew something about the life and death of the previous personality. But Stevenson reasonably addressed this concern as follows:
   a) Many of his subjects were only three or younger when they presented their first apparent memories of a previous existence;

b) Unlike the subjects in many of the classic cases of demonstrated cryptomnesia, they were not hypnotized but in a waking state; and

c) There was no evidence which clearly associated the subject's statements to the source of information.[67]

Neverthess, despite the existing controversial evidence and associated documentation of hypnotic induced memory distortion, it remains difficult to adequately explain the past-life knowledge reportedly confirmed in some hypnotic recall cases.

3. *Genetic Inheritance*: Recent genetic-based research suggests that inherited memory may explain past-life experiences.[68] One unique theory termed "trans-generational epigenetic inheritance" refers to the concept that the parent's life experiences and acquired characteristics may be passed onto their offspring. This concept is supported by evidence, which showed that an aversion to the smell of rose blossoms was passed from the parent onto offspring over multiple generations in mice.[69] Apparently, the genetic makeup induced by the learned aversion to rose blossoms was expressed in the offspring as an inherited aversion to the same smell, even though the offspring never experienced that smell. According to the researchers, "the experiences of a parent, even before conceiving, markedly influence both structure and function in the nervous system of subsequent generations."[70] Additional supportive evidence is provided by the identified associated genetic and neural changes involved in facilitating this inheritance.[71] Consequently, this pattern of inheritance may have potential implications for how psychological disorders and conceptual memories can be acquired from parents and more distant relatives. If proven valid, one must then consider if "past-life recall" represents actual experiences of one's consciousness that may have existed in an alleged previous life, or is instead, facilitated by an inherited memory trait from deceased relatives in some cases. This theory, however, is contradicted by the fact that in about two-thirds of cases the person and the referenced past-life individual are not related.[72]

The concept of "cellular memory" represents another genetic-based explanation for past-life recall. Considered justifiable by several scientists and physicians, cellular memory implies that the brain is not the only physical organ capable of storing memories or personality traits.[73] Apparently, the DNA in the donor organ seems to give rise to fields of consciousness that are received by the recipient. This model, for example, was supported by study results in 150 heart transplant patients who claimed to experience changes in attitude, philosophies, and/or tastes in food and music following surgery.[74] A similar outcome was verified in twenty-one percent of forty-seven heart transplant recipients who experienced a change in personality over a two-year period following surgery.[75] One remarkable documented case was that of a young girl who received the heart of a ten-year-old girl. Following surgery, she experienced nightmares about a murderer and victim that was verified by a psychiatrist as "genuine" memories. Astonishingly, the girl who donated the heart was murdered. But based on the recipient's dreams, she was able to describe the events of that experience that led to the conviction of the murderer.[76] Consequently, if cellular memory in transplanted organs can somehow alter various personal attributes, including memory in the recipient, then can cellular memory also be inherited and later recalled as a past-life experience? If so, the concept of reincarnation may be explained on the basis of pure physical genetics rather than the transference of one's "soul" or consciousness from a prior life to the present one, in some, if not all past-life recall cases.

4. *Extrasensory Perception*: Extrasensory perception (ESP), the alleged ability to sense or perceive information in present or past time not acquired through the physical senses, represents a popular alternative explanation for past-life memory experiences. If valid, can ESP allow one to somehow acquire information of past events from deceased persons, and/or living relatives without their prior knowledge? Although Stevenson dismissed this line of reasoning due to the lack of empirical evidence to prove ESP, he did not exclude the possibility that ESP may explain much of the correct information reported by children in his studies.[77] Accordingly, if an individual can obtain information through ESP, we cannot firmly conclude that past-life recall is directly associated with one's prior existence simply because that information was verified to be true. While controversial in nature, ESP must first be validated and accepted by the scientific community as a distinct aspect of human behavior before accepting it as a contributing factor in such cases.

5. *The Psychology of Past-Life Experiencers*: Studies of the personality and behavioral characteristics of past-life experiencers leave open the possibility that certain predisposing attributes may serve as a confounding variable in reincarnation research. Evidence to support this consideration was provided in a study of thirty children who continuously spoke about their past life.[78] Collectively, they demonstrated higher scores for verbal abilities, memory, daydreaming, attention-seeking, and were more "dissociative, obsessional, and perfectionistic" than a control group who did not report past-life memories.[79] Additionally, a survey study in adults indicated those reporting a past-life experience to be more fantasy-prone and intuitive.[80] In contrast, however, one study reported that children with past-life recall generally did not demonstrate any psychological disorders beyond that exhibited by an "average group" of children.[81] This outcome was also consistent with results from a longitudinal study that showed that almost all children with past-life recall grew up with no outstanding psychological differences from their peers.[82]

One interesting psychological-based explanation for past-life experiences was provided by hypnotherapist L. Tarazi who considered dissociation or multiple personality an outcome of hypnosis that gives rise to "alternate personalities, which can then assume the role of a former life of the subject."[83] She also considered past-life experiences as "fantasies motivated by the unconscious needs of the subject."[84] In a variant of this theory, memories in one's "subconscious that is originally disturbing and anxiety-provoking to the ego is neutralized by being projected onto and integrated into a fabricated personality that lived a previous life and not the present one."[85]

6. *Quantum Physics*: Theories in quantum physics may offer unique insights on past-life experiences. The Quantum Hologram Theory (QHT), for example, which has been advanced to justify ESP and out-of-body and near-death experiences, among other phenomena, provides similar rationale to explain reincarnation.[86] Briefly, according to the QHT, the universe is a self-organizing inter-connected conscious holistic system that retains information of each experience stored in a holographic form.[87] This information, which may be retrieved using focused mental attention, may serve as the basis for past-life memory recall in children. Scientist, astronaut, and founder of the Institute of Noetic Sciences Edgar Mitchell explained how this concept may explain past-life recall in children as follows:

> The person is in a high state of resonance with the quantum hologram of the deceased and is able to retrieve QH information about the deceased from that resonance condition. As the child ages, rational left brain processing begins to dominate and the child is no longer able to resonate with the QH of the deceased unless the child has been trained to maintain that state of altered consciousness.[88]

R. Schild, research astronomer at the Harvard-Smithsonian Center for Astrophysics, also advanced the QHT to explain and support the survival hypothesis. He remarked:

> Consciousness may exist in our space-time and constrain our waking perception. During sleep or death we once again awaken to full consciousness only to discover that we never left that unitary state to begin with. After death we are awake, only to realize yet again, that when we are focused into a physical body with a finite time scale, that is when we are in fact dreaming.[89]

A similar explanation of the QHT-reincarnation relationship was provided by noted counselor and hypnotherapist M. Rodwell who considers that one's "energy consciousness" or "soul essence" is a fundamental aspect of our being. Accordingly, this energy "explores, experiences, and operates in that state as well as material forms in several alternate dimensions at the same time as the same consciousness"; that is, one's soul may be able to relocate from our body to "other living biological containers and then return." Rodwell contends that, "our soul/spirit survives death and continues until it chooses to reincarnate again. So the realities are multiple and can be material, as well as survive and operate in a non-material essence as pure energy."[90]

Support for the perspectives shared by Mitchell, Schild, and Rodwell is provided by several physicists who claim that principles of quantum physics may also explain the distinction between consciousness and the brain; an essential precondition to justify reincarnation and the associated survival hypothesis. In other words, if a quantum code exists for all things, living and dead, then there may be an existence after death. Although definitive evidence to prove the QHT is lacking, several leading physicists believe it to be consistent with general scientific concepts and advancements. Physicist H. Dürr, for example, contends that the brain functions as a computer hard drive which stores all experiences which is then "uploaded" into the "spiritual quantum field."[91] Based on this premise, Dürr proposed that when the body no longer functions, our consciousness still continues to exist in another realm. Thus, our "consciousness" may be "truly immortal."[92] A similar opinion is held by quantum physicist D. Bohm who stated that, "the results of modern natural sciences only make sense if we assume an inner, uniform, transcendent reality that is based on all external data and facts. The very depth of human consciousness is one of them."[93]

Clearly, such concepts within quantum physics serve as a matter of fierce debate within mainstream science.

Hypnotic Regression and Past-Life Recall

Despite the acceptance of hypnosis by the American Psychological Association as a valuable clinical technique in certain cases,[94] hypnotherapy has been criticized for its limited effectiveness recovering lost or hidden memories, and the likelihood of "suggestibility" on those hypnotized.[95] This concern is based on the fact that very few solved regression cases have been reported, inaccurate information in many cases occur,[96] and recall is often attributed to unconscious memories.[97] Accordingly, hypnotic past-life accounts should not be interpreted literally since numerous confounding variables exist:

1. Confabulation;
2. The creation of pseudo-memories;
3. Cueing by the hypnotist; and
4. Preconceptions of the hypnotized subject.[98]

In fact, Stevenson considered past-life memories acquired through hypnosis as unreliable since it "rarely evokes" valid memories and can enable the recall of both "true" and "false" memories.[99] Despite these justified concerns, accurate detailed information has been reportedly verified in some who claimed to have not acquired past-life information by normal means during hypnosis.[100] Consequently, uncertainty exists as to whether one's altered state during hypnosis facilitates an accurate past-life experience or an illusory memory in all cases.

Despite the negative criticisms of hypnosis, some mental health professionals acknowledge the positive behavioral outcomes resulting from past-life regression therapy. For instance, psychologist G. Edelstein realized that, "past-life regressions, for reasons I cannot explain, almost always lead to rapid improvements in the patient."[101] An extension of this position was provided by clinical psychologist E. Fiore who remarked that, "if someone's phobia is eliminated instantly and permanently by remembrance of an event from the past life, it makes logical sense that the event must have happened."[102] Based on similar life regression therapy outcomes in patients, psychiatrist A. Cannon considered reincarnation a valid concept. This position was clarified in his remark that, "for years the theory of reincarnation was a nightmare to me, and I did my best to disprove it. Yet as the years went by one subject after another told me the same story in spite of different and varied conscious beliefs. Now well over a thousand cases have been investigated, and I have to admit that there is such a thing as reincarnation."[103]

Psychotherapist B. Weiss routinely applied hypnotic regression to help patients discover events from supposed previous lives that may contribute towards their abnormal psychological symptoms.[104] One such account of a patient's past-life regression that resulted in a "phobic healing" is represented as follows: "All of my life I was terrified of knives and constantly obsessed about being stabbed to death. During the past-life regression I saw my father lying on the floor of his study, stabbed to death, with constables surrounding him. After this session, I completely and immediately lost my fear of knives and being stabbed to death."[105]

Clearly, the accuracy of past-life memories induced under hypnosis is a concern, especially when the accuracy of recalled information is used as evidence to evaluate the validity of reincarnation. Consequently, the main contribution of hypnotic-induced past-life recall may be to provide therapeutic benefits in some cases, rather than as a reliable technique in reincarnation research.

Future Research

Given the difficulties in establishing whether or not an event actually occurred in this life, let alone in alleged past lives, numerous confounding variables must be controlled in studies that attempt to confirm the authenticity of information reported in previous lives. This daunting concern, concomitant with Stevenson's contention that, "we can never show that reincarnation does not occur; nor are we ever likely to obtain conclusive evidence that it does occur," serves to impede efforts by researchers to study this phenomenon.[106] Despite the apparent limitations associated with methodological and logistical approaches to properly obtain, evaluate, and verify anecdotal testimony, and the skeptical viewpoint by mainstream science of the reincarnation evidence, there still exists a need to research this phenomenon. Consequently, researchers interested in studying children who claim to have conscious recall of past lives should consider adopting the rigorous protocol described by Edelmann and Bernet in their paper, *Setting Criteria for Ideal Reincarnation*

Research.[107] This methodology should serve as a foundation for a multidisciplinary team of researchers to apply as a preliminary step to evaluate the validity of reincarnation evidence and its potential implications for the survival hypothesis. The possible outcome of this research method was summarized in their statement that, "the vast implications of reincarnation for our understanding of mind, memory, and consciousness suggests that such experiments should be beneficial to human knowledge."[108]

Discussion

Given the paucity of compelling evidence to justify reincarnation, we cannot conclude that it does not occur, or that irrefutable evidence will eventually be obtained to conclude that it does. Nevertheless, reincarnation studies have provided ample "suggestive" evidence in the form of verified consciously recalled testimony of claimed previous lives, and positive hypnotic past-life therapy outcomes, for it to be considered worthy of further serious study. While the causative factors associated with verified historically accurate past-life reports remains obscure, the existing unexplained and intriguing evidence reinforces the need to better understand how individuals acquire this knowledge. Consequently, the considerably more questions than answers generated from reincarnation studies should serve as the foundation by which hypotheses may be developed to test in future studies. These include, but are not limited to, the following:

1. Does some aspect of consciousness persist after death?
2. Does a cause-effect relationship exist between the influence of past-life experiences and one's present behavior?
3. Is it possible to access information from past-life experiences and/or from the deceased and living using ESP?
4. Can a reliable reincarnation-based research approach be established to appropriately test the survival hypothesis?

Mainstream science views the concept and associated research implications of reincarnation in the same way it regards near-death and out-of body experiences, apparitions, mediumship, and parapsychology in general; in other words, there exists a lack of objective confirmable evidence to support the survival hypothesis. This steadfast position is primarily based on the fact that most scholars dismiss the question "if reincarnation is true" as impossible to answer or relevant because neuroscientists consider that consciousness and the brain are interdependent physical components of our nervous system. Thus, to accept the concept of reincarnation and the associated survival hypothesis, there must first exist irrefutable evidence that consciousness is a distinct aspect of the brain and is not dependent on normal brain function. Despite this daunting endeavor, researchers must initially develop uniformly accepted experimental protocol and associated defined criteria to be met as "proof" of reincarnation, to more appropriately evaluate the source, accuracy, and validity of conscious past-life recall experiences. Such an endeavor may have potential important implications for understanding the nature of human consciousness and the remote possibility of a form of post-mortem existence. Perhaps the perspective held by internationally renowned astronomer and astrophysicist Carl Sagan best represents the significance of reincarnation research. He wrote, "the study into children who sometimes report the details of a previous life, which upon checking turn out to be accurate and which they could not have known about in any other way than reincarnation, deserves serious study."[109] Time, which we all do not have enough of, may eventually provide a definitive answer.

CHAPTER SIX

MEDIUMSHIP

Introduction

The concept of life after death cannot be appropriately evaluated without considering research in mediums who claim to communicate with the deceased. Mediumship research has addressed the validity of such alleged experiences to determine if one's consciousness can interact with the living and physical world and persist after physical death. Mediumship is certainly controversial and any evidence that supports one's ability to communicate with the deceased certainly provokes debate.

There are two main types of mediumship: mental and physical. In mental mediumship, an individual communicates information from the deceased to others. This may be achieved during a meditative or trance-like state to allow an unknown aspect of the deceased to utilize the medium for this purpose. During this process, the medium's manner of communication, voice quality, and personality may change dramatically.[1] According to psychologist A. Gauld, communication with the alleged deceased is experienced "through interior vision or hearing, or through the spirits taking over and controlling their bodies."[2] In physical mediumship, the communication "proceeds through paranormal physical events in the medium's vicinity,"[3] represented by reports of unexplained voices and sounds, and movement of objects in the environment.[4] Surprisingly, despite the historical prevalence of mediums being stereotyped as charlatans, opinion polls indicate that almost thirty percent of Americans believe in the existence of genuine mediumistic abilities[5], and approximately ten percent of Britons visit mediums to receive messages from the deceased and general guidance.[6]

Anomalous Information Reception by Mediums

The primary objective of mediumship research involves the analysis of information conveyed by mediums from supposed deceased persons to the living (i.e., sitters), and from the living using anomalous information reception (AIR); that is, the reporting of accurate and specific information without prior knowledge, fraud, and in the absence of "normal" sensory input. A vital aspect of this research is to incorporate appropriate experimental control over one's access of information about the deceased and sitters prior to the reading to help determine if AIR by mediums is achieved by non-local means (i.e., perceptual ability extends beyond space and time constraints of sensory systems). Experimental studies designed to evaluate AIR evidence in mediums have revealed both positive[7] and negative[8] outcomes.

- *Positive AIR Outcomes*: In recent years, the most extensive mediumship research has been conducted by J. Beischel and colleagues at the Windbridge Institute for Applied Research in Human Potential.[9] Based on their collective research findings obtained under well-controlled experimental conditions, the researchers considered AIR to be a genuine trait in some individuals.[10] In one study, for example, J. Beischel, co-founder and Director of Research at the Institute, analyzed AIR accuracy of eighty-six readings by twenty Windbridge certified research mediums from "blinded" sitters (i.e., eliminated rater bias, experimenter cueing, and fraud).[11] The reported positive outcomes, considered as valid evidence to support AIR by mediums, led Beischel to conclude that a "non-local source (however controversial) remains the most likely explanation for the accuracy and specificity of their statements."[12] In another study using a more well-controlled triple-blind protocol, the same research group evaluated AIR on individuals not present at the reading (i.e., proxy sitter) who scored target and decoy readings by eight mediums. The results, which indicated that the sitters provided significantly higher scores for target (eighty-one percent of the time) than decoy readings when presented with two or more alternatives, led them to conclude that a form of AIR was "operating during these readings."[13] Collectively, the mediumship research evidence conducted at the Windbridge Institute was summarized by Beischel as follows:

Our data collected under blinded conditions demonstrates that some mediums can demonstrate anomalous information reception. In other words, they have the ability to report accurate and detailed information about a deceased person without any prior knowledge of that person, or about the sitter, the living person wanting to hear from their loved one. The quintuple-blind protocol we use eliminates all the explanations that a skeptic may claim are responsible for a medium's apparent accuracy: fraud, experimenter cueing, information so general it could apply to anyone, rater bias, and "cold reading" (a situation in which a medium uses cues from a present sitter to fabricate an 'accurate' reading).[14]

Support for this conclusion was obtained in a separate study, which evaluated the accuracy of AIR in nine mediums using a blind experimental protocol.[15] The researchers acted as "proxy" sitters to evaluate medium readings without the actual sitter present. Each sitter, presented with both the correct reading and several "decoy" readings given for others in the experimental group, rated each reading on how appropriate it was to them, and commented on why they chose the highest rated reading. According to the researchers, the study results indicated that, "amazingly, fourteen of the thirty-eight readings were correctly chosen and significantly above what would be expected by chance. What's more, one medium in particular stood out above the others: All six of this person's readings were correctly ranked first by each sitter, at quite astronomical odds!"[16] As part of this study, sitters were also asked to cite the specific personal details received from the mediums that was "most meaningful" to them. Two individual accounts are as follows:

1. "The medium referred to a lady that was influential in his [the deceased person's] formative years. So, whether that is mother or whether that is grandmother . . . she can strangle a chicken." The sitter commented that her grandmother (the

deceased person's mother) "killed chickens." She added that, "it freaked me out the first time I saw her do this. I cried so hard that my parents had to take me home. So the chicken strangling is a big deal . . . In fact, I often referred to my sweet grandmother as the chicken killer."[17]

2. "I was given statements from a supposed communicator through the medium that he limped badly in life, that he worked for the Land Registry, that he was an accomplished draughtsman, that his office was in London, and that he supported Arsenal Football Club. All these statements are applicable to my father, who died some years ago."[18].

In an individual case study, the accuracy of AIR by a "very prolific and influential medium," C. Xavier, was evaluated from thirteen letters authored by a deceased personality (J. P.), which was considered "objectively verifiable."[19] The accuracy of the information and the likelihood of Xavier's access to the information via ordinary means were based on documents and interviews with the sister and friends of J. P. Surprisingly, the researchers identified ninety-nine items of "verifiable information" communicated in these letters, of which ninety-eight percent were rated as a "clear and precise fit" with none rated as "no fit."[20] This compelling result led the researchers to conclude that, "ordinary explanations for accuracy of the information (i.e., fraud, chance, information leakage, and cold reading) were only remotely plausible." They also considered that the results "provide empirical support" for consciousness to exist as an entirely physical phenomenon apart from the brain.[21]

Additional evidence to support the validity of AIR by mediums was obtained by psychologist D. Radin, Chief Scientist at the Institute of Noetic Sciences (IONS). The AIR results of nine mediums from forty proxy sitters, who blindly rated their own and five control readings, were considered positive and significant.[22] Interestingly, this finding was consistent with other studies that attempted to mitigate subject bias in their evaluation of medium communications.[23] Similar results were also reported in a large-scale, well-controlled study that employed two groups:

1. A recipient group (N=44) for whom the mediums' messages were intended; and
2. A non-recipient group (N=407) for whom the messages were not intended.[24]

The validity of the study was enhanced by the application of several experimental controls as follows:

1. The mediums were isolated from the sitters;
2. The person for whom the messages were intended was unknown to the medium; and
3. The subjects did not know the group they belonged to or if the messages were intended for them.

The results indicated that the recipient group accepted significantly more of the messages as appropriate to themselves than did individuals in the non-recipient group. According to the researchers, the odds against this positive AIR result occurring by chance were on the "order of a million to one."[25] Interestingly, in July 2016, the IONS announced a five-year, comprehensive research project led by D. Radin to investigate individuals who claim to channel non-human living entities. The IONS research objective is as follows:

> We will use rigorous and systematic methods to study channeling, without preconceived notions about what may or may not be real. We may come to learn that the process is complete "hocus-pocus" and that all mediums are frauds. And then again, we might not. A true scientist is open to either outcome. Through well-designed, blinded, unbiased studies, we will discover which outcome is correct.[26]

Evidence derived from mediumship AIR studies led Professor of Psychology and Medicine G. Schwartz to conclude that mediums can communicate with the deceased.[27] In one study by Schwartz and colleagues, for example, five "well-regarded" mediums were evaluated using one sitter unknown to the mediums who experienced several bereavements. The sitter was allowed to say only "yes" or "no" to questions by the mediums. A control group who did readings on the same sitter based on guesswork was also established. Analysis of the sittings revealed that eighty-three percent of the mediums' statements were rated correct by the sitter as opposed to only thirty-six percent for the control group.[28] According to the researchers, this result represented odds of "ten million to one" that the correct readings occurred by chance. Schwartz believed that the accurate personal AIR by mediums provided compelling evidence that the deceased are capable of communicating with the living.

Despite protocols to control for "fraud, error, and statistical coincidence," and the possible use of ESP by the medium, Schwartz's studies provoked strong methodological criticisms from several researchers (e.g., did not employ blind judging, inappropriate control group, and failure to manage sensory leakage).[29] According to one opponent, psychologist R. Hyman: "Probably no other extended program in psychical research deviates so much from accepted norms of scientific methodology as this one. The studies were methodologically defective in a number of important ways, not the least of which was that they were not double-blind."[30] In response to such criticisms, Schwartz defended the validity of his research by emphasizing that the collective results from his studies, "provided incontrovertible evidence in response to the skeptics' highly implausible argument against the single-blind study that the sitter would be biased in his or her ratings."[31] Despite this justification, the possibility that the positive AIR study outcomes lack sufficient validity and reliability due to methodological problems makes it difficult to conclude with certainty that his research provides convincing evidence to support the survival hypothesis.

- *Negative AIR Outcomes*: The several studies demonstrating positive AIR in mediums were not consistent with the results obtained in a study by psychologists R. Wiseman and C. O'Keeffe.[32] In this study, sitters rated the accuracy of readings from five mediums under tightly controlled experimental conditions as follows:

  1. The sitters were located in a different room and were unknown to the mediums;
  2. The sitters did not know whether the medium's statement was made during their own or another sitter's reading;
  3. Readings were counter-balanced over time to minimize the possibility of any temporal cues; and
  4. Readings were divided into separate statements and given to the sitters for evaluation.

A quantitative risk analysis of medium accuracy revealed no significant difference between the ratings that sitters assigned to their own readings and those assigned to other sitters' readings.[33] This negative outcome is consistent with several studies which also failed to support AIR by mediums.[34]

- *Anecdotal Case Reports*: Individual case studies of alleged medium communications with the deceased have served to support the possible existence of an afterlife. One such account was provided by philosopher M. Sudduth of a Rev. D. Kennedy who documented supposed medium AIR from his deceased wife, Ann.[35] According to Kennedy, on one occasion a medium telephoned him that Ann had "impressed" her to call at that moment to tell him, "get out now and use the old notes." Apparently, he was asleep and would have been late for his service if not awakened by that call. On another occasion, an assumed message from Ann concerned the location of clerical collars, which Kennedy was looking for at the time of the medium's phone call. He contends that Ann knew the location of the collars and the person he was to give a memorial service for on that day.[36]

Of all the mental mediums subjected to study by members of the Society for Psychical Research (SPR), L. E. Piper was the first to provide compelling evidence for AIR. While there are certainly many charlatans who contend they can communicate with the deceased, psychologist W. James stated that it takes only "one white crow to prove that all crows aren't black." Accordingly, L. E. Piper was his "white crow."[37] Initially skeptical of Piper, he became convinced of her honesty and integrity, as reflected in his remark that, "My later knowledge of her sittings and personal acquaintance with her has led me absolutely to reject the latter (lucky coincidence) explanation, and to believe that she has supernormal powers."[38] While the alternative explanation of telepathy has been proposed to account for such ability, this consideration is largely negated when correct information is given, which is not at the time known to the sitter. Piper's unique ability was reinforced by psychologist

A. Gauld who concluded that, "the records of her case are still unsurpassed in quantity and detail and she is one of the very few mediums whose trance speech and writings have been subjected to a serious and extensive psychological analysis."[39] Added support was provided by former SPR President, psychologist D. Fontana who remarked that, "the real stars come along quite rarely. Mrs. Piper was probably the best example, because she was investigated by such careful and well-known researchers."[40] Even lawyer and debunker of spiritual mediums Richard Hodgson, who considered that "nearly all the professional mediums are a gang of vulgar tricksters in league with one another"[41], acknowledged the validity of her abilities after observing hundreds of Piper's sittings. He concluded that, "Frankly, I went to Mrs. Piper twelve years ago with the aim of unmasking her. I entered her house profoundly materialistic, not believing in the continuance of life after death. Now, I say, I believe. The truth has been given to me in such a way as to remove the possibility of a doubt."[42]

The Scole Experiment

The Scole Experiment, conducted by members of the SPR in the late 1990s in Scole, England, constitutes one of the most extensive investigations of mediumship. While controversial in nature, the considerable number and consistency of unexplained incidents observed during the séances by investigators over several years have led many researchers to consider the Scole Experiment as the best evidence to support AIR ability by mediums and the survival hypothesis.

The Scole Report, authored by three investigators from the SPR who participated in the experiment, documented numerous reported phenomena during the experiments. These included lights traveling about the room, accurate personal information from medium communications, images imprinted on unopened rolls of film inside a locked box, materialization of people and objects, being touched, levitation of a table, and disembodied voices, among others. Coauthor of the Scole Report D. Fontanna concluded: "If Scole was genuine—and no one has demonstrated anything to the contrary—it thus provides us with further evidence that some intelligent source of unknown energy is occasionally at work within our material world."[43] Speaking on behalf of the investigators who wrote the report, plant scientist M. Keen stated:

> Our objective was to obtain evidence of a permanent nature which could be experienced or examined independently outside the séance room and which was not wholly reliant on subjective assessment, experience, memory, or feeling: evidence which had been produced under circumstances which precluded human interference and which would satisfy external critics. None of our critics has been able to point to a single example of fraud or deception.[44]

Considered one of the most interesting phenomena of the Scole Experiment was the reported materialized lights that would emit beams, pass through solid objects, move in time to music, produce a physical sensation, and move from one hand to the other. According to Keen, "the light phenomena were the most immediately impressive because of what we considered to be the impossibility of a natural origin or mechanism."[45] One SPR investigator described this phenomena as follows: "There was a small ball of white light which moved around the room in all directions, sometimes at great speed, leaving a trail like a firework by persistence of vision . . . At times the light hovered in mid-air, and then touched some of the sitters, giving them a small electric shock."[46] D. Fontanna, who participated in several experiments as a sitter in the Scole Experiment concluded that, "These phenomena do not conclusively demonstrate the reality of survival, but it would be hard to argue that they do not add materially to the case in its favor."[47] This perspective was based on several phenomena he and other participants experienced as follows:

> Lights ranging in size from a pea to a grape would land on the table in front of us and appear to roll forward towards us before moving swiftly back into the air. Sometimes this would happen in response to requests. They would land upon the palms of our hands, exerting a gentle pressure, as if they carried weight, and allowing us to examine them from close quarters. Hands frequently materialized, sometimes visible as dark silhouettes in the illumination from the spirit lights. Hands caught hold of both mine and lifted them high into the air, and pulled hard at the sweater I sometimes wore. Sometimes we asked the hands to place certain objects taken from the table onto our palms, and this also was unerringly done in the darkness.[48]

A common theme among those who defend the Scole Experiment is that no evidence of hoaxing was ever confirmed. This notion was emphasized by SPR investigator, electrical engineer A. Ellison who emphasized that, "No serious student of the Scole investigation can reasonably conclude that their four years' work and some 500 sittings, most of them closed to outsiders, warrants the assumptions (of fraud) implicit in such a practice. None of our critics has been able to point to a single example of fraud or deception."[49] The validity of the Scole Experiment was also supported by parapsychologist and lawyer V. Zammit who stated:

> For the thinking open-minded skeptic, the evidence for the afterlife produced by the Scole experiments is abundant, legitimate, definitive, and positively conclusive. Once again the hard-core skeptics/critics came up with their anticipated response by claiming fraud or "hoaxing" or deceit of some sort by the Scole Experimenters' Group and refuse to acknowledge that science has once more proved the existence of the afterlife.[50]

The controversy pertaining to the Scole Experiment methodology, results, and associated conclusions has generated many opposing viewpoints as summarized by A. Gauld, who wrote:

> All of the Scole phenomena can be explained by reference to well-established principles of human motivation and action—without any necessary appeal to

spirits of the dead. And, in broad terms, on the basis of previous experience of hoaxing in this area, we can see the sorts of "physical manifestations" in this case as precisely the sorts of things that might have been expected from contemporary hoaxers.[51]

Investigator B. Dunning also questioned the validity of the Scole Experiment due to the perceived lack of adequate experimental protocols. For example, the mediums banned the use of still or video cameras, and the séances were carried out in a room provided by the mediums, not the researchers. Consequently, he considered the Scole Experiment to be, ". . . hampered by a set of rules which explicitly *prevented* any scientific investigation of the phenomena. They (SPR investigators) followed the mediums' instructions to the T and acted as an audience only and not as investigators. The Scole Report details the authors' *perceptions* of what happened in the room; no reader has cause to believe it describes what *actually* happened in the room."[52] The controversy surrounding the Scole Experiment may best be summarized by SPR Communications Officer Tom Ruffles who remarked that, "Scole will put most outside observers such as myself, who never visited and now have to assess the products second hand, in a quandary: impossible to accept all of it, difficult to reject some of it. It is possible that we will never come to a definitive conclusion over what happened in that Norfolk cellar."[53]

Clearly, the strong conflicting arguments pertaining to the validity of the Scole Experiment indicates the need to replicate the study using more well-controlled research protocols established by leading behavioral research scientists. Until then, if ever, evidence from the Scole Experiment will continue to be debated with little, if any, progress made to understand the nature of the phenomena experienced and their associated implications.

Theories

Theories to explain AIR must be considered before firmly concluding that the positive mediumship research outcomes noted prior provide any degree of support for the survival hypothesis. The over-arching question, for instance, remains as to whether the medium is in fact capable of receiving information telepathically from the sitter of the deceased and/or directly from the deceased. Several theories advanced to address this concern include the following:

1. Parapsychological;
2. Super-ESP;
3. The Survival Hypothesis;
4. Combined Super-Psi and Survival-Psi;
5. The Akashic Records;
6. The Psychology of Sitters;
7. The Psychology of Mediums; and
8. Neurobiology.

1. *Parapsychological*: Parapsychology, an interdisciplinary study of human experiences, employs research methods of the social sciences to acquire and analyze data on paranormal experiences. Many parapsychologists who advocate for the continuity of consciousness after physical death do so, in part, on the belief that consciousness is non-local. This notion, which violates established scientific laws that govern known sensory and cognitive abilities, include the broad spectrum of phenomena associated with extra-sensory perception (ESP) which incorporates telepathy (communication between minds); precognition (prediction of future events); clairvoyance (perception without the use of known physical senses); and psychokinesis (manipulation of physical objects by mental influence). Despite the questionable validity of ESP, many scholars from various disciplines consider one or more forms of ESP as the source of AIR by mediums from both the living and deceased.

2. *Super-ESP*: An alternative explanation for the reported authenticity of communication by the medium with the deceased is based on telepathy or clairvoyance from living people by the medium.[54] However, since the survival hypothesis requires an aspect of ESP to facilitate information between the deceased and living, the medium may acquire knowledge of the deceased by telepathy, the deceased telepathically sends information to the medium, or by means of an alternative unknown explanation.[55] Leading parapsychology researcher J. B. Rhine, who founded scientific research in parapsychology as a branch of psychology stated: "There is nothing as yet on record from the studies of mediumship that cannot be explained by the sort of 'omnibus hypothesis' into which we have expanded the old counter-hypothesis of telepathy."[56]

The Super-ESP hypothesis presents a major dilemma. That is, if mediumship evidence to support the survival hypothesis is to be proven, it must be confirmed by consulting records and/or surviving individuals that the information given by the communicator was accurate. However, if these sources are not present, they might in theory be telepathically or clairvoyantly accessible to the medium or percipient. And since we do not know the parameters and boundaries of ESP, we can never say for certain that ESP is not possible.

The possibility that mediums may utilize super-ESP in their representations of supposed communication from the dead was evidenced in one case by A. Gauld.[57] This involved a communicator calling himself G. Davis during his sittings with B. Cooper, a direct voice medium.[58] Davis referred correctly to matters relating to past acquaintances, used forms of words characteristic of the real G. Davis, and the medium described detailed features of Davis's house. Subsequently, a researcher who learned that G. Davis was still alive, visited him and learned that much of the medium's information about the house was correct despite the fact that Davis had not moved in until a year after the sittings. According to Gauld, this case represents an example of the "construction of a mediumistic communicator by means of telepathy with the sitter plus precognitive telepathy or clairvoyance relating to a distant living person."[59] If true, then it represents evidence of information obtained telepathically from living persons whose existence was unknown to the medium.

The Super-ESP theory is not without controversy. One major criticism is the absence of compelling well-controlled experimental evidence that confirms one's ability using ESP to obtain accurate information from sitters they do not know, and from deceased individuals who were unknown to them in life. Unfortunately, this reported common but very weak ability, is difficult, if not impossible to test empirically.[60] In fact, many psychologists consider Super-ESP untestable because, "it postulates an omniscient and omnipotent capacity that cannot be falsified by the scientific method."[61] This same conclusion, however, can certainly apply to the survival hypothesis. Philosopher and parapsychologist S. Braude, for example, contends that it is, "exceedingly difficult, if not impossible, to defend the survival hypothesis against the hypothesis of living-agent psi."[62]

Support for the survival hypothesis was formulated by A. Gauld based on evidence provided by some mediumistic communications of reincarnated personalities which provide "so many correct and detailed apparent memories of a former existence on earth that ESP by medium or reincarnated subject scarcely seems a possible explanation."[63] Although Gauld did not exclude the possibility of "Super-ESP," he discounted this theory due to the inability to justify other aspects of the evidence for survival represented by the demonstration of "skills, personality traits, purposes, a whole point of view, and characteristic of the formerly living person."[64] Consequently, he considered that the Super-ESP hypothesis "suffers from a large credibility gap."

3. *The Survival Hypothesis*: The survival hypothesis, which alleges that the deceased are capable of providing accurate information significant to them during their previous life to the living, promotes the continuity of consciousness after physical death. Collectively, research in AIR by mediums, and near-death and out-of-body experiences led J. Beischel to conclude that, "the survival of consciousness after physical death ('life after death') is the theory that best explains all of that data."[65] Support for the survival hypothesis was also advanced by psychologist and leading researcher in reincarnation studies. I. Stevenson who stated that, "Since the Super-ESP theory assumes that discarnate personalities do not exist, it has to attribute motive for a particular mediumistic communication or apparitional experience to the subject. But evidence of such a motive is not always available, and we should not assume that one exists in the absence of such evidence."[66]

An opposing viewpoint of accurate AIR mediumship evidence, suggestive of the survival of consciousness after physical death, is that it is due to chance coincidence, sensory cues, and/or cheating by the medium, rather than communication from the deceased. This consideration is reinforced by those who contend that the acquisition of the information by mediums arise through ESP with the living who knew the deceased and not from the deceased.[67] J. B. Rhine, who considered the survival hypothesis untestable, suggested that the question of survival requires a better understanding of ESP abilities of the living.[68] A reasonable perspective, consistent with my position, is represented by Rhine's statement that, "For one thing, it is necessary to know the limits and conditions of the operation of the psi process before we can design adequate experiments dealing with the survival hypothesis. It is only when we have evidence of something beyond the range of explanation by ESP that a case for survival begins."[69]

Successful proxy sittings present a challenge to opponents of the survival hypothesis. It is very difficult to explain, for example, how the medium is able to locate sources of accurate information remote from the environment, and from the sitter who may be unknown to the medium. One theory is that the medium obtains information of the identity of the person acting as proxy from the sitter's mind, and the associated information from the proxy's mind. Proxy sittings also provide a means of addressing the other major normal explanation for mediumistic statements, which is that most of the statements are general or vague enough that they can apply to many people or be interpreted in a variety of ways by different sitters. Consequently, successful mediumistic sittings have been generally regarded as the result of chance, and the biased selection of statements that is consistent with the sitter's wishful thinking. A strong criticism of this non-local ESP-based process was expressed by A. Gauld, who wrote:

> One has only to ask oneself in detail what would be involved here to see that the proposed process is grotesquely implausible. Proper names, addresses, dates, and so forth—details which identify a person uniquely—are notoriously among the most difficult of all items for sensitives to obtain; and yet such uniquely identifying details (or their equivalents) would have to be obtained in a proxy case before the medium could pinpoint the right source of information to tap; and in some cases they would have to be obtained from several sources as the medium's mind so to speak moved along the chain of clues.[70]

4. *Combined Super-ESP and Survival-ESP*: This theory proposes that mediums obtain information using both Super-ESP and Survival-ESP from the deceased. According to one medium, this information "comes in" from the deceased (i.e., Survival-ESP) rather than having to "reach out" (i.e., Super-ESP) to acquire the information.[71] M. Sudduth summarized this theory by stating that, "the best explanation for the survival evidence is that some interaction with discarnate souls is involved," and that ESP of the living "serves as the basis of mediumship information at times."[72]

5. *The Akashic Records*: One highly controversial theory is that the medium accesses information not from the living or deceased but rather from the theoretical existence of the Akashic Records. This information field has been described symbolically as a universal computer which contains, "energetic records of all souls about their past lives, the present lives, and possible future lives."[73] Accordingly, it has been proposed that each soul has its Akashic

Records, "like a series of books with each book representing one lifetime; that is, the Akashic Records is where "all souls are stored energetically."[74] This elusive theory, therefore, suggests that both past-life recall and medium communication with the deceased is allowed for by one's consciousness, which in some way not fully understood, retrieves the memory of a deceased individual from this information field and assumes them as its own. This abstract and unconfirmed concept is described by D. Fontanna:

> It might be that the medium's mind does not need to travel clairvoyantly to wherever this evidence exists, and that he or she accesses it from some paranormal data bank (e.g., the Akashic Records). However, since there is not a scrap of evidence that this supposed data bank exists in physical space, in order to access it the medium's mind would have to operate outside space-time.[75]

6. *The Psychology of Sitters*: All of us have at one time or another sought out and assigned more weight to evidence or information that confirms our beliefs or desires. This error in inductive reasoning is termed "confirmation bias," i.e., the inherent tendency to search for or interpret information that confirms one's preconceptions. Research psychologists maintain that one's belief in mediumship readings is primarily associated with such biased reasoning. The notion that the psychology of some sitters may contribute to their acceptance of information by mediums was explained by social psychologist D. J. Bem, who wrote: "The problem with such subjective validations, of course, is that sitters—who are typically highly motivated believers in the afterlife hypothesis are free to selectively interpret ambiguous or multiple-choice statements (e.g., 'I am getting a name that starts with an 'M' or an 'R.'") to fit any of several of their deceased friends or relatives."[76]

Psychologists have identified factors in language itself which make vague readings by mediums seem very definite and accurate. Inappropriate decisions facilitated by "confirmation bias" associated with language was evidenced in one study whereby one third of the subjects who participated in a fake seance believed one's suggestion that a table had moved when it remained stationary.[77] The researchers also confirmed a significant relationship between the reported movement of the table and belief in the paranormal. This conclusion was based on results, which showed that a significantly greater percentage of believers than disbelievers concluded that the table had moved, and that approximately one fifth of the subjects considered that the fake seances comprised actual paranormal phenomena. Apparently, believers were more susceptible to suggestion than disbelievers, but only when the suggestion was consistent with their confidence in the paranormal.[78]

7. *The Psychology of Mediums*: A psychosocial model of mediums was developed by psychologist E. de O Maraldi based on an analysis of dissociation (i.e., detachment from reality), paranormal beliefs, and self-esteem in eleven mediums.

The results of this study, which indicated that one of the main characteristics of the source of automatic writing is the acknowledgment by mediums that it is facilitated by an alleged spirit, led him to conclude that mediums exhibit dissociative behavior.[79] In contrast, evidence that mediumship is not associated with dissociation or other forms of psychological pathology was provided in a cross-sectional psychological survey study.[80] This incorporated a psychological profile of mediums, analyzed by comparing the psychological well-being of 159 mental mediums to seventy-nine non-mediums on measures of dissociation, fantasy-proneness (i.e., difficulty differentiating between fantasy and reality), and personality characteristics. The researchers concluded that the mediums: 1) scored significantly higher than non-mediums on psychological well-being; 2) reported lower "psychological distress," and 3) were not found to manifest a dissociation or fantasy-proneness disorder.[81]

One commonly held theory to account for accurate AIR is that mediums are capable of leading the people being read to believe the information received; that is, no meaningful information is conveyed by either Super-ESP or Survival-ESP; the medium employs unique skills to obtain information by normal perceptual means, guesswork, and deceit.

8. *Neurobiology*: Researchers have employed brain scanning techniques to better understand the possible contribution of physiologic brain activity responsible for supposed accurate AIR mediumship ability. The theory that if ESP exists, brain activity should differentiate ESP from non-ESP stimuli, was tested in a study which presented participants ESP and non-ESP visual stimuli.[82] The stimuli were identical with the exception that the ESP stimuli were not only presented visually, but also telepathically, clairvoyantly, and precognitively to participants. The neuroimaging results, which showed that participants' brains responded identically to ESP and non-ESP stimuli, led the researchers to consider this as the "best evidence to date against the existence of ESP." In contrast, support for a neurological correlate of AIR was demonstrated in a study by which psychometric and electrophysiology data were collected from six individuals who had reportedly provided accurate AIR of the deceased under well-controlled experimental conditions.[83] These data were obtained while the subjects were asked to achieve each of the following mental states: 1) thinking about a known living person; 2) listening to a biography; 3) thinking about an imaginary person; and 4) interacting mentally with a known deceased person. The results indicated statistically significant differences among these states in all subjects, primarily in the Gamma brain wave. Interestingly, an enhanced presence of this brain wave is considered to contribute towards expanded consciousness and spiritual emergence, although its role in subjective awareness remains unknown.[84] Based on this finding, the researchers suggested that, "the impression of communicating with the deceased may be a distinct mental state different from ordinary thinking or imagination."[85] Clearly, additional research

is needed to determine the underlying contributing factor(s) for the reported change in the Gamma brain wave, and if this outcome is facilitated by the brain itself or an unknown artifact.

Another physiological study of brain activity measured during a mediumship process was conducted by clinical psychologist and neuroscientist J. Peres using photon emission computed tomography (i.e., provides three dimensional cross-sectional information of the brain).[86] This activity was measured in five "less expert" and five "experienced" mediums while performing psychography (i.e., the deceased purportedly writes through the medium's hand) during both dissociative trance and non-trance states. The results indicated that the experienced mediums had reduced activity in several brain regions during psychography and higher averaged complexity scores for psychographed content compared to their normal (non-trance) writing. The researchers concluded that, "the fact that subjects produced complex content in a trance dissociative state suggests that relaxation is an unlikely explanation for the under-activation of brain areas specifically related to the cognitive processing being carried out."[87] The reason(s) for this physiologic state remains unknown.

Discussion

For more than a century, researchers have evaluated AIR by mediums. Despite claims to the contrary, there exists a lack of compelling evidence to support the notion that some individuals are capable of communicating with the deceased. Consequently, a daunting, if not impossible task for researchers is to resolve whether reported accurate AIR by mediums is obtained from the non-local consciousness of the deceased (i.e., Survival Hypothesis), through ESP with the living (i.e., Super-ESP Hypothesis), from their combination (i.e., Survival Hypothesis and Super-ESP hypothesis), or from other possible sources (e.g., confirmation bias, deception, and/or fraud).

The conflicting research evidence, combined with the limited number (if any) of experiments that employ stringent accepted scientific methodology, have contributed to mainstream science's skepticism of both Super-ESP and mediumistic communication with the deceased. Although controversial, the preliminary evidence should serve as a basis for continued mediumship research to address several unresolved issues that pertain to one's ability to obtain valid information using non-local processes and the associated survival hypothesis. This is especially important since mediumship is the only phenomenon directly relevant to the survival hypothesis given that it can be produced and observed under well-controlled experimental conditions. Consequently, an initial imperative step is for researchers to develop mediumship criteria and appropriate experimental protocol to define and evaluate the possible characteristics of what it is that may survive death. In other words, how can the survival hypothesis be adequately tested if there lacks consensus of what constitutes proof in mediumship research? While it is one thing to possibly demonstrate accurate AIR by mediums, it is another thing entirely to conclude that such information represents irrefutable evidence of communication from the deceased. This is apparent since the reported accurate AIR evidence, while suggestive of post-mortem survival, does not exclude the influence of Super-ESP. To possibly resolve this over-arching concern, the following methodological issues proposed by established mediumship investigators A. Rock and J. Beischel should be considered as a foundation to build upon in future investigations as follows:

1. Evaluation of the mediums' "report that they are communicating directly with the deceased," and
2. Evaluation of the mediums' "alleged ability to differentiate between that communication and their use of ESP."[88]

The distinction between the concepts of survival after death and ESP may be made if these two experiences differ under controlled conditions.

This research protocol, concomitant with the experimental strategies proposed by R. Wiseman and C. O'Keeffe,[89] should also be considered by researchers to help answer two fundamental questions:

1. Is consciousness a localized product of the brain as theorized by materialist neuroscientists or is consciousness non-local?
2. Does positive AIR medium evidence represent valid communication with the deceased and/or living, ESP, or psychological factors in sitters and mediums?

And if consciousness is eventually proven to be non-local in nature, then what are its' potential implications for life after death? Thus, despite the existing highly controversial experimental and anecdotal evidence suggestive of the survival of consciousness after physical death, it is still premature to conclude whether the origin of the experience lies in the Super-ESP of the medium, in the intentions of a potential discarnate being, or from other potential sources. Consequently, research which employs more well-controlled experimental protocol and defined criteria, that is uniformly approved by the scientific community, should be employed to evaluate the source, accuracy, and validity of AIR by mediums.

CHAPTER SEVEN

CONNECTING THE DOTS

Introduction

What we typically find in the literature pertaining to the survival hypothesis is an accumulation of evidence, consisting largely of testimonial claims, descriptions of the methods of their verification, and associated conclusions. And the conclusion most often drawn is that the survival hypothesis is the best explanation. But while many scholars firmly contend to have compelling evidence to prove "life after death," I often feel misled by the corresponding lack of scientifically derived justifiable evidence and associated rationale to support this astonishing decision. All too often, this is the case in topic areas associated with life after death research as evidenced by the extraordinary controversial research procedures and associated analyses and interpretations made by many researchers. After all, skepticism is incorporated in the scientific method.

The scientific method integrates the observation of a phenomenon, the development of a hypothesis about the phenomenon, experimentation designed to demonstrate the truth (or not) of the hypothesis, and a conclusion that supports or amends the hypothesis. That is, a hypothesis becomes a fact when confirmed by strict scientific standards, which is of course, subject to challenge. So when we hear extraordinary claims of seeing and communicating with deceased relatives, having lived before this life, perceiving reality beyond the confines of one's physical body, and experiencing another realm of existence during a period of no detectable brain activity, I say "great, prove it." In other words, skeptical analysis of such claims serves as a necessary component to refining theories and initiating the continuation of related investigations to seek verification, or not, of experimental results and conclusions.

The application of the scientific method, however, is likely impossible to adequately apply to test if the survival hypothesis is true or not since it lacks tangible, objective based evidence to study. A reliable, widely accepted test that can yield persuasive evidence in support of either outcome simply does not exist since science lacks the accepted principles and required methodology needed to evaluate the concept of life after death. Yet, despite these significant limitations, the reported anecdotal and experimental research findings addressed prior are regarded by many as compelling evidence in support of this concept.

All the theories that attempt to explain life after death can't be correct and maybe they are all incorrect. But how do we know who and what to believe when the preponderance of evidence is hearsay, anecdotal, and lacking in hard, verifiable, undisputable facts? The difficulty incurred from diverse opinions tend to leave us confused about who and what to believe. Much of this problem is struggling to filter sense from nonsense especially since skeptics often adopt the position that those who believe in immortality consider that because their claims have not been disproved. But while I take serious notice of the perspectives on life after death by prodigious minds, it is still a belief and not a conclusion formulated using scientific principles applied under well-controlled experimental conditions. After all, the greatest intellects and spiritual leaders do not necessarily hold the truth on everything, especially something as elusive and seemingly impossible to prove as some form of conscious existence after death. Within this context, consider the perspectives held by some of the greatest minds of our times as follows:

Perspectives on Life after Death

Quantum consciousness begins to dissipate into the cosmos as the quantum processes in the brain terminate, but it returns to the brain once the physical body is revived. The individual may recall an out-of-body experience, seeing their dead relatives, or walking towards a light or tunnel, as a result of quantum consciousness reentering the brain with new information.[1]

S. Hameroff, anesthesiologist

Aspects of a personality might be able to survive bodily death and persist for a while as an enduring mental entity, existing somewhere in Descartes' world of mental things, but capable on rare occasions of reconnecting with the physical world. Quantum mechanics would both allow our conscious efforts to influence our own bodily actions, and also allow certain purported phenomena such as "possession," "mediumship," and "reincarnation" to be reconciled with the basic precepts of contemporary physics.[2]

H. Stapp, mathematical physicist

Death "cannot exist in any real sense" . . . "when we die our life becomes a perennial flower that returns to bloom in the multiverse."[3]

R. Lanza, physician and chief scientific officer
at the Astellas Institute for Regenerative Medicine

What we consider the here and now, this world, it is actually just the material level that is comprehensible. The beyond is an infinite reality that is much bigger which this world is rooted in. In this way, our lives in this plane of existence are encompassed, surrounded by the afterworld already . . . The body dies but the spiritual quantum field continues. In this way, I am immortal.[4]

H. Peter Dürr, physicist and former head
of the Max Planck Institute for Physics in Munich

If we were to apply Occam's Razor to the total set of data collected over the past hundred years, there is a straightforward hypothesis that is elegant in its simplicity. This is the simple hypothesis that consciousness continues after death. This hypothesis accounts for all the data.[5]

G. Schwartz, psychologist

I accept reincarnation as the best explanation for a case only after I have excluded all others—normal and paranormal. I conclude, however, that all the other interpretations may apply to a few cases, but to no more than a few. I believe, therefore, that reincarnation is the best explanation for the stronger cases.[6]

I. Stevenson, psychiatrist

The soul takes nothing with her to the next world but her education and her culture. At the beginning of the journey to the next world, one's education and culture can either provide the greatest assistance, or else act as the greatest burden, to the person who has just died.[7]

Plato, philosopher and mathematician

I believe that the soul of man is immortal and will be treated with justice in another life, respecting its conduct in this. "I look upon death to be as necessary to the constitution as sleep. We shall rise refreshed in the morning."[8]

Ben Franklin, political theorist, politician, scientist, and inventor

My life often seemed to me like a story that has no beginning and no end. I had the feeling that I was an historical fragment, an excerpt for which the preceding and succeeding text was missing. I could well imagine that I might have lived in former centuries and there encountered questions I was not yet able to answer; that I had been born again because I had not fulfilled the task given to me.[9]

Carl Jung, psychiatrist and psychotherapist
who founded analytical psychology

I am confident that there truly is such a thing as living again, that the living spring from the dead, and that the souls of the dead are in existence.[10]

Socrates, one of the founders of Western philosophy

Souls are poured from one into another of different kinds of bodies of the world.[11]

Jesus Christ in Gnostic Gospels: Pistis Sophia,
central figure of Christianity, whom the teachings of most
Christian denominations hold to be the Son of God

Immortality? There are two kinds. The first lives in the imagination of the people, and is thus an illusion. There is a relative immortality which may conserve the memory of an individual for some generations. But there is only one true immortality, on a cosmic scale, and that is the immortality of the cosmos itself. There is no other.[12]

Albert Einstein, theoretical physicist

I have lived with the prospect of an early death for the last forty-nine years. I'm not afraid of death, but I'm in no hurry to die. I have so much I want to do first. I regard the brain as a computer which will stop working when its components fail. There is no heaven or afterlife for broken down computers; that is a fairy story for people afraid of the dark.[13]

Stephen Hawking, theoretical physicist
and director of research at the Centre for Theoretical Cosmology
at the University of Cambridge

I would love to believe that when I die I will live again, that some thinking, feeling, remembering part of me will continue. But as much as I want to believe that, and despite the ancient and worldwide cultural traditions that assert an afterlife, I know of nothing to suggest that it is more than wishful thinking.[14]

C. Sagan, astrophysicist

I don't believe in an afterlife, so I don't have to spend my whole life fearing hell, or fearing heaven even more. For whatever the tortures of hell, I think the boredom of heaven would be even worse. [15]

I. Asimov, author and professor of biochemistry

Super-ESP or Life after Death?

The survival hypothesis is primarily defended by the notion that consciousness can function while the body is clinically dead. And if consciousness is not of the body and of something else (e.g., Super-ESP), it is not surprising that some consider a form of mind-body dualism as authentic. This conclusion is based largely on the NDE evidence that involves veridical OBEs, i.e., lucid consciousness and perceptual capacities despite a severely compromised brain.[16] According to the Super-ESP hypothesis, the primary argument against the survival hypothesis, during a conscious OBE, one's telepathic ability enables the observation of events remote from the body. Extending this concept to the NDE, proponents of Super-ESP contend that one's fear of dying facilitates their psychic ability to allow for veridical information to be obtained from the memories of living persons. Accordingly, this process "stimulates a hallucinatory experience that is incorporated into their NDE," which acts as an inherent psychological coping mechanism in the form of a "meeting with deceased spirits" that provides comfort when facing death.[17] Consequently, the terror experienced awaiting impending death somehow triggers psychic events that mitigate fear in the form of palliative illusory perceptions. Thus, the Super-ESP refutes the NDE as evidence of life after death.

Mediumship and reincarnation evidence, which imply that an individual may exhibit knowledge about the deceased, have largely contributed to the Super-ESP/ life after death debate. Some of the best examples are represented by mediumship evidence in which "drop-in" communicators provide accurate information about themselves that are later found to be true. Researchers who support the survival hypothesis also claim to have ruled out other hypotheses (e.g., Super-ESP, psycho-cultural, dissociative phenomena, rare cognitive skills, fraud, etc.) by arguing that they cannot adequately explain the apparent accurate knowledge some mediums and young children who claim to remember past lives exhibit. Psychologist S. Braude, who contends that mediums use exceptional psychic powers to gather information of the deceased from living witnesses (e.g., telepathy) or from documents (e.g., clairvoyance), has argued for cases sufficiently rich in detail as evidence to support the survival hypothesis, but believes no such evidence exists.[18] I. Stevenson explained this issue succinctly by stating: "Since the [Super-ESP] theory assumes that discarnate personalities do not exist, it has to attribute motive for a particular mediumistic communication or apparitional experience to the subject. But evidence of such a motive is not always available, and we should not assume that one exists in the absence of such evidence."[19] Philosopher M. Sudduth also argued that while ESP among the living is sometimes a component of mediumship evidence, it is not sufficient to show that this is "Super-ESP at work or that nothing else is going on."[20] A similar position is held by Director of the Centre for Systems Philosophy" D. Rousseau, who remarked that, "The Super-ESP theorist may in fact be sympathetic to the ideas of dualism and/or survival, but I just don't think that discarnate interactionism is the best explanation for the evidence suggestive of survival."[21] Such assumptions, which cannot be adequately tested using established scientific principles and accepted test protocol, make it impossible to interpret explanations of evidence in support (or not) of communication from the deceased with confidence.

There exists a key question at hand which must be addressed to help explain the possibility of life after death. That is, do mediums who claim to communicate with the deceased, individuals who claim past-life experiences, and those who display extraordinary skills (e.g., child prodigies, speak a different language, or play a musical instrument, etc.) without prior knowledge or training, provide compelling evidence to reject the Super-ESP hypothesis and accept the survival hypothesis? According to the Super-ESP hypothesis, successful mediums obtain much of their information about deceased persons by somehow accessing and retrieving the memory of the living. However, since past experience from the brain's coded representations of such experience is dependent on normal brain function, this widely accepted principle is challenged by those who consider that memory may exist after death of the body. The question, therefore, emerges as to how one can have conscious recall of a claimed past life if memory representations are dissolved along with the brain after death? Consequently, in the absence of post-mortem memory representations, how can mediums telepathically access the deceased? The Super-ESP hypothesis, therefore, is weak unless we assume that memory storage manifests not only in the brain but also externally to the brain, as some propose in the form of what is referred to as a collective unconscious memory bank, (i.e., the Akashic records, or "the mind of God").[22] The key questions advanced from mediumship and reincarnation evidence, therefore, is whether or not information about the deceased is accessed through either:

a. Communication exchange with an aspect of consciousness associated with another body at an earlier period of time, which presently exists in an incarnated person;

b. A memory trace of the deceased person's life experiences; or

c. The memory from the survival of the person's consciousness?

Since the validity of accurate past life reincarnation and mediumship evidence to support a living consciousness of the deceased is unconfirmed, the survival hypothesis is seriously challenged by the inadequacy of existing explanations of such questions.

This similar concern may extrapolate to apparitional experiences, especially the collectively perceived crisis apparition. This "crisis" case, which is considered to be facilitated by the dying person who is its original, may also be produced by a "living person (one of the percipients) in response to extrasensorially acquired information about his death."[23] Cases of veridical apparitions of the dead have also been explained as a manifestation enabled somehow from the mind of a living person grieving about the referenced deceased person. Psychical researcher F. Myers, however, considers this evidence to support the survival hypothesis since the creator of the apparition cannot be among the percipients of it. That is, the apparition is veridical to the extent that it "contains details and conveys information unknown to the witnesses, represents a person with whom they were not acquainted, and ostensibly pursues a goal which they do not consciously entertain, etc."[24] If Myers is correct, veridical post-mortem apparitions are not created in the mind of the percipient since there is no person known to be thinking or grieving over the deceased. So, is it Super-ESP or life after death?

The Holographic Concept of Reality, Quantum Consciousness, and Life after Death

The theories and associated experiments in quantum physics, (e.g., law of entanglement, double-slit, non-locality, and the "observer effect"), concomitant with unexplained anecdotal evidence from studies in NDE, OBE, mediumship, past-life recall, apparitions, super-psi, among other phenomena, lend indirect evidence to support the concept that our consciousness may influence and give rise to various phenomena that seem to exist in the physical world. Theories developed from studies in quantum physics may provide the foundation to eventually explain the relationship between scientific principles, paranormal events, and the concept of life after death.

Advancements in quantum theory aiming to join together all physical processes have opened the door to a profoundly new vision of reality, where observer, observed, and the act of observation are somehow connected. The observation, for instance, that our conscious perception compels an electron to assume a definite position, acknowledges that we create of our own reality (i.e., the "observer effect"). Taking this a step further, many physicists conclude on this basis that the universe is a "mental" construction and that the interconnectedness of everything is particularly evident in the non-local interactions of the quantum universe.[25] Theoretical physicist Fred Alan Wolf sums up this view as follows:

> There is evidence (i.e., quantum physics) that suggests the existence of a non-material, non-physical universe that has a reality even though it might not as yet be clearly perceptible to our senses and scientific instrumentation. When we consider out-of-body experiences, shamanic journeys and lucid dream states, though they cannot be replicated in the true scientific sense, they also point to the existence of non-material dimensions of reality.[26]

- *The Holographic Concept of Reality*: The "Holographic Concept of Reality," first suggested by Miller, Webb, and Dickson[27] and advanced by many noted scientists[28] considers the Universe as one dynamic holomovement—a grand Unity. In other words, there is a more fundamental reality represented by an invisible fluidity comprised of an inseparable interconnectedness of reciprocal patterns of meaningful information about the universe. More specifically, our universe instead of being a three-dimensional spatial construct, is actually more like a holographic image built up by interacting vibratory waves, like colliding ripples on the surface of a pond. Within this context, some physicists suggest that the nature of reality is fundamentally analogous to that of a holographic projection associated with a form of 3-D photography where objects to be photographed are illuminated by a laser beam; that is, lightwaves bouncing off the objects collide and form "interference patterns" which encode the spacial information about the illuminated objects. Consequently, any fragment of a holographic picture contains all the information to reproduce the entire original 3D scene, despite the fragment size. Thus, the term "holographic" refers to a condition where a fragment contains all of the information to reconstruct the whole of which it was a part. In this paradigm, all potential information about the universe is holographically encoded in the spectrum of frequency patterns constantly bombarding us. If so, reality may consist of embedded holograms which somehow gives rise to our existence and perceptual experiences. Related to this perspective are both the controversial Superstring Theory, which proposes the existence of an additional six dimensions beyond our three-dimensional reality where the concept of other possible dimensions of existence arises,[29] and the Quantum Hologram Theory (QHT), which describes the universe as a self-organizing inter-connected conscious holistic system.[30]

Noted scientists such as D. Bohm, K. Wilber, B. Greene, and K. Pribram consider that biological and physical phenomena associated with theories of consciousness may also be explained by quantum theory.[31] In fact, K. Pribram considers that brain activity and memory are facilitated by holographic principles that convert incoming physical energy received by the senses into perceptions. This potential information, therefore, is holographically encoded in the spectrum of frequency patterns, which influence our experiences. Taking this complex concept to the next level, physicists contend that our brains construct "concrete" reality by interpreting such frequencies from another dimension, which transcends time and space. Thus, the brain may behave as a hologram by interpreting a holographic universe and their interrelatedness, which somehow gives rise to our existence and sensory images. This "holonomic brain theory" of quantum consciousness or "holistic" view of reality (i.e., a whole system being more than just the sum of its parts) has gained increasing support among neurophysiologists such as J. Hayward, who emphasized that "some scientists belonging to the scientific mainstream frankly say that consciousness next to space, time, matter, and energy could be one of the basic elements of the world."[32] But don't interpret this perspective too literally since it stands in sharp contrast to the founder of the general theory of relativity, Dr. A. Einstein, who believed that quantum mechanics is "not a complete or holistic science."[33] In support of Einstein's viewpoint, physicist R. Feynman remarked that quantum mechanic explanations of reality are, "marred with multiple unresolved paradoxes" and "no one understands it."[34]

The most significant theoretical consideration of the Quantum Hologram Theory (QHT) is that at the subatomic scale of matter everything in the universe is interconnected. In other words, all objects in the universe retain evidence of each event that has occurred to them, which is stored in a holographic form that can be retrieved by the mind when it "attends" to an object.[35] The QHT, which allows for distinctions that occur in our consciousness, and those that can manifest on a physical scale, may provide the foundation for understanding how things interact with one another such as thoughts in telepathic experiments and consciousness with the brain. For example, if a person's consciousness is shared with another in the QH field and they are in close contact throughout space-time, telepathy may occur (i.e., non-locality). In fact, many physicists apply the QHT to explain the nature by which the consciousness of the deceased may communicate with the living non-locally.

- *Quantum Consciousness and Non-Locality*: The apparent enigma with the concept of "consciousness" is that it is difficult to define and implicates many different things. According to the QHT, consciousness is an essential component of the universe, and all matter possesses subjective characteristics of consciousness (i.e., the foundation of everything). The QHT, which considers consciousness non-local in the same sense that quantum objects behave in a non-local manner, has potential significant implications for understanding death. In other words, upon death, we may no longer exist in space-time but instead behave outside the constraints of our 3-D space-time continuum. Despite the many unresolved questions associated with how the information of the QH may be transmitted over vast distances, many physicists, such as Nobel Prize recipient E. Wigner, are realizing the implications of quantum mechanics for possibly explaining the nature of life after death and anomalous events. For example, Wigner considers theories in quantum mechanics as proof of "the existence of 'God' or some form of "cosmic consciousness," while physicist and brain researcher C. Hellwig advocates that consciousness is a quantum state, and that "our thoughts, our will, our consciousness, and our feelings show properties that could be referred to as spiritual properties."[36] Support for this complex notion may be evidenced, in part, by reported ESP experiments which tend to illustrate that "telepathy" is not affected by distance (outside space) and "precognition," which provides information of future events (outside time). Through extrapolation of such evidence, therefore, it may be possible for a characteristic of consciousness to remain unaffected by death and to continue to function, in some capacity, in some undefined realm of existence beyond our 3-D space-time continuum.

The consistency of reported near-death and out-of body experiences may be critical for understanding the relationship between the brain and consciousness. Although our current medical and scientific concepts are inadequate to explain all aspects of the NDE, however, certain features of an NDE/OBE appear to correspond with some of the basic principles from quantum theory, such as non-locality and coherence or interconnectedness, and instantaneous information exchange in a timeless and placeless dimension. The perplexing aspect of the NDE/OBE, concomitant with the experimental results in non-local intuition, also suggests that our consciousness may be separate from our physical body and capable of affecting events remote from our body. More specifically, if sensory information processing is in fact "non-local" it may explain the reported altered perception and the life review and images often described as a dimension without time and space associated with an NDE/OBE.

Reciprocal OBE cases represent especially intriguing evidence to support the consciousness-brain distinction and the associated survival hypothesis. This is represented by one who goes through an OBE and finds himself/herself at a distant location from their physical body, and is observed by another person at that same location. One documented case of a reciprocal OBE is of M. Johnson, who described a dream in which she traveled "by walking or floating" to her mother's home more than 900 miles away on January 27, 1957. Her account is as follows:

> After a little while I seemed to be alone going through a great blackness. Then all at once way down below me, as though I were at a great height, I could see a small bright oasis of light in the vast sea of darkness. I started on an incline towards it as I knew it was a small house by the school where my mother lives. After I entered, I leaned up against the dish cupboard with folded arms, a pose I often assume. I looked at my mother who was bending over something white

and doing something with her hands. She did not appear to see me at first, but she finally looked up. I had a sort of pleased feeling and then after standing a second more, I turned and walked about four steps.[37]

She awoke from her dream at 2:10 a.m. (1:10 a.m. Minnesota time). A paraphrased account of her mother's experiences were provided in two letters to her daughter by A. Gauld:

I believe it was Saturday night, 1:10 a.m., January 26 or the 27th. It would have been 2:10 a.m. your time. I was pressing a blouse here in the kitchen. I looked up and there you were by the cupboard just standing smiling at me. I started to speak and you were gone. I forgot for a minute where I was. I think the dogs saw you too. They got so excited and wanted out—just like they thought you were by the door—sniffed and were so tickled. Your hair was combed nice—just back in a ponytail with the pretty roll in front. Your blouse was neat and light—seemed almost white.[38]

If both M. Johnson's and her mother's account represent accurate details of their experiences, the existence of a duplicate "astral" body as a vehicle for an aspect of her consciousness or product of it, cannot be entirely dismissed. This evidence, which lacks verification, tentatively suggests that the instrument required for our surviving "I" (i.e., memories, personality, etc.) manifests in an "astral" secondary body whose manner and nature of function have yet, if ever, to be realized. If we extrapolate this evidence to the apparitional phenomenon of the dead and of living projectors, one may infer that apparitions of both the living and dead represent the same "astral" vehicle for one's consciousness.

• *The Synchronized Universe Model and Zero Point Field*: The nature of many unexplainable experiences may possibly be justified by the Zero Point Field (ZPF) (i.e., the lowest possible energy of a quantum mechanical physical system) postulated by physicist C. Swanson, who considers the ZPF to offer "much promise if we are to understand paranormal phenomena."[39] Consequently, anomalous events such as ESP, apparitions, reincarnation, and OBE and NDE, among others, may be explained by Swanson's Synchronized Universe Model (S.U.M.) of which the ZPF is a part. More specifically, photons created by "distant matter" contain almost all the matter of the universe and interact with one another over long distances (i.e., non-locality). Therefore, every "zig and zag of a local electron is really a communication between it and the distant matter."[40] If factual, the synchronous interaction of particles across great distances and times may explain ESP, whereby, "the sender can cause energy or information to refocus at some other point in space-time using the 4-D holographic principle."[41] By extension, the S.U.M may also provide the underlying principle(s) to explain:

1. How our consciousness may leave the body and travel in space and time;

2. The NDE and OBE in which one describes reality apart from the body; and

3. The foundation to explain life after death and paranormal phenomena.

According to Swanson, the S.U.M can "explain how paranormal effects can be seemingly immune to time and space displacements. It may help us understand how two minds can be linked when separated by vast distances of space and time. And it offers a way to connect paranormal effects to changes in quantum noise, which is one of the central mysteries facing the new physics."[42]

Accordingly, the S.U.M, QHT, and ZPF, among other theories within quantum physics, have the potential to explain the reported connection between one's own consciousness and that of other living persons or deceased relatives. This relationship has drawn the attention of several well respected scientists such as astrophysicist R. Schild who proposed that, "consciousness exists in our space-time and constrains our waking perception."[43] Schild and Leiter provided additional support to the potential infinite capacity of our universe to store "quantum holograms," by the existence of "black holes" (i.e., "super-dense, massive, collapsed, evolved stars and galaxy-center quasars").[44] Because of its' "relativistically-continuous contraction and continuous acquisition of more mass," they contend that "black holes" may function as "nature's hard-drives," holding copies of the quantum holograms generated by each new moment of human experience, as well as by each new event which occurs to non-living objects.[45] The existing paradox of how all information (past, present, and future) may be accessed by an individual via ESP may potentially be explained by theoretical physicist Stephen Hawking's research on "black holes." In 2016, for example, Hawking and his colleagues proposed that it is possible that information is encoded as a two-dimensional hologram and stored in the form of "super translations" (i.e., a hologram of the in-going particles). According to Hawking, "The information is not stored in the interior of the black hole as one might expect, but in its boundary—the event horizon. Thus they contain all the information that would otherwise be lost."[45a] Consequently, the quantum information of every occurrence is stored in this hologram record on the surface of the black hole and emitted in the form of "quantum fluctuations." If valid, the question arises as to whether information about matter is fundamentally conserved and can be retrieved by one's mind? If so, this theorized holographic information store may provide a scientific explanation (albeit highly debatable) of the so-called "Akashic records, "the mind of God," and/or non-locality. In other words, can such an existing information field, accessible without the use of one's sensory systems, account for ESP, non-local intuition, and past-life recall? Assuming that the universe may actually be permeated with intelligence of information experienced at all scales, the QHT suggests that different expressions of consciousness are integrated in a unified psychic network; interconnected in ways unrestricted by space-time (non-locally). More specifically, studies in ESP and mental intuition, among others in parapsychology noted prior such as the quantum double slit experiment (i.e., an experiment used to examine how consciousness and our physical material world are intertwined) represent examples of how consciousness and our physical material world may be connected. Thus physicists are being forced to admit that the universe is a "mental" construction. Related to this concept is the perspective held by cardiologist P. Lommel who stated, "It seems to be possible to have a non-local connection with other people's consciousness as well as with thoughts and feelings of deceased friends and family and to communicate with them by way of thought transfer."[46] The implications of these yet, if ever, to be confirmed perspectives, may hold the key to the many mysteries of our time, especially life after death.

- *The Quantum Brain and DNA*: Quantum mechanics postulates that each of the approximately eighty-seven billion neurons in the brain, of which one-hundred times as many microtubules exist in every neuron, either contains or supports consciousness. Physicist H. P. Stapp's viewpoint that the brain operates in accordance with the uncertainty principle of quantum mechanics is supported by physicist R. Penrose's theory that "microtubules," which form the cytoskeleton in neurons both within and between brain cells, may be sites of quantum effects enabling entanglement (i.e., the quantum state of each particle cannot be described independently).[47] Penrose teamed with anesthesiologist S. Hameroff to formulate the controversial "orchestrated objective-reduction" (Orch-OR) theory, which states that brain neurons behave as "quantum computers." They considered every synapse, which is where two nerves come together and do their "decision making," as a quantum system and the source of information computation. Accordingly, quantum activity within the neuron interact non-locally with other neurons and, along with the quantum hologram, facilitate a "conscious event." In fact, they believe that the Orch-OR theory serves as the foundation for the human "soul," NDEs, OBEs, and may even account for one's perception of reality after physical death.[48] Hameroff wrote, "The connection to space–time geometry also raises the intriguing possibility that Orch-OR allows consciousness apart from the brain and body, distributed and entangled in space–time geometry," and that "quantum information can exist outside the body, perhaps indefinitely, as a soul."[49] Related to this concept, physicists J. McFadden and J. Al-Khalili proposed that the brain's electromagnetic field may couple to quantum-coherent (i.e., entanglement) ions moving through microtubules, enabling the "binding" of cortical processes and the "emergence of consciousness."[50] Similarly, physicist D. Zohar contends that biological quantum coherence serves as an organizing principle which may explain a "quantum relationship" between consciousness and the body.[51] Physicist W. Tiller also advanced the idea that the holographic properties of space are key to understanding the effects of consciousness and how ESP can take place in single living cells.[52] C. Swanson summarizes these perspectives as follows:

These large-scale, coherent, resonant processes, where trillions of molecules in the body are in communication with one another and can function in resonance, brings up a new possibility: Maybe the body is a macroscopic quantum system with a set of coherent quantum states all vibrating in step? If so, then some of the weird phenomena we have called "paranormal" might really be just quantum mechanics working its strange magic on the large scale of everyday life.[53]

Indirect support for the Orch-OR theory was provided by S. Berkovitch, who calculated that the brain has an "inadequate capacity to produce and store all the informational processes of our memories."[54] He based this conclusion on the fact that the brain would need to perform "1024 operations per second" which he considered to be "absolutely impossible for our neurons."[55] A similar perspective is held by neurobiologist H. Romijn who stated, "One should conclude that the brain has not enough computing capacity to store all the memories with associative thoughts from one's life, has not enough retrieval abilities, and seems not to be able to elicit consciousness."[56]

Testimonials from prominent physics researchers from institutions such as Cambridge University, Princeton University, and the Max Planck Institute for Physics claim that quantum mechanics predicts some version of life after death; in other words, a person may possess a body-soul duality that is an extension of the wave-particle duality of subatomic particles.[57] Physicist H. Peter Dürr, for instance, believes in an existence after death based on the opinion that the dualism of the smallest particles is not "restricted to the subatomic world" and that a "universal quantum" code exists for all living and dead matter.[58] He explains this concept as follows: "What we consider the here and now, this world, it is actually just the material level that is comprehensible. The beyond is an infinite reality that is much bigger which this world is rooted in. In this way, our lives in this plane of existence are encompassed, surrounded by the afterworld already. The body dies but the spiritual quantum field continues. In this way, I am immortal."[59]

The DNA molecule, composed of nucleotides with a double helix structure, is arranged into twenty-three pairs of chromosomes, defines 30,000 genes, and contains about three billion base pairs.[60] Many mysteries surround human DNA, one of which is that about ninety-five percent is termed "junk DNA" due to its unknown function. According to computer scientist S. Berkovich, a possible functional significance of "junk DNA" may be to facilitate "hereditary information and memories from the past," i.e., it acts as the "receiver and transmitter of our evolving consciousness.[61] Related to this concept is the perspective of noted quantum physicist E. Schrödinger who considers DNA a "statistic molecule" which behaves as a quantum mechanical process with non-local communication.[62] S. Hameroff also proposed that DNA behaves as a chain of quantum bits which functions similarly to a quantum computer with quantum superposition.[63] According to P. Lommel, the potential role of the "person-specific DNA" in our cells may serve as the "place of resonance, or the interface across which a constant informational exchange takes place between our personal material body and phase-space, where all fields of our personal consciousness are available as fields of possibility."[64] In fact, Lommel contends that DNA molecules in chromosomes throughout the body may be linked non-locally by enzymatic action in the cell since they exist in a quantum state of "substance-wave duality."[65]

Quantum theories on the nature and role of DNA has provoked speculation about phenomena like past life recall and genetic immortality. In fact, professor of pedagogy A. Szyszko-Bohusz proposed a theory of genetic immortality in which parental consciousness and hereditary information is transmitted to children.[66] This viewpoint is supported by psychiatrist J. Tucker from his studies with children who report past life recall, and the concept in quantum physics that consciousness creates our physical world and doesn't require a brain to exist. Consequently, he concluded that reincarnation may be based on the possibility that "consciousness requires no physical binding to pass on through the generations."[67] According to Tucker, "I understand the leap it takes to conclude there is something beyond what we can see and touch." But there is this evidence here that needs to be accounted for, and when we look at these cases carefully, some sort of carry-over of memories often makes the most sense."[68]

It is well documented that experiences necessary for survival of a species are learned and that this knowledge is passed on to subsequent generations. But what other kinds of experiences might be saved in our DNA over the many thousands of years when our ancestors were born, lived, and died? Is it possible that our DNA contains coded memories of ancestors who had life-changing experiences that were passed on to future generations which can be accessed by us now and possibly exert influence on present behaviors? In other words, can memories be inherited by DNA, or is some other mechanism responsible for past life recall yet to be realized? In fact, some paranormal phenomena may even have holographic characteristics. Bohm and Pribram, for instance, noted that phenomena such as ESP may be explained by this model which allows for individual brains to be interconnected parts of the greater hologram (i.e., information is exchanged between minds regardless of distance stored non-locally in the ZPF).[69] That is, the brain's holographic structure may enable it to both send and receive holographic wave patterns as represented in thoughts. Evidence to support this concept is supported by the behavior of light in a hologram, whereby, if one observes the radiation flowing into and out of it, "the light is coming from the past, flowing through the image, and then on out into space where it is absorbed in the future."[70] Interestingly, biophysicist Pjotr Garjajev and his colleagues, who studied the vibrational behavior of DNA, believe that the DNA molecule may also generate waves that perform in a similar manner. Based on their findings, they concluded that chromosomes function like a holographic computer using "endogenous DNA laser radiation" which alter "DNA frequency and associated genetic information."[71]

Physiological evidence to support the theory that the brain operates like a hologram, and that memory and visual perception are governed by the holographic principle, was provided by neurosurgeon K. Pribram, who showed that even without most of the brain, organisms can function almost normally. His research in cats, for example, demonstrated their continued ability to perform complex visual tasks despite a loss of ninety percent of the primary visual cortex.[72] A similar result was obtained by neuroscientist R. Galambos, who severed up to ninety-eight percent of the optic tract of cats without seriously impairing the cats' "ability to perform skillfully on tests requiring them to differentiate between highly similar figures."[73] One theory to explain such maintained normal functioning is related to the recovery of memory from a brain even after much of it has been destroyed. This is based on the notion that a hologram contains the entire image, in this case the entire memory. According to C. Swanson, this effect is "consistent with the holographic structure of the brain," which allows for "the direct and instantaneous communication of images and other anomalies which occurs in paranormal events."[74] Supportive evidence for this aspect of function has also been advanced in the form of competent mental functioning in those with severely compromised brain function. This has been documented in approximately fifty cases of so-called "terminal lucidity" where mental abilities are restored before death despite severe brain disorders in those with Alzheimer's and schizophrenia;[75] about eighty cases of normal cognitive function despite severe brain developmental disorders such as hydroenencephaly;[76] and cases of serious brain degeneration without associated cognitive deficits.[77] The question remains, therefore, if normal function in severely compromised physiological states, as in those who report an NDE, may it be facilitated by holographic-based brain and associated DNA activity? And, if so, what are its possible implications for the continuity of consciousness and memory after death?

- *The Multiverse Theory*: An extension of the Holographic Concept of Reality is represented by the "Multiverse Theory" proposed by physicist H. Everett. This theory states that there are a couple of multiverses, whereby, we may be living in one dimension while other surfaces with other beings on it exist. According to Everett, all possible alternate histories and futures are real, with each representing an actual "world" and "everything that could possibly have happened in our past, but did not, occurred previously in another universe."[78] That is, when an action occurs having more than one possible outcome, separate universes emerge to accommodate each possible outcome. Everett saw his theory as guaranteeing life after death in which at each "branching of universes between death and living," a being's "consciousness endures"; that is, upon death, you are still alive in other universes and will be born again in other universes.[79] A similar viewpoint by R. Lanza is that, "Multiple universes allow for the possibility that in one universe the body can be dead while in another it continues to exist, absorbing consciousness which somehow entered into this universe."[80] J. Bockris, known for his creation of physical electrochemistry, also concluded that we live in a synchronized universe, which enables us to experience our "real" universe, which coexists with "other universes just as real as this one."[81] Accordingly, Bockris concluded that this model provides the means to understand how "the soul, the center of human consciousness, can exist in a permanent form, surviving human death."[82]

The controversial existence of multiple universes has also been promoted as a possible explanation for various phenomena by many leading physicists such as S. Hawking, M. Kaku, D. Bohm, and D. Greene, among others. S. Hawking, for instance, proposed that one can have different universes in one existence called a "multiverse."[83] He wrote: "Down at the smallest of scales, smaller even than molecules, smaller than atoms, we get to a place called the quantum foam. This is where wormholes exist. Tiny tunnels or shortcuts through space and time constantly form, disappear, and reform within this quantum world. And they actually link two separate places and two different times."[84]

Scientists continue to search for a mathematical solution to explain levels of human consciousness that correspond well with the laws of nature and the quantum field theory. In fact, the deep meditative states and associated level of awareness produced by yogic masters may actually represent a universal aspect of pure consciousness that may even correspond with theories in quantum physics (e.g., Superstring theory, M theory) and the unified field theory. Devised by Einstein, the unified field theory attempts to integrate known phenomena (e.g., gravity, space-time, electricity, electromagnetism, etc.) using a single comprehensive set of equations to explain on the macroscopic level (things that are visible to the naked eye) what governs and regulates all matter and energy in existence. In contrast, quantum theory explains the nature and behavior of all phenomena on the microscopic (atomic and subatomic) level.

Given this context, the persistence of a form of one's consciousness after bodily death cannot be entirely ruled in or out since it is not known if the nature of consciousness itself represents an aspect of the physical universe. A fundamental question associated with this overarching concept pertains to how the brain, which resides within our 3 +1 dimensional space, behaves as a quantum system. In other words, are quantum correlations occurring within the neurons of the brain in the form of entangled microtubules, as described by string theory and wormholes developed on those strings, as higher dimensional (4 +1) space-time? If valid, then consciousness is a quantum mechanical system, represented as a fundamental aspect or phenomenon of the unified field. As such, both the string and unified field theories may indeed be a fundamental property of brain activity. And if true, then one's consciousness may in fact be part of one universal consciousness. That is, our emotions, sensations, and stream of conscious thought represent the essence of experience as a subjective aspect of our physical world. But while these aspects of consciousness give life meaning, one must ask two simple yet unanswerable questions: Why am I conscious, and am I the brain? As far as I know, there are no answers. But when we look to the objective world of science for an answer to our subjective conscious experiences we find surprisingly little research in this area.

Only in the past few decades have scientists begun to correlate areas of the brain, which may govern and regulate aspects of consciousness, to determine if consciousness is indeed a fundamental neurophysiological brain event. Consciousness may actually represent the collection of correlated neurophysiological brain states of emotion and perception as interpreted into a meaningful whole by another yet to be identified region of the brain. This complex integrative process, in turn, may then facilitate our subjective experience. Or not. After all, while areas of the brain have been found to correlate with various states of emotion and perception, science still cannot explain why we all experience subjective consciousness. Is there a scientific-based answer to this elusive question, a purely philosophical or religious explanation, or is the question simply unanswerable, and just is? The question, therefore, remains as to whether or not consciousness is a different manifestation of a single fundamental field. In fact, the answer to what is consciousness may very well be analogous to the question: Why did our universe begin? We simply do not have an accepted uniform answer of how to integrate consciousness into our physical reality. And that answer may be the key towards unlocking the mystery of whether or not an aspect of our consciousness persists after bodily death.

For lack of a precise explanation of the principles which may govern and regulate such enigmatic concerns, several scholars adopt the century old theory of panpsychism; that is, consciousness is a universal feature of all things. Subsequently, the idea has been advanced that consciousness exists in molecules and atoms, perhaps as some kind of quantum mechanical effect. In fact, physicist M. Tegmark proposed that there is a state of matter, like solid, liquid and gas whereby atoms are somehow capable of processing information which gives "rise to subjectivity." This concept, referred to as the perceptronium theory, was inspired in part by neuroscientist G. Tononi whose integrated information theory (IIT) has become a popular notion in the science of consciousness. This theory predicts that simple physical devices like an iPhone or thermostat may actually possess aspects of consciousness; a subjective self.

Fundamental laws of physics, which include space and time, have been applied to address consciousness with limited success. So what are the laws of consciousness if it cannot be explained by physicists and neuroscientists? Maybe consciousness is fundamental like our known physical laws of space, time, and gravity? If so, consciousness may represent a universal fundamental construct whereby all physical matter is actually conscious in varying ways or levels of sophistication or information integration. The consciousness-based ideas addressed prior by Tegmark, Lanza, and Tononi (i.e., panpsychism, biocentrism, IIT), suggest that all physical matter may be capable of processing information that gives rise to subjectivity and associated consciousness. In fact, Tononi's popularized IIT theory of consciousness implies that panpsychism may be valid and measureable by a quantifiable unit of the level of consciousness (i.e., how much the system exists). This so-called "consciousness measure" of any living or non-living physical system is represented by its phi, i.e., a high quantified level of phi represents a high level of consciousness. Thus, humans would expect to have a higher level of phi than other lower order species and non-biological systems. The questions remain, however, as to whether "phi" actually integrates consciousness into the physical world, and represents a sufficiently valid condition of consciousness. And if we extrapolate this concept to that of a deceased body, one would expect this quantized level of consciousness to register a value above zero (i.e., it is conscious). Thus, according to this theorized model, a dead body is as conscious as any non-biological system. And if true, a certain level of consciousness may persist after bodily death. So if one accepts the IIT literally, then one may conclude that there is a form of conscious awareness when the so-called hard drive crashes and the screen fades to black. That is, there may indeed be a form of "life after death." But before celebrating, keep in mind that this tenuous notion remains a theory and should not be accepted as fact. At least, not yet.

Discussion

If we assume that one's consciousness somehow survives physical death, then where and how does it exist, and what principles may explain the nature which regulates its continued functioning? And if an aspect of one's personality continues on, that aspect must not have been entirely dependent on normal brain function since the brain, once functional, ceases at some point in time. Consequently, to prove there is a form of life after death, there must be irrefutable evidence that a form of consciousness and/or a, yet to be discovered subtle energy, operates independently of the brain and remains unaffected following bodily death. Despite the absence of supporting evidence, numerous scientific concepts have been advanced to support their independence (e.g., quantum physics, psychic factors and Super-ESP, the collective unconscious, quantum brain activity and DNA, holographic principles, and the Multiverse, among others). Or, it is the popular notion that a second "astral" body (i.e., consciousness, soul, or spirit), which operates at a higher vibrational frequency, persists after physical death? We can only conjecture if this non-local aspect of one's consciousness, personality, and memory exists, or maybe the abstract answer is that it just "is" and persists through a vacuum where there is no time or space within an intradimensional reality.

The scientific approach to the concept of life after death should be a required methodology for research in reincarnation, mediumship, NDE/OBE, apparitions, consciousness, and quantum physics, among others, which could enhance its relevance and potential implications. Although associated hypotheses have been advanced to explain the nature of past-life evidence and associated phenomena, there remains no consensus within the scientific community about the nature of such events, nor the possible functional mechanisms of human consciousness that could be responsible for such phenomena and persist after death. An inherent factor that impedes our further understanding of such elusive concepts is that the survival hypothesis fails to define exactly what criteria are needed to delineate the essential features of whatever it is that may survive death.

An associated research limitation is that although consciousness has been acknowledged to affect quantum systems noted prior, it has never been integrated into physics in a quantitative theory. Consequently, consciousness is largely ignored as a contributing variable for NDE/OBE, apparitions, past-life recall, and UFO-based encounters, despite the possibility that these experiences may be interrelated with and/or facilitated by an aspect of one's mind.

The most significant argument against accepting the survival hypothesis is that the evidence represents a form of Super-ESP among the living. And if valid, it would imply that some characteristic of a deceased person may exist, which can affect our consciousness. This may explain how people report experiencing a deceased personality in the form of apparitions, NDEs, after death communication, mediumistic communication, and past-life recall, etc. And if such a characteristic of the deceased can somehow be experienced, we can only speculate as to what form of energy and associated principles of operation it is that interrelates with one's consciousness. That is, communication may be either occurring with the mind of a present person and not with the deceased, or alternatively, discarnate souls can, via their psychic abilities, interact with the living and physical world.

Results supporting the validity of psi phenomena continue to be published in peer-reviewed, academic journals in fields from psychology to neuroscience to physics noted prior. Since such studies with experimental controls have not eliminated or even decreased significant support for the existence of psi phenomena, it is apparent that supportive evidence of psi phenomena cannot reasonably be accounted for by chance. In fact, in 2017, a psi trial registry was established to improve research psi practice by the Koestler Parapsychology Unit based in the Psychology Department at the University of Edinburgh. The need for such continued research is reinforced by the fact that most of the founding fathers of quantum physics all spoke of something outside of our physical realm that influences aspects of consciousness, like measurement, observation, and intention. Maybe this is why noted scientist Nicolas Tesla stated, "The day science begins to study non-physical phenomena, it will make more progress in one decade than in all the previous centuries of its existence."[84a] And maybe Tesla is correct. After all, in human studies addressed previously, a meta-analysis of experiments demonstrates compelling statistical evidence that the perception of non-local information is indeed a strong possibility.

Even if one accepts that the survival hypothesis is supported by the present evidence of the observed phenomena, many issues remain ambiguous, unresolved, and complicated by existing evidence that can be interpreted as a convincing case either for or against some form of survival. Since the general life-after-death-related evidence is largely based on anecdotal testimony, it is very difficult to either reject or confirm this hypothesis through a validation process. The problem is that the approaches used have not consistently conformed to the expected scientific method and standards routinely applied by research scientists. The evidence presented, therefore, cannot sufficiently explain and justify the continuity of consciousness after death.

CHAPTER EIGHT

CONCLUSION

The concept of life after death is one of the most fundamental issues of our existence. But as much as I want to believe, I can't, not because I don't have a faith-based belief in Heaven and Hell, nor is it because science has yet to develop and apply uniformly accepted criteria of what constitutes "proof," but rather because no compelling empirical evidence exists to unconditionally accept the survival hypothesis. My research career has trained me to test hypotheses using established scientific principles and research protocol, verified by independent research investigations. But since this approach has not been applied in studies associated with life after death, my skepticism will remain until a rigorous scientific endeavor yields, if ever, valid and reliable evidence to resolve the most ethereal question of humankind: *Is death the end?*

The certainty that "I" am an independent essence of the physical body, unchanged by its mortality, and which may influence the way we view ourselves, relate to others, and provide a foundation for the purpose of life, is tenuous at best. But while most trust religious teachings of immortality, I am unable to accept that if I'm good I enter the pearly gates of Heaven, and if not, I don't. The idea that consciousness exists apart from the body and continues beyond its lifetime will remain conceptually implausible until evidence justifies an individual "will" that can transcend the confines of the body. But despite this apparent steadfast left-brain conviction, my intuitive "gut feeling," which may provide a more accurate viewpoint than my logical mindset, tells me not to dismiss the prospect that science may eventually provide convincing evidence to shock the world at its deepest core.

The broad continuum of unproven theories, controversial perspectives, and associated tenuous research evidence on the nature of consciousness and how it may persist in a post-mortem existence, raises considerably more scientific, philosophical, and spiritual related questions than answers. Despite the many perspectives that consciousness is independent of human matter and persists after death, and the similarity of perplexing anecdotal experiences and research outcomes addressed prior, there exists little more than unsubstantiated conclusions and associated diatribe to either accept or reject the survival hypothesis with confidence. And so, despite decades of research, we are left wondering if a post-mortem existence can be rationalized only by certainty in one's faith-based belief, intuition, or logic. At the very least, however, the collective evidence clearly indicates that *something* significant is occurring in varying ways that cannot be adequately explained using traditional scientific principles. And researching what governs and regulates that *something* should be considered an important endeavor by mainstream science. But despite the many unresolved questions and theories noted previously, there exists the remote possibility that death may serve as a transition from one state of consciousness to another.

If death is just a phase on the natural continuation of life, it cannot be appropriately rationalized by science since such an outcome is not considered a part of the natural world. As humans, we experience different perceptions and emotions, which from a strictly scientific point of view are explained as a result of nothing more than the complex and poorly understood neuroelectric and chemical processes within our central nervous system. Consequently, those who believe that once the chemical reactions in our brains stop, so does consciousness and our life. This prevailing concept may be why the survival hypothesis remains largely out of the realm of scientific study; it incorporates variables that cannot be objectively measured in the same way you can measure electrophysiological activity from the brain. In fact, an idealized research approach may not even be possible using current theories known to science today, if ever. Evidence to support this hypothesis from studies in reincarnation, NDEs/OBEs, mediumship, consciousness, intention and non-locality, after-death communication, and apparitions, may, therefore, be non-provable. And if any one of these phenomena is valid, it is not subjected to scientific scrutiny since mainstream science cannot explain, let alone, accept it even exists. The apparent enigma is that science is the empirical measurement of the natural world, but our consciousness or "soul" may be a non-physical entity existing beyond the natural world.

Despite the numerous documented studies addressed, science still has no method of including the subjective experience into the scientific method of inquiry. Consequently, there currently is no broadly acceptable or consistent way for science to validate the survival hypothesis. Despite this limitation, increasing circumstantial evidence from NDEers, and research into the nature of consciousness and quantum physics, has led some researchers to support the survival hypothesis.

The great challenge for science is to determine whether or not consciousness is distinct from the brain and can perceive a form of reality beyond the limited space-time continuum of our physical world when the body ceases to function. It is very difficult, if not impossible, to develop this concept into testable hypotheses since current scientific principles and associated methodology don't apply. The answer may, therefore, have to be based more on one's personal viewpoints developed from teachings, experiences, and possibly a touch of "gut feeling." Thus, there exists a need to dramatically alter the way, if at all possible, to evaluate the survival hypothesis. As theories in physics, neuroscience, and psychology evolve, our increased understanding of the brain, consciousness, and physical universe, combined with the associated application of newly developed principles and associated multidisciplinary research models, may offer greater potential to adequately test hypotheses associated with the concept of life after death. But is it even necessary to do so? After all, life after death exists if you view life as a cycle, with dead cells serving as building blocks for new cells, and with remnants of genetic material passed on through inheritance over generations. But is there more than just our cells and genes that continue beyond death, or are we just a biological system which ascribes to the phrase "ashes to ashes, dust to dust," used sometimes to denote total finality? This paradox has led "skeptics" to often adopt the position that those who believe in life after death do so because their claims have not been disproved. In contrast, the "believers" contend that because skeptics have not adequately explained evidence from studies which reject the survival hypothesis, there must be an afterlife. Maybe leading astronomer and astrophysicist Carl Sagan's perspective best captures the essence of this enigma as follows: "With insufficient data it is easy to go wrong.

Human beings have a demonstrated talent for self-deception when their emotions are stirred. What counts is not what sounds plausible, not what we would like to believe, not what one or two witnesses claim, but only what is supported by hard evidence rigorously and skeptically examined. Extraordinary claims require extraordinary evidence."[1]

Related to this theme is an old joke that comes to mind: *The good news is that there is baseball in Heaven. The bad news is that you're pitching this weekend.* Or does the game go on forever but without us at some inescapable point in time? Knowing our life will end has led many to search for proof that this game is eternal. And religion, which has provided an answer in the form of the soul's immortality to millions over the centuries, may inspire you to live each moment with dignity, hope, meaning, a connection to others, and a way to better confront the inevitability of death. And if an aspect of consciousness survives to continue in another realm is proven valid, I can't help but wonder if memory of our prior existence is also maintained. After all, if I am unable to recall my family and experiences, then the concept of life after death loses much of its appeal. Do we reunite with deceased loved ones and possess an expanded consciousness of existence in paradise, or do some of us struggle to fend off evil entities in a hellish-like environment for eternity? Maybe it is best not to know our fate after the last breath. That knowledge will likely have both significant positive and negative implications for how we lead our lives in the present. And maybe if we were supposed to possess that knowledge, we would, intuitively.

The conclusion that at the time of physical death consciousness will continue to be experienced in another invisible and immaterial dimension is difficult to form with certainty. While comforting on many levels, the absence of verification, in combination with the tenuous, albeit intriguing evidence and associated contrasting and unresolved viewpoints, contributes to that elusive so-called "smoking gun" needed for me to accept an "everlasting existence" as a valid concept. Consequently, our understanding of the many topics addressed prior would greatly benefit from collaborative multidisciplinary research efforts, which may eventually discover that consciousness can be experienced independently of brain function. This discovery might well provide the needed foundation to support the possibility that death may represent a transition from one realm of existence to another. Despite this objective, however, there regrettably exists a lack of qualified scientists interested in seeking ways to study the fundamental concerns associated with such an enigmatic concept. Consequently, a discernable answer to this intangible concern will likely remain until we may eventually discover the truth the moment after our last breath.

Thousands of papers written on consciousness have been generated by scholars across many disciplines resulting in an overwhelming mass of information with no resulting uniformly accepted conclusion as to what it actually is. One strong possibility is that there may simply be only a few levels of consciousness: 1) the realization of our orientation in physical space, 2) the realization and response to other people's physical and emotional behaviors, and one's own social behavior within the context of environmental situations, and 3) intuition or knowing possible future events relative to one's knowledge of personal and non-personal situations, events, and laws governing the universe.

We constantly sense, interpret, and make predictions based on information received. This cyclic internal brain event, which incorporates a possible non-physical aspect of consciousness of "free will" enables one to synthesis and understand complex multi-sensory information. This integration of information into a meaningful whole is then acted upon in a careful mindful way through a process of reasoning and abstract thought with the intent to create expected future outcomes that may be beneficial to oneself and/or others. One's response to an external event may also be reflexive, conducted without sufficient reasoning that may facilitate unexpected and possible adverse consequences.

Given this context, we simply do not understand how our extraordinary brain's conscious-like behaviors, a sophisticated biological learning machine that constantly learns by re-wiring its neural networks in response to experiential activity over time, can produce abstract thought, intuition, and one's sense of "self." The elusive critical question is whether or not the brain possess an aspect of consciousness termed the "soul." If there is indeed a soul, or some "thing" that may persist after bodily death, how can it be quantified using current scientific principles and techniques? Unfortunately, this possible aspect of one's brain, if present, is not testable (i.e., measureable, reproducible, and falsifiable) since it does not conform to current accepted scientific principles and methodologies. But even though the existence of a "soul" eludes current scientific minds, it may indeed exist. But until it is testable and proven valid, if ever, the existence of an aspect of one's self that persists after bodily death must remain a mystery. I simply do not know. Do you?

The question whether or not the concept of life after death exists at the scientific, spiritual, or philosophical level has left millions over the centuries confused about who and what to believe, and left wondering what possible theory or perspective may provide the answer. Now theories within the mysterious world of quantum physics tell us that we must consider consciousness to understand the nature of reality, and that a higher information field of consciousness in the universe exists. Do such theories explain the nature of consciousness, and can a better understanding of consciousness take quantum physics to the next level of confirming life after death? In this era of discovery, as we continue to realize the inner working of our universe, we may someday answer the perplexing concept of what lies beyond our demise. But since death eventually captures all of us, the only thing I can tell the approximately 150,000 people who die every day with certainty, is that their physical body will remain here. Maybe the answer will continue to remain at the philosophical, spiritual, and theoretical levels until science, in some inconceivable way, may provide a definitive answer. Until then, if ever, the concept of life after death will remain a personal dilemma. And time alone, which we may not have enough of, might eventually determine if it is true that, "you can't take it with you" when you die. Or, *should I believe* that I can?

Endnotes

Chapter One: Introduction

1. Colwyn Vulliamy, *Immortality* (London: Random House, 1997).
2. Arnold Toynbee and Arthur Koestler, eds., *Life after Death* (London: Weidenfeld and Nicolson, 1996).
3. Philippe Ariès, *The Hour of Our Death* (Melbourne: Penguin, 1983), 189.
4. The Austin Institute for the Study of Family and Culture. www.austin-institute.org/ (accessed March 12, 2016).
5. News Poll, "Americans' Views on Death," November 6, 2013, www.cbsnews.com/news/cbs-news-poll-americans-views-on-death/ (accessed March 8, 2016).
5a. Science Daily, "Humans 'predisposed' to believe in gods and the afterlife," *Science Daily*, July 14, 2011. www.sciencedaily.com/releases/2011/07/110714103828.htm (accessed June 12, 2017).
5b. Carr D, and S. Sharp, "Do afterlife beliefs affect psychological adjustment to late-life spousal loss?" *Journal of Gerontology Psychol Sci*, 69, no. 1 (2014): 103-112.

Chapter Two: Consciousness

1. David Chalmers, "The Puzzle of Conscious Experience," Scientific America, no. 92 (2001): 21.
2. Max Velmans and Susan Schneider, eds., *Consciousness* (London: Blackwell, 2007).
3. John Wheeler and Zurek Wojciech, eds., *Quantum Theory and Measurement* (Princeton: Princeton University Press, 1983), 167.
4. Roger Penrose and Karl Giberson, "The Man Who Fell to Earth," Science and Spirit, 25, no, 34 (2003), 189.
5. Louis Menard, "What Comes Naturally: Does Evolution Explain Who We Are?" *The New Yorker*, November 25, 2002, www.newyorker.com/magazine/2002/11/25/what-comes-naturally-2 (accessed May 12, 2016).
6. Steve Paulson, "God Enough." *Salon*, November 19, 2008. www.salon.com/2008/11/19/stuart_kauffman/ (accessed February 18, 2016).
7. Amit Goswami, *Physics of the Soul: The Quantum Book of Living, Dying, Reincarnation, and Immortality* (New York: Hampton Roads Publishing, 2001), 24.
8. David Pratt, "John Eccles on Mind and Brain." *Theosophy*, June 1995, www.theosophy-nw.org/theosnw/science/prat-bra.htm/ (accessed January 8, 2016).
9. Big Think Editors, "Max Planck: I Regard Consciousness as Fundamental," *The Observer*, January 2016, http://bigthink.com/words-of-wisdom/max-planck-i-regard-consciousness-as-fundamental (accessed January 10, 2016).

10. Bob Davis, "Consciousness, the Brain, and Quantum Physics," *The Foundation for Research into Extraterrestrial Encounters*, February, 30, 2016, www.experiencer.org (accessed August 23, 2016).

11. Ibid., 2.

12. UCLA Newsroom, "UCLA Psychologists Report New Insights on the Human Brain and Consciousness," October 17, 2013, http://newsroom.ucla.edu/releases/ucla-psychologists-report-new-248299 (accessed March 3, 2016).

13. Francis Crick and Christof Koch, "Consciousness and Neuroscience," June, 1995, www.paradise.caltech.edu/cook/Workshop/Conscious/crick-koch-cc-97.html (accessed March 3, 2016).

14. The Center for Sleep and Consciousness, "Neural Substrates for Consciousness," September 14, 2015, www.centerforsleepandconsciousness.med.wisc.edu/ (accessed March 10, 2016).

15. Bernard Baars, "The Conscious Access Hypothesis: Origins and Recent Evidence," *Trends in Cognitive Sciences*, 12, no. 6 (2002): 47.

16. UCLA Newsroom. "UCLA Psychologists Report New Insights on the Human Brain and Consciousness," *UCLA*, http://newsroom.ucla.edu/releases/ucla-psychologists-report-new-248299 (accessed March 7, 2016).

17. Steven Nelson, et al. "Evidence Accumulation and Moment of Recognition: Dissociating Perceptual Recognition Processes Using fMRI," *Journal of Neuroscience*, no. 2 (2007): 27.

18. Cell Press, "Neurorobotics Reveals Brain Mechanisms of Self-Consciousness." *Cell Press*, April 27, 2016. www.sciencedaily.com/releases/2011/04/110427131818.htm (accessed March 19, 2016).

19. Ibid., 23.

20. IFLScience, "Consciousness, Science, and Life after Death. Researchers May Have Discovered The Consciousness On/Off Switch," *IFL Science*, June 10, 2016. www.iflscience.com/brain/researchers-may-have-discovered-consciousness-onoff-switch (accessed March 3, 2016).

21. Ibid., 2.

22. Goswami, *Physics of the Soul: The Quantum Book of Living, Dying, Reincarnation, and Immortality*, 132-133.

23. Ibid., 133.

24. Henry Romijn, "About the Origin of Consciousness. A New Multidisciplinary Perspective on the Relationship between Brain and Mind," *Proc Kon Ned Akad v Wetensch*, 5, no. 100 (1997): 181.

25. Eugene Wigner, *Symmetries and Reflections* (Cambridge: M.I.T Press, 1970), 126.

26. Erwin Schrödinger, "Discussion of Probability Relations between Separated Systems," *Mathematical Proceedings of the Cambridge Philosophical Society*, 6, no. 31 (1935): 555.

27. Robert Nadeau and Kafatos Menus, *The Non-Local Universe* (New York: Oxford University Press, 1999), 245.

28. Dean Radin, *The Conscious Universe* (San Fransisco: HarperCollins, 1997).

29. Louis Menard, "What Comes Naturally," *New Yorker*, August 2, 2016, www.newyorker.com/magazine/2002/11/25/what-comes-naturally-2 (accessed March 14, 2016).

30. Janey Tracey, "Physicists Claim that Consciousness Lives in Quantum State After Death," *Outerplaces*, June 17, 2014, www.outerplaces.com/science/item/4518-physicists-claim-that-consciousness-lives-in-quantum-state-after-death (accessed March 22, 2016).

31. Paul Davies and John Gribbin. *The Matter Myth: Discoveries That Challenge Our Understanding of Physical Reality.* (New York: Simon and Schuster), 2007.

32. Barbara Mango, email message to author, March 22, 2016.

33. *New York Times*, "What is Consciousness," *Anomalist*, August 12, 2016, http://mobile.nytimes.com/2016/07/05/science/what-is consciousness. html?r=2&referer=www.anomalist.com/ (accessed March 13, 2016).

34. Ibid., 18.

35. Bob Berman and Robert Lanza, *Biocentrism: How Life and Consciousness are the Keys to Understanding the True Nature of the Universe* (New York: BenBella Books, 2010), 127.

36. Jessica Utts, "Replication and Meta-Analysis in Parapsychology," *Statistical Science*, 12, no. 16 (1991): 363.

37. Robert Jahn and Brian Dunne, "On the Quantum Mechanics of Consciousness, with Application to Anomalous Phenomena," *Foundations of Physics*, 7, no. 16 (1986): 721.

38. David Bohm, *Quantum Theory* (Englewood Cliffs: Prentice-Hall, 1951).

39. T. Ethan, "Scientists Find Hints for the Immortality of the Soul," *Skeptiko*, August 3, 2014, www.skeptiko-forum.com/threads/scientists-find-hints-for-the-immortality-of-the-soul.1124/ (accessed March 23, 2016).

40. Nick Herbert, "Nick Herbert Home Page," August 28, 2013. www2.cruzio.com/~quanta/ (accessed April 3, 2016).

41. Henry Stapp, "Henry Stapp," August 30, 2012, www-physics.lbl.gov/~stapp/Compatibility.pdf (accessed March 12, 2016).

42. Carlos Alvarado, "Compelling Evidence for the Afterlife," *Afterlife*, May 12, 2015, http://compellingevidencefortheafterlife.com/?p=273 (accessed March 8, 2016).

43. Leanna Standish et al. "Evidence of Correlated Functional MRI Signals between Distant Human Brains," *Alternative Therapies. Health and Medicine,* 2, no. 9 (2003): 122.

44. Carlos Alvarado, "New Study of Electroencephalographic Detection of ESP," April 6, 2016, https://carlossalvarado.wordpress.com/2016/08/06/new-study-of-electroencephalographic-detection-of-esp/ (accessed March 8, 2016).

45. Menus Kafatos and Robert Nadeau, *Over a Distance and In "No Time": Bell's Theorem* (New York: Oxford University Press, 1999), 126.

46. Dean Radin, "Event-Related EEG Correlations between Isolated Human Subjects," *Journal of Alternative and Complementary Medicine,* 6, no. 10 (2004): 315.

47. Dean Radin, "Testing Nonlocal Observation as a Source of Intuitive Knowledge," *Explore*, Jan–Feb: (2008): 23.

48. Daily Grail, "Quantum Mind: Can Experienced Meditators Influence the Movement of Atomic Particles?" April 23, 2016, www.dailygrail.com/Mind-Mysteries/2016/6/Quantum-Mind-Can-Experienced-Meditators-Influence-the-Movement-Atomic (accessed April 3, 2016).

49. Ibid., 145.

50. Benjamin Libert, "Unconscious Cerebral Initiative and the Role of Conscious Will in Voluntary Action," *Behavioral and Brain Sciences*, 4, no. 8 (1985): 529.

51. Dean Radin, "Unconscious Perception of Future Emotions: An Experiment in Presentiment," *Journal Scientific Exploration*, 8, no. 11 (1997): 163.

52. Saeed Rezaei, "Nonlocal Intuition: Replication and Paired-Subjects Enhancement Effects," *Global Adv Health Med*, 5, no. 4 (2014): 23.

53. Dick Bierman, "Exploring Correlations between Local Emotional and Global Emotional Events and the Behavior of a Random Number Generator," *Journal of Scientific Exploration*, 7, no. 10 (1996): 363.

54. L. Vanier, "Global Consciousness the Mind Blowing Effects of Mass Meditation," *Collective Evolution*, July 12, 2016, www.collective-evolution.com/2015/10/07/ (accessed April 12, 2016).

55. Roger Nelson et al. "Field REG: Consciousness Field Effects: Replication and Explorations," *Journal of Scientific Exploration* 6, no. 12 (1998): 425.

56. Ibid., 427

57. Nelson, "Field REG: Consciousness Field Effects: Replication and Explorations," 428.

58. Nelson, "Field REG: Consciousness Field Effects: Replication and Explorations," 429.

59. Peter Fenwick, "Compelling Evidence for the Afterlife," November 12, 2014, http://compellingevidencefortheafterlife.com/?p=273 (accessed March 12, 2016).

60. Chris Clark, "A-Quantum Theory and Consciousness," *Schumacher College*, January 23, 2012, www.schumachercollege.org.uk/resources/audio-video-archive/chris-clarke%3A-quantum-theory-and-consciousness (accessed March 23, 2106).

61. Ibid., 23.

62. R. Byrd, "Positive Therapeutic Effect of Intercessory Prayer in a Coronary Care Population," *Southern Medical Journal*, 7, no. 81(1998): 826.

63. Ibid., 828.

64. B. Grad, B "Some Biological Effects of the "Laying-On of Hands: A Review of Experiments with Animals and Plants," *Journal of the American Society for Psychical Research*, 7, no. 59 (1965): 95.

65. Luke Hendricks, William Bengston and Jay Gunkelman, "The Healing Connection: EEG Harmonics, Entrainment, and Schumann's Resonances," *Journal of Scientific Exploration*, 3, no. 24 (2010): 655.

66. William Tiller, "How the Power of Intention Alters Matter," *Spirit of Matter*, February 23, 2014, www.spiritofmaat.com/archive/mar2/tiller.htm (accessed April 5, 2016).

67. Marco Bischof, "Biophotons," *Bibliotecapleyades,* March 2005, www.bibliotecapleyades.net/ciencia/ciencia_fuerzasuniverso06.htm (accessed April 23, 2016).

68. Roger Sheldrake, *Seven Experiments That Could Change the World* (New York: Riverhead Books, 1995).

69. William Tiller, "William Tiller," *The Tiller Institute*, March 2016, www.tillerinstitute.com/ (accessed April 6, 2016).

70. P. Rosch, ed., *Bioelectromagnetic Phenomena* (New York: Dekker, 2004)175.

71. Ibid., 176.

72. Tara Maclsaac, "Quantum Mechanics Has Reached Limit," *Epoch Times*, May 29, 2016, www.theepochtimes.com/n3/2078501-quantum-mechanics-has-reached-limit-says-stanford-scientist-who-offers-alternative/ (accessed March 18, 2016).

73. Janey Tracey, "New Theory Claims Quantum Weirdness Only Exists in Our Imaginations," *Outerplaces*, December 1, 2015, www.outerplaces.com/science/item/10547-new-theory-claims-quantum-weirdness-only-exists-in-our-imaginations (accessed March 14, 2016).

74. Ibid., 1.

74a. Jon Klimo, *Channeling: Investigations on Receiving Information From Paranormal Sources,* Los Angeles: (St. Martin's Press, 1987).

Chapter Three: The Near-Death Experience

1. Hubert Knoblauch, Ina Schmied, and Bernt Schnettler, "Different Kinds of Near-Death Experience: A Report on a Survey of NDEs in Germany," *Journal of Near-Death Studies,* 12, no. 20 (2001): 15.

2. J. Pope, "Near Death Experiences and Attitudes towards Life, Death, and Suicide," *Australian Parapsychological Review,* 4, no. 19 (1994): 23.

3. E. S. Cardena and S. Krippner, eds., *American Psychological Association* (New York: Harper Collins, 2000).

4. Sam Parnia, "Near Death Experiences During Cardiac Arrest," *Goldsmith's London*, February 2000, www.horizonresearch.org/video_case/near-death-experiences-during-cardiac-arrest/ (accessed May 12, 2016).

5. Enrico Facco and Christian Agrillo, "Near-Death-Like Experiences without Life-Threatening Conditions or Brain Disorders: A Hypothesis from a Case Report," *Front. Psychology,* 6, no. 3 (2012): 490.

6. Design leave this in red; Missing number 6 Robert!

7. Raymond Moody and Paul Perry, *Glimpses of Eternity.* New York: Guideposts, 2010.

8. Bruce Greyson, "The Incidence of Near-Death Experiences," *Med Psychiatry* 8, (1998): 92.

9. Raymond Moody, *Life After Life: The Investigation of a Phenomenon-Survival of Bodily Death* (Covington: Mockingbird Books, 1975), 125.

10. Kenneth Ring, "Precognitive and Prophetic Visions in Near-Death Experiences," *Anabiosis*, 12, no. 2 (1982): 47.

11. Bruce Greyson, "Incidence and Correlates of Near-Death Experiences in a Cardiac Care Unit," *Gen Hosp Psychiatry*, no. 25 (2003): 269-277.

12. Christian Agrillo, "Near-Death Experience: Out-of-Body and Out-of-Brain?" *Rev. Gen. Psychology*, 5, no. 1 (2011): 1.

13. Raymond Moody, *Reflections on Life After Life* (Covington: Mockingbird Books, 1977).

14. David Rousseau, "Near-Death Experiences and the Mind-Body Relationship: A Systems-Theoretical Perspective," *Journal of Near-Death Studies*, 6, no. 3 (2011): 29.

15. Kenneth Ring, "Solving the Riddle of Frightening Near-Death Experiences," *Journal of Near-Death Studies*, 8, no. 13 (1994): 5.

16. Pim Van Lommel, *Consciousness Beyond Life* (New York: HarperOne, 2010).

16a. Ibid., 137.

17. Harvey Irwin, *An Introduction to Parapsychology* (Jefferson: McFarlend and Company, 2003).

18. Kenneth Ring, *Life at Death* (New York: Coward, McCann and Geoghegan, 1980).

19. Ibid., 156.

20. Michael Sabom, *Recollections of Death* (New York: Harper and Row, 1982).

21. P. M. H. Atwater, *Beyond the Light* (New York: Birch Lane, 1994).

22. Allan Kellehear, *Experiences Near Death: Beyond Medicine and Religion* (New York: Oxford University Press, 1996).

23. Michael Sabom, *Light and Death: One Doctor's Fascinating Account of Near-Death Experiences* (Grand Rapids: Zondervan, 1998).

24. Stephen Braude, "Out-of-Body Experiences and Survival After Death," *Journal of Parapsychology*, 7, no. 12 (2001): 83.

25. Bruce Greyson, "The Near-Death Experience as a Focus of Clinical Attention," *Journal of Nervous and Mental Disease*, 6, no. 185 (1997): 327.

26. Etzel Cardeña, Jay Lynn, and Stanley Krippner, eds., *Varieties of anomalous experience: Examining the Scientific Evidence* (Washington: Charles C. Thomas, 2000).

27. Esalen, "Mediumship," Esalen Institute, July 2015, www.esalen.org/ctr-archive/mediumship.html (accessed May 30, 2016).

28. Kenneth Ring and Christopher J. Rosing, "The Omega Project: An Empirical Study of the NDE-Prone Personality," *Journal of Near-Death Studies*, 12, no. 8 (1990): 211.

29. Michael Potts, "The Evidential Value of Near-Death Experiences for Belief in Life after Death," *Journal of Near-Death Studies*, 6, no. 20 (2002): 233.

30. Dell 'Olio, "Do Near-Death Experiences Provide a Rational Basis for Belief in Life After Death?" *Sophia 2*, no. 49 (2010): 113.

31. Marie Thonnard et al., "Characteristics of Near-Death Experiences Memories as Compared to Real and Imagined Events Memories," *PLOS ONE* 1, no. 8 (2013): 1.

32. Marie Thonnard et al., "Characteristics of Near-Death Experiences Memories," *PLOS ONE* 1 no. 8: (2013) 12.

33. Emily Kelly, A. Crabtree, A. Gauld, M. Grosso and Bruce Greyson, eds., *Irreducible Mind: Toward a Psychology for the 21st Century* (Lanham: Rowman and Littlefield, 2007).

34. Jean-Pierre Jourdan, "Near Death Experiences and the 5th Dimensional Spatio-Temporal Perspective," *Journal of Cosmology,* 6, no. 14 (2011): 23.

35. Brian Josephson, "String Theory, Universal Mind, and the Paranormal. Department of Physics," December 2003, www.tcm.phy.cam.ac.uk/~bdj10 (accessed June 12, 2016).

36. Jeffrey Long, "Dr. Jeff's Corner," *NDERF,* 1999, www.nderf.org/NDERF/Articles/jeff_corner.htm (accessed May 2, 2016).

37. Alan Batthyany, "Complex Visual Imagery and Cognition during Near-Death Experiences, *Journal of Near-Death Studies,* 4, no. 34 (2015): 232.

38. Bruce Greyson, "Biological Aspects of Near-Death Experiences," *Perspective in Biology and Medicine,* 6 no. 42 (1998): 14.

39. Jeffrey Long, *Evidence of the Afterlife* (New York: HarperCollins, 2011).

40. Ibid., 112.

41. Raymond Moody and Paul Perry, *Coming Back: A Psychiatrist Explores Past Life Journeys* (New York: Bantam Books, 1991).

42. Emily Kelly, "Near-Death Experiences with Reports of Meeting Deceased People," *Death Studies,* 7, no. 25 (2001): 229.

43. Melvin Morse, *Parting Visions* (London: Piatkus Books, 1994).

44. Janice Holden, Bruce Greyson, and D. James, eds., *The Handbook of Near-Death Experiences: Thirty Years of Investigation* (Westport: Praeger Publishers, 2009).

45. Melvin Morse, *Transformed by the Light: The Powerful Effect of Near-Death Experiences on People's Lives* (New York: Villard Books, 1992).

46. Holden et al., *The Handbook of Near-Death Experiences: Thirty Years of Investigation.*

47. Penny Sartori, "A Prospective Study to Investigate the Incidence and Phenomenology of Near-Death Experiences in a Welsh Intensive Therapy Unit," *Unpublished doctoral dissertation* (University of Wales, 2005).

48. Eben Alexander, *Proof of Heaven: A Neurosurgeon's Journey into the Afterlife* (New York: Simon and Schuster, 2012).

49. Ibid., 39.

50. Near Death Research Foundation, "NDERF," May 2015, www.nderf.org/ (accessed May 16, 2016).

51. David Rousseau, "Centre for Systems Philosophy," *Center for Systems Philosophy,* May 27, 2014, http://systemsphilosophy.org/david-rousseau.html (accessed June 2, 2016).

52. Larry Dossey, *Healing Beyond the Body* (New York: Time Warner, 2002).

53. Sabrina Golonka and Andrew Wilson, "Ecological Representations," *Ecological Representation's*, June 15, 2016, http://biorxiv.org/content/early/2016/06/15/058925 (accessed May 23, 2016).

54. Bruce Greyson, "NDE Scale," IANDS, July 2007, https://iands.org/research/important-research-articles/698-greyson-nde-scale.html (accessed May 23, 2016).

55. Bruce Greyson, "Dissociation in People who Have Near-Death Experiences: Out of their Bodies or Out of Their Minds?" *Lancet* 17, no. 355 (2000): 460.

56. Sam Parnia et al., "AWARE—AWAreness during REsuscitation-A Prospective Study," *Resuscitation* 6, no. 85 (2014): 1799.

57. Ibid., 1802

57a. Robin Marantz Henig, "Crossing Over: How Science Is Redefining Life and Death," *National Geographic*, April 2016. www.nationalgeographic.com/magazine/2016/04/dying-death-brain-dead-body-consciousness-science/ (accessed June 12, 2017).

58. Bruce Greyson and C. P. Flynn, eds., *The Near-Death Experience* (Springfield: Charles C. Thomas, 1984).

59. Kelly Emily, Bruce Greyson, and Ian Stevenson, "Can Experiences Near Death Furnish Evidence of Life after Death?" *Omega* 2, no. 40 (2000): 513.

60. Kenneth Ring and M. Lawrence, "Further Evidence for Veridical Perception During Near-Death Experiences," *Journal of Near-Death Studies* 3, no. 11 (1993): 223.

61. David Fontanna, *Is There an Afterlife?* (Park Lane: O Books, 2005).

62. Ibid., 223.

63. Michael Sabom, "Dr. Michael Sabom's Near-Death Experience Research," *Near Death*, 2014. www.near-death.com/science/experts/michael-sabom.html (accessed May 18, 2016).

64. Ibid., 2.

65. Penny Sartori, *The Near-Death Experiences of Hospitalized Intensive Care Patients: A Five-Year Clinical Study* (Lewiston: Edward Mellen Press, 2008).

66. Ibid., 102.

67. Holden et al., *The Handbook of Near-Death Experiences: Thirty Years of Investigation*, 127

68. Ibid., 310.

69. Henry Hart, "ESP Projection: Spontaneous Cases and the Experimental Method," *Journal of the American Society for Psychical Research* 3, no. 48 (1954): 121-132.

70. Janice Holden, "Response to "Is it Rational to Extrapolate from the Presence of Consciousness During a Flat EEG to Survival of Consciousness After Death?" *Journal of Near-Death Studies* 4, no. 29 (2010): 362.

71. Bruce Greyson, "Telepathy in Mental Illness." *Journal of Nervous and Mental Disease* 6, no. 16 (1977): 184.

72. Pim van Lommel, et al., "Near-Death Experience in Survivors of Cardiac Arrest: A Prospective Study in the Netherlands," *Lancet* 4, 358 (2001): 2039.

73. Ibid., 2041.

74. Charles Cook, Bruce Greyson, and Ian Stevenson, "Do Any Near-Death Experiences Provide Evidence for the Survival of Human Personality after Death?" *Journal of Scientific Exploration* 7, no. 12 (1998): 377.

75. Pim Van Lommel, "About the Continuity of Our Consciousness," *Adv Exp Med Biology* 2 no. 550 (2004): 115.

75a. Ibid., 197.

76. Michael Sabom, *Recollections of Death* (New York: Harpercollins, 1981).

77. Ibid., 221.

78. Kenneth Ring and Sharon Cooper, *Mindsight: Near-Death and Out-of-Body Experiences in the Blind* (Institute of Transpersonal Psychology: William James Center for Consciousness Studies, 1999), 32.

79. Ibid., 78.

80. Ring and Cooper, *Mindsight*, 79.

81. Ring and Cooper, *Mindsight*, 82.

82. Ring and Cooper, *Mindsight*, 85.

83. Tara Maclsaac, "In-Near-Death Experiences Blind People See for First Time," *The Epoch Times*, July 30, 2016, www.theepochtimes.com/n3/2128726-in-near-death-experiences-blind-people-see-for-first-time/?utm_expvariant=D001_01&utm_expid=21082672-11.b4WAd2xRR0ybC6ydhoAj9w.1 (accessed June 11, 2016).

84. Near Death, "Evidence People Can Experience Someone Else in NDE," *Near Death*, July 2014. www.near-death.com/science/evidence/people-can-experience-someone-elses-nde.html (accessed May 18, 2016).

85. Penny Sartori, "Empathic or Shared Death Experiences How Do We Explain Them," *Dr. Penny Sartori*, November 8, 2011, https://drpennysartori.wordpress.com/2011/11/08/empathic-or-shared-death-experiences-how-do-we-explain-them/ (accessed May 14, 2016).

86. Ibid., 18.

87. P. M. H. Atwater, "Near-Death Experiences of Groups of People," *Near Death*, 2016, www.near-death.com/experiences/group.html (accessed May 10, 2016).

88. Near-Death Experience Research Foundation, "Out of Body Research Experience," *NDERF*, June 2015, www.nderf.org (accessed May 20, 2016).

88a. Debra L. Luczkiewicz et al., "End-of-Life Dreams and Visions: A Qualitative Perspective From Hospice Patients," *American Journal of Hospice and Palliative Care*, January (2014): 1.

89. Sam Parnia, K. Spearpoint, and Peter, Fenwick, "Near Death Experiences, Cognitive Function and Psychological Outcomes of Surviving Cardiac Arrest," *Resuscitation* 3, no. 74 (2007): 215.

90. Ibid., 217.

91. Margot Grey, *Return from Death: An Exploration of the Near-Death Experience* (London: Arkana, 1985).

92. Ibid., 130.

93. Pim van Lommel, *Consciousness Beyond Life: The Science of the Near-Death Experience* (New York: Harper Collins, 2010).

93a. Ibid., 178.

94. Charles Sutherland, *Transformed by the Light: Life after Near-Death Experiences* (Sydney: Bantam Books, 1992).

95. Casandra Musgrave, "The Near-Death Experience: A Study of Spiritual Transformation," *Journal of Near-Death Studies* 6, no. 15 (1997): 187.

96. Michael Sabom, "The Near Death Experience," *Journal American Medical Association* 11, no. 244 (1980): 29.

97. Kenneth Ring, *The Omega Project: Near Death Experiences, UFO Encounters and Mind at Large* (New York: William Morrow, 1992).

98. P. M. H. Atwater, *Beyond the Light, What Isn't Being Said About Near Death Experience: from Visions of Heaven to Glimpses of Hell* (Kill Devil Hills: Transpersonal Publishing, 2009).

99. Ibid., 127.

100. Ring, *The Omega Project*, 231.

101. Bruce Greyson, "Near-Death Experiences: Clinical Implications," *Archives of Clinical Psychiatry* 6, no. 34 (2007): 1–10.

102. Ibid., 2.

103. Kenneth Ring and Evelyn Valarino, *Lessons from the Light* (Needham: Moment Point Press, 2000).

104. Darrah Brustein, "This Entrepreneur's Near-Death Experience Revealed Her True Purpose," Entrepreneur, December 8, 2015, www.entrepreneur.com/article/253350 (accessed May 19, 2016).

105. Jeffrey Long, "Stories of God's Love Common among Those who Almost Die," *The Washington Post*, June 29, 2016, www.washingtonpost.com/news/acts-of-faith/wp/2016/06/29/people-who-had-near-death-experiences-consistently-report-one-thing-gods-love/ (accessed July 8, 2016).

106. Ibid., 24.

107. Long, "Stories of God's Love Common among Those who Almost Die," 25.

107a. *Ring. The Omega Project*, 157–189.

107b. Reinerio Hernandez, Robert Davis, Rudolph Schild, Claude Swanson, Jon Klimo, and Giorgio Piacenza, "The Quantum Hologram Theory of Consciousness and the Multi-Dimensional Nature of Contact with Non-Human Intelligence," *Proceedings of the 2nd International Congress on Consciousness, Journal of Consciousness,* 19, no. 62 (2017).

108. J. Pope, "Near Death Experiences and Attitudes towards Life, Death, and Suicide," *Australian Parapsychological Review* 12, no. 19 (1994): 23.

108a. Ibid., 27.

109. Crick, Francis, *The Astonishing Hypothesis: The Scientific Search for the Soul.* London: Simon and Schuster, 1994.

110. Istvan Bókkon, Birendra Mallick, and Jack Tuszynski, "Near Death Experiences: A Multidisciplinary Hypothesis," *Front. Hum. Neuroscience* 4, no. 7 (2013): 533.

111. Susan Blackmore, *Dying to Live* (Amherst: Prometheus Books, 1993).

112. Pim Van Lommel, "Nonlocal Consciousness. A Concept Based on Scientific Research on Near-Death Experiences during Cardiac Arrest," *Journal of*

Consciousness Studies 8, no. 20 (2013): 7.

113. Bruce Greyson Bruce and Ian Stevenson, "The Phenomenology of Near-Death Experiences," *Am J Psychiatry* 2, no. 137 (1980): 1193.

114. Edward et al., *Irreducible Mind: Toward a Psychology for the 21st Century*, 87

115. P. K. Bhattacharya, "Is There Science Behind the Near-Death Experience: Does human Consciousness Survive after Death?" *Ann Trop Med Public Health* 2, no. 6 (2013): 151.

116. Sam Parnia and Peter Fenwick, "Near Death Experiences in Cardiac Arrest," *Resuscitation* 3, no. 52 (2002): 5.

117. Pim van Lommel, et al. "Near-Death Experiences," *Lancet* 4, no. 350 (2001): 2024.

118. Bruce Greyson, "Near-Death Experiences and Personal Values," *American Journal of Psychiatry* 7, no. 140 (1983): 618.

119. Michael Sabom, *Light and Death: One Doctor's Fascinating Account of Near-Death Experiences* (Grand Rapids: Zondervan, 1998).

120. Ibid., 110.

121. Adam Hoffman, "Lazarus Phenomenon," *Smithsonian*, March 31, 2016, www.smithsonianmag.com/science-nature/lazarus-phenomenon-explained-why-sometimes-deceased-are-not-dead-yet-180958613/?no-ist (accessed May 12, 2016).

122. Ibid., 1.

123. Vriens et al., "The Impact of Repeated Short Episodes of Circulatory Arrest on Cerebral Function," *Electroencephalography and Clinical Neurophysiology* 6, no 98 (1996): 236.

124. Susan Blackmore, "Near-Death Experiences: In or Out of the Body?" *Skeptical Inquirer* 6, no. 16: (1991) 34.

125. Sam Parnia, D. G. Waller, R. Yeates, and Peter. Fenwick, "A Qualitative and Quantitative Study of the Incidence, Features and Aetiology of Near Death Experiences in Cardiac Arrest Survivors, *Resuscitation* 6, no. 48 (2001): 149.

125a. Pim van Lommel, "Continuity of Consciousness," IANDS, April 25, 2015, http://iands.org/research/nde-research/important-research-articles/43-dr-pim-van-lommel-md-continuity-of-consciousness.html?showall=&start=3 (accessed June 12, 2017).

126. Melvin Morse, D. Venecia, and J. Milstein, "Near-Death Experiences: A Neurophysiologic Explanatory Model," *Journal of Near-Death Studies* 4, no. 8 (1989): 45.

127. G. Roberts and J. Owen, "The Near-Death Experience," *British Journal of Psychiatry* 4, no. 153 (1988): 607.

128. Glen Gabbard and S. Tremlow, *With the Eye of the Mind* (New York: Prager, 1984).

129. Ibid., 202.

130. J. S. Cheyne, Rueffer, and I. Newby-Clark, "Hypnagogic and Hypnopompic Hallucinations during Sleep Paralysis: Neurological and Cultural Construction of the Night-Mare," *Conscious Cognition* 4, no. 8 (1999): 319.

131. Ibid., 322.
132. American Academy of Neurology, "People With Near Death Experiences Can Differ in Sleep-Wake Control," *ScienceDaily*, April 17, 2006, www.sciencedaily.com/releases/2006/04/060417110256.htm (accessed June 23, 2016).
133. Kevin Nelson, "Out-of-Body Experiences May Be Caused by Arousal System Disturbances in Brain," *University of Kentucky*, March 6, 2007, www.sciencedaily.com/releases/2007/03/070305202657.htm (accessed August 3, 2016).
134. Ibid., 2.
135. Nelson, "Out-of-Body Experiences May Be Caused by Arousal System Disturbances in Brain," 3.
136. P. Maquet et al., "Functional Neuroanatomy of Human Rapid Eye Movement Sleep and Dreaming," *Nature* 4, no. 383 (1996): 163.
137. Olaf Blanke, C. Mohr, and C. Michel, "Linking Out-of-Body Experience and Self Processing to Mental Own-Body Imagery at the Temporoparietal Junction," *Journal of Neuroscience* 7, no. 25 (2005): 550.
138. Ibid., 552.
139. T. A. Stephan, A. Deutschlander, and A. Nolte A, "Functional MRI of Galvanic Vestibular Stimulation with Alternating Currents at Different Frequencies," *Neuroimage* 2, no. 26 (2005): 721.
140. F. Sang et al., Depersonalisation/Derealisation Symptoms in Vestibular Disease," *Journal of Neurology and Neurosurgical Psychiatry* 8, no. 77 (2006): 760.
141. Saavedra-Aguilar and J. Gomez-Jeria, "A Neurobiological Model for Near-Death Experiences," *Journal of Near-Death Studies* 4, no. 7 (1989): 205.
142. Keith Osis and Ermund Haraldsson, *At the Hour of Death* (New York: Hastings House, 1986).
143. Susan Blackmore, *Beyond the Body: An Investigation of the Out-of-Body Experience* (London: Heinemann, 1982).
144. Ibid., 187.
145. Blackmore, *Beyond the Body: An Investigation of the Out-of-Body Experience*, 190.
146. Bruce Greyson, "A Typology of Near-Death Experiences," *Am J Psychiatry* 2, no. 142 (1985): 967.
147. John McGrath, Sukanta Saha, and Ali Al-Hamzawi, "Psychotic Experiences in the General Population: A Cross-National Analysis Based on 31,261 Respondents From 18 Countries," *JAMA Psychiatry* 8, no. 72 (2015): 697.
148. Ibid., 698.
149. Jimo Borjigin et al., "Surge of Neurophysiological Coherence and Connectivity in the Dying Brain," *Edited by Solomon Snyder*, July 9, 2013, www.pnas.org/content/110/35/14432.abstract (accessed June 2, 2016).
150. Ring, *Mindsight*, 89.
151. J. Arnette, "On the Mind/Body Problem: The Theory of Essence," *Journal of Near-Death Studies* 5, no. 11 (1992): 5.
152. Amit Goswami, "The Paranormal Perception of Color," *Parapsychological* 7, no. 16 (1993): 1.

153. Michael Talbot, *The Holographic Universe* (New York: HarperCollins, 1991).

154. Lommel, *Consciousness,* 34.

155. Femilab. "Fermi Lab Center," *Hogan,* January 20, 2016, http://astro.fnal.gov/people/hogan-nguyen/ (accessed May 12, 2016).

156. Jean-Pierre Jourdan, "Near Death Experiences and Temporal Perspectives," *Journal of Cosmology* 6, no. 14 (2011): 236-245.

157. J. Smythies, "Space, Time and Consciousness," *Journal of Consciousness Studies* 2, no. 10: (2003) 47.

158. B. Carr, "Worlds Apart?" *Proceedings of the Society for Psychical Research* 1, no. 59 (2008): 1.

159. T. Droulez, "Conscience, Espace, Réalité. Implications d'une Critique du Réalisme Perceptuel Direct," *Cahiers Philosophiques de Strasbourg* 6, no. 28 (2010): 23.

160. Fred Wolf, "The Yoga of Time Travel and Dr. Quantum's World," *Fred Alan Wolf,* November 9, 2012, http://fredalanwolf.blogspot.com/ (accessed June 8, 2016).

161. Lisa Smart, "Final Words Can Heal," *Final Words Project,* 2015, www.finalwordsproject.org/healing.html (accessed June 12, 2016).

162. Talbot, *The Holographic Universe,* 143.

163. Stuart Hameroff, "Through The Wormhole," Interview by the Science Channel, October, 2012.

164. Ibid., 23.

165. Hugh Everett, "Relative State Formulation of Quantum Mechanics," *Reviews of Modern Physics* 8, no. 29 (1957): 454.

166. Ibid., 457.

167. Karen Schaeffer, "Near Death Experience," *Near Death,* 2016, www.near-death.com/experiences/notable/karen-schaeffer.html (accessed May 24, 2016).

168. Alexander, *Proof of Heaven,* 202.

169. Pim van Lommel, "Near-Death Experiences: The Experience of the Self as Real and Not as an Illusion," *Annals NY Academy of Sciences* 4, no. 1234 (2011): 19.

170. David Baudoin, "Curious Dissociation between Cerebral Imaging and Clinical Findings," *The Lancet* 14, no. 347 (1996): 965.

Chapter Four: Apparitions

1. Julia Assante, *The Last Frontier* (Novato: New World Library, 2012).

2. Ibid., 24.

3. Henry Sidgwick, "Report on the Census of Hallucinations," *Proceedings of the Society for Psychical Research* 3, No. 10 (1894): 25.

4. David West, "A Mass-Observation Questionnaire on Hallucinations," *Journal of the Society for Psychical Research* 12, no. 34 (1948): 187.

5. William McCready and Andrew M. Greeley, *The Ultimate Values of the American Population* (Beverly Hills: Sage Publications, 1976).

6. Ibid., 23.

7. George Nygent and Merle Tyrrell, *Apparitions* (New York: Collier, 1963).

8. Celia Green and Charles McCreery, *Apparitions* (London: Hamish Hamilton, 1975).

9. Henry Sidgwick et al., "Report on the Census of Hallucinations." *Proceedings of the Society for Psychical Research 4, no. 10 (1894)*, 25.

9a. Ibid., 28.

10. Ibid., 26.

11. J. D. Morris, W. G. Roll, and R. L. Morris, eds., *Research in Parapsychology* (Metuchen: Scarecrow Press, 1976).

12. Harvey Irwin, "Parapsychological Phenomena and the Absorption Domain," *Journal of the American Society for Psychical Research 6, no.79* (1985): 1.

13. Erlendur Haraldsson, "Survey of Claimed Encounters with the Dead," *Omega 1, no. 19* (1988): 14.

14. Irwin, *Parapsychological Phenomena*, 1985, 1

15. Ibid., 2.

16. Nygent, *Apparitions*, Collier, 13.

17. Ibid., 15.

18. Henry Sidgwick, "Report on the Census of Hallucinations," 1894, 26.

19. Ian Stevenson, "Are Poltergeists Living or Are They Dead?" *Journal of the American Society for Psychical Research 7, no. 66* (1972): 233.

20. Ibid., 235.

21. B. B. Wolman, ed., *Handbook of Parapsychology* (New York: Van Nostrand Reinhold, 1977).

22. J. Assante, *The Last Frontier*, 35.

23. F. W. Myers, *Human Personality and its Survival of Bodily Death* (London: Longmans, 1903).

24. Hornell Hart, "Six Theories about Apparitions," *Proceedings of the Society for Psychical Research 4, no. 50* (1956): 153.

25. Survival After Death, "Is there Life Beyond Death?" *Survival After Death*, 2014, www.survivalafterdeath.info/articles/sargent/beyond.htm (accessed January 23, 2016).

26. Ibid., 2.

27. Lois Duncan and William Roll, *Psychic Connections* (New York: Bantam Doubleday, 1995).

28. Michael Persinger, "The Neuropsychiatry of Paranormal Experiences," *Journal of Neuropsychiatry and Clinical Neuroscience 14, no. 13* (2001): 515.

29. Pehr Granqvist, "Sensed Presence and Mystical Experiences are Predicted by Suggestibility, Not by the Application of Transcranial Weak Complex Magnetic Fields. Randomized Controlled Trial," *Neuroscience Letters 8, no. 23* (2005): 34.

30. Richard Wiseman, Caroline Watt, and Paul Stevens, "An Investigation into Alleged Hauntings," *British Journal of Psychology 12, no. 94* (2003): 95.

31. Livingston Gearhart and Michael Persinger, "Geophysical Variables and Behavior: Onsets of Historical and Contemporary Poltergeist Episodes Occurred with Sudden Increases in Geomagnetic Activity," *Perceptual and Motor Skills 7, no. 62* (1986): 440.

32. Sarah Krapton, "Ghosts Created by Scientists," *The Telegraph*, 2014, www.telegraph.co.uk/news/science/science-news/11214511/Ghosts-created-by-scientists-in-disturbin g-lab-experiment.html (accessed January 18th, 2016).

33. Pehr Granqvist, "Sensed Presence," *Neuroscience Letters* 1, no. 23 (2005): 34.

34. Michael Persinger, "Vectorial Cerebral Hemisphericity as Differential Sources for the Sensed Presence, Mystical Experiences and Religious Conversations," *Perceptual and Motor Skills* 4, no. 76 (1993): 915.

35. Michael Persinger and Katherine Makarec, "The Feeling of a Presence and Verbal Meaningfulness in Context of Temporal Lobe Function: Factor Analysis Verification of the Muses?" *Brain and Cognition* 4, No. 20 (1992): 217.

36. Kristen Barnes and Nicholas Gibson, "Supernatural Agency: Individual Difference Predictors and Situational Correlates," *The International Journal for the Psychology of Religion* 5, no. 23 (2013): 1

37. Edward Kelly et al., *Irreducible Mind* (New York: Rowan and Littlefield, 2007).

38. Hornell Hart, "Six Theories," 1956, 154.

39. Ibid. 155.

40. James Houran, "Toward a Psychology of "Entity Encounter Experiences," *Journal of the American Society for Psychical Research* 12, no. 64 (2000): 141.

41. James Alcock, *Science and Supernature. A Critical Appraisal of Parapsychology* (Buffalo: Prometheus Books, 1990).

42. John Yuille and John Cutshall, "A Case Study of Eyewitness Memory of a Crime," *Journal of Applied Psychology* 12, no. 7 (1986): 1.

43. Carla Brandon, *One Last Hug Before I Go: The Mystery and Meaning of Deathbed Visions* (Deerfield Beach: HCI, 2010).

44. Charles McCreery and Celia Green, "A Follow-Up Study of People Reporting Apparitional Experiences," *Society for Psychical Research* 2, no 12 (1986): 134.

45. Susan Datson and Samuel Marwitt, "Personality Constructs and Perceived Presence of Deceased Loved Ones," *Death Studies* 5, no. 21 (1997): 131.

46. A. Sheik, ed., *Imagery: Current Theory, Research, and Applications* (New York: Wiley, 1983).

47. Edmund Gurney, F. W. Myers and Frank Podmore, *Phantoms of the Living* (London: Trubner, 1886).

48. John Palmer, "A Community Mail Survey of Psychic Experiences," *Journal of the American Society for Psychical Research* 16, no. 73 (1979): 221.

49. Scott Rogo, "Psychical Research and the Survival Controversy: Apparitions and the Case for Survival," London Guild Publishing, 1986, www.survivalafterdeath. info/articles/rogo/apparitions.htm (accessed February 12, 2016).

50. Joe Nickell, "Haunted Inns Tales of Spectral Guests," *Committee for Skeptical Inquiry* 6, no. 12 (2009): 23.

51. David Fontanna, *Is there an Afterlife?* (London: O Books, 2005).

52. Ian Stevenson, "The Contribution of Apparitions to the Evidence of Survival," *Journal of the American Society for Psychical Research* 2, no. 76 (1982): 341.

53. Ibid., 344.

54. Bill Guggenheim and Judy Guggenheim, *Hello from Heaven! A New Field of Research ~ After-Death Communication* (New York: Bantam Books, 1996).

55. Ian Stevenson, "Are Poltergeists Living or are they Dead?" *Journal of the American Society for Psychical Research* 4, no. 66 (1972): 233.

56. F. W. H. Myers, "On Recognized Apparitions Occurring More than a Year after Death," *Proceedings for the Society for Psychical Research* 7, no. 6 (1889): 13.

57. Celia Green and Charles McCreery, *Apparitions* (The University of Virginia: Hamilton, 1985).

58. B. B. Wolman, ed., *Handbook of Parapsychology*, 137.

59. F. W. H. Myers, "Case of the Will of James L. Chaffin," *Proceedings of the Society for Psychical Research*, 6, no. 36 (1927): 517.

60. Ibid., 518.

61. Irwin, *An Introduction to Parapsychology*, 35

62. Irwin, *An Introduction to Parapsychology*, 128.

63. Irwin, *An Introduction to Parapsychology*, 134.

64. B. B. Wolman, ed., *Handbook of Parapsychology*, 137.

65. Irwin, *An Introduction to Parapsychology*, 167.

66. The Professor Forum, "The Professor Forum," August 11, 2007, http://z6.invisionfree.com/The_Professor_Forum/ar/t1226.htm (accessed February 13, 2016).

67. Scott Rogo and Raymond Bayless, *Phone Calls from the Dead* (Englewood Cliffs: Prentice Hall, 1979).

68. Victor Zammit, "Victor Zammit," 2006, www.victorzammit.com/book/4thedition/chapter19.html (accessed January 12, 2016).

69. Julia Assante, *The Last Frontier*, 154.

70. Hornell Hart, "ESP Projection: Spontaneous Cases and the Experimental Method," *Journal of the American Society for Psychical Research*, 9, no. 48 (1954): 121.

71. Larry Dossey, Bruce Greyson, Peter Sturrock and Jim Tucker, "Consciousness—What Is It?" *Journal of Cosmology* 11, no. 14 (2011): 84.

72. Guy Lyon Playfair, *This House is Haunted: An Investigation of the Enfield Poltergeist* (London: Souvenir Press, 1980).

73. Irwin, *An Introduction to Parapsychology*, 169.

74. Ryan Sprague, "The Most Haunted Theater on Broadway," *Paranormal Braintrust*, March 8, 2016, http://jimharold.com/haunted-theater-broadway-mr-belasco/ (accessed June 15, 2016).

75. Stevenson, "Are Poltergeists Living or are they Dead?" 238.

76. Ernst Senkowski, *Instrumentelle Transkommunikation* (Frankfurt: F. G. Fischer, 1989).

77. Bill Guggenheim and Judy Guggenheim, *Bantam Books*, 1996, http://eternea.org/ADC_Definition.aspx (accessed February 13, 2016).

78. Michael Nees and Charlotte Phillips, "Auditory Pareidolia: Effects of Contextual Priming on Perceptions of Purportedly Paranormal and Ambiguous Auditory Stimuli," *Applied Cognitive Psychology* 6, no. 12 (2014): 134.

79. James Alcock, "Electronic Voice Phenomena: Voices of the Dead?" *The Committee for Skeptical Inquiry*, December 21, 2004. www.csicop.org/specialarticles/show/electronic_voice_phenomena_voices_of_the_dead (accessed September 2, 2016).

80. Tom Butler, "Transcommunication," *Etheric Studies*, October 10, 2014, http://ethericstudies.org/concepts/transcommunication.htm (accessed March 12, 2016).

81. Sinesio Darnell, *Voces sin Rostro* (Barcelona: Fausi, 1979).

82. Karen Stollznow, "Skepticism and Blogging," *Skeptical Inquirer* 14, no. 33 (2009): 33.

83. Hans Bender, "Mediumistic Psychoses," *Parapsychology* 7, no. 23 (1966): 574.

84. Brian Regal, *Pseudoscience: A Critical Encyclopedia* (New York: Greenwood 2009).

85. Imants Baruss, "Failure to Replicate Electronic Voice Phenomenon," *Journal of Scientific Exploration* 15, no. 6 (2001): 355.

86. Craig Klugman, "Dead Men Talking: Evidence of Post Death Contact and Continuing Bonds," *Journal of Death and Dying* 53, no. 2 (2006): 249.

87. Louis LaGrand, "The Nature and Therapeutic Implications of the Extraordinary Experiences of the Bereaved," *Journal of Near-Death Studies* 24, (2005): 3.

88. Melvin Morse, *Parting Visions.* (New York: Villard Books, 1995).

89. Christopher Kerr, "End-of-Life Dreams and Visions: A Longitudinal Study of Hospice Patients' Experiences," *Journal of Palliative Medicine* 7, no. 14 (2014): 43.

90. Diane Arcangel, *Afterlife Encounters: Ordinary People, Extraordinary Experiences* (Charlottesville, VA: Hampton Roads, 2005).

91. Ecstacy, "Afterlife Encounters Survey Phase 3," *ECSTASY*, June 2012, http://ae.kfancher.com/survey2k7.html (accessed May 12, 2016).

92. M. Barbato et al., "Parapsychological Phenomena Near the Time of Death," *Journal of Palliative Care* 15, no 3 (1999): 30.

93. Sandra Dannenbaum and Richard Kinnier, "Imaginal Relationships with the Dead: Applications for Psychotherapy," *Journal of Humanistic Psychology* 49, (2009): 100.

94. Julie Beischel, "Assisted after-Death Communication: A Self-Prescribed Treatment for Grief," *Journal of Near-Death Studies* 32, (2014): 161.

95. Arcangel, *Afterlife Encounters*, 112.

96. Ibid., 114

97. Guggenheim, *Hello from Heaven*, 43.

98. Ibid., 45.

99. Guggenheim, *Hello from Heaven*, 74.

100. Guggenheim, *Hello from Heaven*, 134.

101. Ernest Bozzano, *Phénomenes Psychiques au Moment de la Mort.* (Paris, France: JMG, 1998).

102. Sir William Barrett, *Death Bed Visions* (London, UK: Methuen, 1926).

103. Bozzano, *Phénomenes Psychiques*, 45.

104. Karlis Osis and Erlendur Haraldsson, *At the Hour of Death* (Norwalk, CT: Hastings House, 1995).

105. John Lerma, *Into the Light: Real Life Stories about Angelic Visits, Visions of the Afterlife, and other Pre-Death Experiences* (Franklin Lakes, NJ: Career Press, 2007).

106. Osis, *At the Hour of Death*, 67.

107. Assante, *The Last Frontier*, 87.

108. Arcangel, *Afterlife Encounters*, 114.

109. Cheryl Nosek, "End-of-Life Dreams and Visions: A Qualitative Perspective from Hospice Patients," *Am Journal Hospital Palliative Care* 8, (2015): 235.

110. David Sunfellow, "Parting Visions," January 6, 1995, www.nhne.com/articles/sapartingvisions.html (accessed March 20 2016).

111 Ibid., 3.

112. Peter Fenwick and Elizabeth Fenwick, *The Art of Dying: A Journey to Elsewhere* (London, UK: Continuum, 2008).

113. Bruce Greyson, "Seeing Dead People Not Known to Have Died: Peak in Darien Experiences," *Anthropology and Humanism* 35, (2010): 159.

114. Emily W. Kelly, "Near-Death Experiences with Reports of Meeting Deceased People," *Death Studies* 25, (2001): 229.

115. Ibid., 232.

Chapter Five: Reincarnation

1. Ian Stevenson, *Twenty Cases Suggestive of Reincarnation* (Charlottesville: University Press of Virginia, 1974).

2. Ibid., 32.

3. Ian Stevenson, *Cases of the Reincarnation Type. II: Ten Cases in Sri Lanka* (Charlottesville: University Press of Virginia, 1977a)

4. Ian Stevenson, *Cases of the Reincarnation Type. Ill: Twelve Cases in Lebanon and Turkey* (Charlottesville: University Press of Virginia, 1980).

5. Stevenson, *Twenty Cases Suggestive of Reincarnation*, 12.

6. Ian Stevenson, *Where Reincarnation and Biology Intersect* (Westport: Praeger, 1997).

7. Ian Stevenson, "The Explanatory Value of the Idea of Reincarnation," *Journal of Nervous and Mental Disease* 12, no. 164 (1977): 305.

8. Ibid., 310.

9. Stevenson, *Where Reincarnation and Biology Intersect*, 23.

10. Ian Stevenson, *Cases of the Reincarnation Type. I: Ten Cases in India* (Charlottesville: University Press of Virginia, 1975b).

11. Based on Ian Stevenson Research, "Past Forward," *Past Forward*, January 12, 2014, www.healpastlives.com/future/rule/ruevplif.htm (accessed July 12, 2016).

12. Ian Stevenson, "Birthmarks and Birth Defects Corresponding to Wounds on Deceased Persons," *Journal of Scientific Exploration* 7 no. 3 (1993): 403.

13. B. B. Wolman, ed., *Handbook of Parapsychology* (New York: Van Nostrand Reinhold, 1977).

14. Ibid., 231.

15. Stevenson, *Cases of the Reincarnation Type. I: Ten Cases in India,* 132.

15a. Ibid., 147.

16. Ian Stevenson, *Reincarnation and Biology: A Contribution to the Etiology of Birthmarks and Birth Defects. Volume 1* (Westport: Praeger, 1997a).

17. Ibid., 28.

18. Stevenson, *Birthmarks and Birth Defects*, 408.

19. Antonia Mills, "A Replication Study: Three Cases of Children in Northern India Who are said to Remember a Previous Life," *Journal of Scientific Explanation* 3, no. 4 (1989): 133.

20. Erlendur Haraldsson, "Birthmarks and Claims of Previous Life Memories I. The Case of Purnima Ekanayake." Journal of the Society for Psychical Research 64 (2000a): 16.

21. Stevenson, *Reincarnation and Biology*, 32.

22. A. Mills, "Modern Cases of the Reincarnation Type in Northern India: A test of the Hypothesis of Imposed Identification. Part 1: Analysis of 26 Cases." Journal of Scientific Explanation 4 (1990): 171.

23. Ian Wilson, *Reincarnation? The Claims Investigated* (Harmondsworth: Penguin, 1982).

24. Harvey Irwin, *An Introduction to Parapsychology* (Jefferson: McFarland and Company, 2003).

25. Stevenson, *Twenty Cases Suggestive of Reincarnation,* 241.

26. Paul Cunningham, "An Experimental Investigation of Past-Life Experiences by Dr. Paul F. Cunningham," August 2009, www.rivier.edu/faculty/pcunningham/Research/Web%20Page%20Past-Life%20Experiences%204-29-11.pdf (accessed July 20, 2016).

27. Eugene Brody, "Review of Cases of the Reincarnation Type: Ten Cases in Sri Lanka," *Journal of Nervous and Mental Disease* 12, no. 4 (1979): 769.

28. Jurgen Keil, "New Cases in Burma, Thailand, and Turkey: A Limited Field Study Replication of Some Aspects of Ian Stevenson's Research," *Journal of Scientific Explanation* 5 no. 6 (1991): 27.

29. Antonia Mills, Erlendur Haraldsson and H. Keil, "Replication Studies of Cases Suggestive of Reincarnation by Three Independent Investigators," *Journal of the American Society for Psychical Research* 88, no. 2 (1994): 207.

29a. Jesse Bering, "Ian Stevenson's Case for the Afterlife: Are We 'Skeptics' Really Just Cynics?" *Scientific American*, November 2, 2013, www.blogs.scientificamerican.com/bering-in-mind/ian-stevensone28099s-case-for-the-afterlife-are-we-e28098skepticse28099-really-just-cynics/ (accessed June 13, 2017).

30. Bruce Leininger, "Was a World War II Pilot Reincarnated in a Body of a Little Boy?" *Soul Survivor: The Reincarnation of a WW II Fighter Pilot*, November 22, 2010, www.wanttoknow.info/a-world-war-II-pilot-reincarnated-little-boy

(accessed August 3, 2016).

31. K. S. Raivat, "The Case of Shanti Devi," *Venture Inward Magazine*, March 1997, www.carolbowman.com/dr-ian-stevenson/case-shanti-devi/ (accessed July 20, 2016).

32. Chris Carter, *Science and the Afterlife Experience* (Rochester: Inner Traditions, 2012).

33. Stevenson, *Twenty Cases Suggestive of Reincarnation*, 42.

34. Stevenson, *Cases of the Reincarnation Type. II*, 12.

35. Ian Stevenson and S. Pasricha, "A Preliminary Report on an Unusual Case of the Reincarnation Type with Xenoglossy," *Journal of the American Society for Psychical Research* 74, no. 4 (1980): 331.

36. Lisa Miller, "Remembrances of Lives Past," *New York Times*, August 27, 2010, www.nytimes.com/2010/08/29/fashion/29PastLives.html?pagewanted=all&_r=2& (accessed June 20, 2016).

37. Julia Assante, *The Last Frontier* (Novato: New World Library, 2012).

38. Morris Netherton and Nancy Shiffrin, *Past Life Therapy* (New York: Ace Books, 1978).

39. Ibid., 23.

40. Netherton, *Past Life Therapy*, 24.

41. Stevenson, *Twenty Cases Suggestive of Reincarnation*, 3.

42. Julia Assante, *The Last Frontier*, 121.

43. B. B. Wolman, ed., *Handbook of Parapsychology* (New York: Van Nostrand Rheinhold, 1977).

44. Ibid., 137.

45. B. B. Wolman, ed., *Handbook of Parapsychology, 139.*

46. Joanne Ruthsatz, "The Cognitive Bases of Exceptional Abilities in Child Prodigies," *Intelligence* 43, no. 2 (2014): 14.

47. Larry Vandervert, "The Emergence of the Child Prodigy 10,000 years ago: An Evolutionary and Developmental Explanation," *The Journal of Mind and Behavior* 30, no. 7 (2009): 15.

48. Ibid., 17.

49. S. Krippner, ed., *Advances in Parapsychological Research* (Jefferson: McFarland, 1990).

50. Fabrice Bartolomei, J. Emmanuel and Barbeau Rhinal, "Hippocampal Interactions During déjà vu," *Clinical Neurophysiology* 123, no. 3 (2012): 489.

51. Ibid., 492.

52. Harvey Irwin, *An Introduction to Parapsychology* (Jefferson: McFarland and Company, 2003).

53. The Harris Poll, "The Religious and Other Beliefs of Americans," *Gallup News Service*, Feb 26, 2003, www.theharrispoll.com/ (accessed July 12, 2016).

54. E. Cardeña, S. J. Lynn and S. Krippner, eds., *Varieties of Anomalous Experience: Examining the Scientific Evidence* (Washington: American Psychological Association, 2000).

55. Stevenson, *The Explanatory Value*, 308.

56. Stevenson, *Reincarnation*, 27.
57. Ian Stevenson, "American Children Who Claim to Remember Previous Lives," *Journal of Nervous and Mental Disease* 71, no. 6 (1983a): 742.
58. Ibid., 743.
59. Stevenson, "American Children Who Claim to Remember Previous Lives," 745.
60. Jurgen Keil, "New Cases in Burma, Thailand, and Turkey," 29.
61. Irwin, *An Introduction to Parapsychology*, 134.
62. Leonard Zusne and Warren Jones, *Anomalistic Psychology: A Study of Extraordinary Phenomena of Behavior and Experience* (Hillsdale: Lawrence Erlbaum Associates, 1982).
63. Ibid., 143.
64. Carter, *Science and the Afterlife*, 251.
65. Jane Dywan and K. S. Bowers, "The Use of Hypnosis to Enhance Recall," *Science* 222, no. 12 (1983): 184.
66. F. Frankel and H. Zamansky, eds., *Hypnosis at Its Bicentennial* (New York: Plenum, 1978).
67. Stevenson, *Reincarnation: Field Studies*, 23.
68. Brian G. Dias and Kerry Ressler, "Parental Olfactory Experience Influences Behavior and Neural Structure in Subsequent Generations," *Nature Neuroscience* 17, no 3 (2014): 89.
69. Ibid., 92.
70. Dias, "Parental Olfactory Experience Influences Behavior and Neural Structure in Subsequent Generations," 93.
71. Ibid., 95.
72. Irwin, *An Introduction to Parapsychology*, 144.
73. Theophanes, "Cellular Memories in Organ Transplant Recipients," *Theophanes*, January 25, 2013, http://hubpages.com/health/Cellular-Memories-in-Organ-Transplant-Recipients (accessed July 14, 2016).
74. About Paul Pearsall, "Paul Pearsall," 2015, www.paulpearsall.com/info/about.html (accessed August 2, 2016).
75. Lizelte Borreli, "Can An Organ Transplant Change A Recipient's Personality? Cell Memory Theory Affirms 'Yes,'" *Medical Daily*, July 9, 2013, www.medical-daily.com/can-organ-transplant-change-recipients-personality-cell-memory-theory-affirms-yes-247498 (accessed July 30, 2016).
76. Ibid., 3.
77. Stevenson, *Where Reincarnation and Biology Intersect*, 25.
78. Stevenson, *Twenty Cases Suggestive of Reincarnation*, 14.
79. Ibid., 15.
80. K. M. Gow and S. Robertson, "Do Fantasy Proneness and Personality Affect the Vividness and Certainty of Past-life Experience Reports II?" *Austalian Journal of Clinical and Experimental Hypnosis* 27, no. 2 (1999): 149.
81. Irwin, *An Introduction to Parapsychology*, 176.
82. Gauld, Discarnate Survival, 215.

83. Linda Tarazi, "An Unusual Case of Hypnotic Regression with Some Unexplained Contents," *Journal of the American Society for Psychical Research* 84, no. 5 (1990): 309.

84. Ibid., 311.

85. Ibid., 312.

86. Edgar D. Mitchell and Robert Staretz, "The Quantum Hologram and the Nature of Consciousness," *Journal of Cosmology* 14 (2011): 143.

87. Rudy Schild and D. Leiter, "Black Hole or MECO?: Decided by a Thin Luminous Ring Structure Deep within Quasar," *Journal of Cosmology* 6 (2010): 1400.

88. Mitchell, *The Quantum Hologram and the Nature of Consciousness*, 145.

89. Schild, *Black Hole or MECO*, 1403.

90. Mary Rodwell, e-mail message to author, June 12, 2016.

91. Janey Tracey, "Physicists Claim that Consciousness Lives in Quantum State after Death," *Outerplaces*, June 17, 2014, www.outerplaces.com/science/item/4518-physicists-claim-that-consciousness-lives-in-quantum-state-after-death (accessed July 18, 2016).

92. Ibid., 2.

93. David Bohm, *Wholeness and the Implicate Order* (Routledge: London, 1980).

94. American Psychological Association, "Hypnosis," *APA*, June 12, 2015, www.apa.org/topics/hypnosis/ (accessed August 18, 2016).

95. Terrence Hines, *Pseudoscience and the Paranormal* (Amherst: Prometheus Books. 2003).

96. J. Venn, "Hypnosis and the Reincarnation Hypothesis: A Critical Review and Intensive Case Study," *Journal of the American Society for Psychical Research* 80, no. 12 (1986): 409.

97. Hines, *Pseudoscience and the Paranormal*, 218.

98. H. M. Pettina, ed., *Hypnosis and Memory* (New York: Guilford Press, 1988).

99. Jane Dywan and K. S. Bowers, "The Use of Hypnosis to Enhance Recall," *Science* 222, no. 4 (1983): 184.

100. Tarazi, "An Unusual Case of Hypnotic Regression with Some Unexplained Contents," 312.

101. Joe Fisher, *The Case for Reincarnation*. (London: Granada, 1986).

102. Ibid., 24.

103. Fisher, *The Case for Reincarnation*, 27.

104. Brian Weiss, *Many Lives, Many Masters*. (New York: Warner, 1988).

105. Ibid., 163.

106. Stevenson, *Reincarnation: Field Studies*, 45.

107. Jonathan Edelmann and William Bernet, "Setting Criteria for Ideal Reincarnation Research," *Journal of Consciousness Studies* 14, no. 3 (2007): 92.

108. Ibid., 96.

109. Carl Sagan, *The Demon-Haunted World: Science as a Candle in the Dark* (New York: Random House, 1995).

Chapter Six: Mediumship

1. Michael Tymn, "Mediumship: Direct Connection to a level of the Afterlife, Telepathy or Fraud?" *International Survivalist Society*, 2002, www.survivalafterdeath.info/articles/other/tymn.htm (accessed December 8, 2015).
2. Alan Gauld, *Mediumship and Survival: A Century of Investigations* (London: Heinemann, 1982), 176.
3. Alan Gauld, "A Series of "Drop-In" Communicators," *Proceedings of the Society for Psychical Research* 55, no. 4 (1971): 273.
4. David Fontana, *Is There an Afterlife? A Comprehensive Overview of the Evidence* (Oakland: O Books, 2005), 87.
5. Frank Newport and Maura Strausberg, "Americans' Belief in Psychic and Paranormal Phenomena is up Over Last Decade," *Report by The Gallup Organization*, (2001): 4.
6. Chris Roe, "Belief in the Paranormal and Attendance at Psychic Readings," *Journal of the American Society for Psychical Research* 92, no. 5 (1998): 25.
7. Guy Playfair, *This House is Haunted: An Investigation of the Enfield Poltergeist* (London: Souvenir Press, 1980), 74.
8. Andrew Mackenzie, *Apparitions and Ghosts: A Modem Study* (London: Arthur Barker, 1971).
9. The Windbridge Institute, "The Windbridge Institute," 2015, www.windbridge.org/about-us/ (accessed January 3, 2016).
10. Ciaran O'Keeffe and Richard Wiseman, "Testing Alleged Mediumship: Methods and Results," *British Journal of Psychology* 96, no. 5 (2005): 165.
11. Julie Beischel, "Anomalous Information Reception by Research Mediums under Blinded Conditions II: Replication and Extension," *Explore* 2, (2015): 13.
12. Ibid., 25.
13. Julie Beischel and Gary Schwartz, "Anomalous Information Reception by Research Mediums Demonstrated Using a Novel Triple-Blind Protocol," *Explore* 3 (2007): 23.
14. Kim Nash, "Investigating Mediums: Interview with Dr. Julie Beischel," Januuary 19, 2016, www.theresacheung.com/investigating-mediums-interview-with-dr-julie-beische/ (accessed January 14, 2016).
15. Beischel, "Anomalous Information Reception by Research Mediums under Blinded Conditions II: Replication and Extension," 26.
16. Beischel, "Anomalous Information Reception by Research Mediums under Blinded Conditions II: Replication and Extension," 28.
17. Beischel, "Anomalous Information Reception by Research Mediums under Blinded Conditions II: Replication and Extension," 29.
18. Beischel, "Anomalous Information Reception by Research Mediums under Blinded Conditions II: Replication and Extension," 32.
19. Alexandre Rocha, "Investigating the Fit and Accuracy of Alleged Mediumistic Writing: A Case Study of Chico Xavier's Letters," *Explore* 7, (2014): 15.
20. Ibid., 167.

21. Rocha, "Investigating the Fit and Accuracy of Alleged Mediumistic Writing: A Case Study of Chico Xavier's Letters," 169.

22. Emily Kelly, "Some Directions for Mediumship Research," *Journal of Scientific Exploration* 24, no. 4, (2010): 247.

23. Gary Schwartz, L. Russek, L. A. Nelson, and C. Barentsen, "Accuracy and Replicability of Anomalous After-Death Communication across Highly Skilled Mediums," *Journal of the Society for Psychical Research* 65, no. 3 (2001):1.

24. Archie Roy and Ttricia Robertson, "Results of the Application of the Robertson-Roy Protocol to a Series of Experiments with Mediums and Participants," *Journal Society Psychical Research* 68, no 5 (2004): 161.

25. Ibid., 163.

26. David Weatherly, "IONS to Study Channeling," *Two Crow Paranormal*, August 1, 2016, http://twocrowsparanormal.blogspot.com/2016/08/ions-to-study-channeling.html?m=1 (accessed August 8, 2016).

27. Gary Schwartz, *The Afterlife Experiments: Breakthrough Scientific Evidence of Life After Death*. (NY: Atria Books. 2002), 165.

28. Ibid., 162.

29. Richard Wiseman and Ciaran O'Keeffe, "A Critique of Schwartz et al.'s After-Death Communication Studies," *Skeptical Inquirer* 25, no. 6 (2001): 24.

30. Ray Hyman, "How Not to Test Mediums: Critiquing the Afterlife Experiments," *Skeptical Inquirer* 27, no. 1 (2003): 24.

31. Gary Schwartz, "Accuracy and Replicability of Anomalous After-Death Communication across Highly Skilled Mediums," 23.

32. Richard Wiseman and Ciarán O'Keeffe, "Testing Alleged Mediumship: Methods and Results," Paper presented at the annual meeting for the Parapsychological Association, New Orleans, November 3–5, 2004).

33. Ibid., 167.

34. Emily Kelly and D. Arcangel, "An Investigation of Mediums who Claim to Give Information about Deceased Persons," *Journal Nervous Mental Disorders* 199, no. 4 (2011): 11.

35. Michael Sudduth, "Super-Psi and the Survivalist Interpretation of Mediumship," *Journal of Scientific Exploration* 23, no. 4 (2009): 167.

36. Ibid., 169.

37. Sudduth, "Super-Psi and the Survivalist Interpretation of Mediumship," 169.

38. Alson Smith, *The Psychic Source Book* (New York: Creative Age Press, 1951), 27.

39. Gauld, *Mediumship and Survival: A Century of Investigations*, 145–156.

40. Fontana, Is There an Afterlife? 178.

41. Ibid., 179.

42. Ibid., 180.

43. Ibid., 181.

44. M. Keen, "The Scole Investigation: A Study in Critical Analysis of Paranormal Physical Phenomena." Journal of Scientific Exploration 15 (2001): 167.

45. Ibid., 169.

46. Fontana, *Is There an Afterlife? A Comprehensive Overview of the Evidence*, 178.

47. Fontana, *Is There an Afterlife? A Comprehensive Overview of the Evidence*, 179.
48. Fontana, *Is There an Afterlife? A Comprehensive Overview of the Evidence*, 187.
49. Victor J. Zammit, "Victor Zammit," Zammit, April 2001, www.victorzammit.com/articles/scole1.html (accessed August 23, 2016).
50. Ibid., 1.
51. The Scole Experiment, "The Scole Experiment," SCOLE, 2006, www.thescoleexperiment.com/article_05.htm (accessed July 12, 2016).
52. Brian Dunning, "The Scole Experiment," *Skeptoid Media* 10, (2015): 4.
53. Tim Coleman, "The Afterlife Investigations: Has Science Proved the Afterlife?" June 2010, www.spr.ac.uk/publication/afterlife-investigations-has-science-proved-afterlife-dvd (accessed June 18, 2016).
54. David Rousseau, "The Implications of Near-Death Experiences for Research into the Survival of Consciousness," *Journal of Scientific Exploration* 26, no. 4 (2012): 43.
55. Ibid., 46.
56. Eterna, "Mediumship," *Eterna*, July 2, 2015, http://eternea.org/Mediumship.aspx (accessed December 2, 2015).
57. Gauld, *Mediumship and Survival: A Century of Investigations*, 145–156.
58. Samuel Soal, "A Report on Some Communications Received through Mrs. Blanche Cooper," *Proceedings of the Society for Psychical Research* 35, no. 2 (1925): 471.
59. Ibid., 472
60. Joseph B. Rhine, *The Reach of the Mind* (New York: William Sloane, 1947), 275.
61. Carlos Alvarado and Alfonso Martinez-Taboas, "The Super-Psi Hypothesis: A Review," *Theta* 11, no 1 (1983): 57.
62. Stephan Braude, "Survival or Super-Psi?" *Journal of Scientific Exploration* 6 (1992): 127.
63. Gauld, *Mediumship and Survival: A Century of Investigations*, 153.
64. Ibid., 156.
65. Beischel, "Anomalous Information Reception by Research Mediums under Blinded Conditions II: Replication and Extension," 35.
66. Ian Stevenson, *Unlearned Language: New Studies in Xenoglossy* (Charlottesville, VA: University Press of Virginia, 1984), 145.
67. Gauld, *Mediumship and Survival: A Century of Investigations*, 157.
68. Fontana, *Is There an Afterlife? A Comprehensive Overview of the Evidence*, 204.
69. Mediumship: Direct Connection, 3.
70. Gauld, *Mediumship and Survival: A Century of Investigations*, 175.
71. Beischel, "Anomalous Information Reception by Research Mediums under Blinded Conditions II: Replication and Extension," 42.
72. Sudduth, "Super-Psi and the Survivalist Interpretation of Mediumship," 174.
73. Akemi Gaines, "Akashic Records," 2014, www.akashicrecordsofsouls.com/ (accessed March 11, 2016).
74. Ibid., 2.
75. Fontana, *Is There an Afterlife? A Comprehensive Overview of the Evidence*, 217.

76. Daryl J. Bem, "The Afterlife Experiments: Breakthrough Scientific Evidence of Live After Death," *The Journal of Parapsychology* 69, no. 3 (2005): 173.

77. Richard Wiseman, "Belief in the Paranormal and Suggestion in the Seance Room," *British Journal of Psychology* 23 (2003): 37.

78. Ibid., 39.

79. Everton de O Maraldi, "Medium or author?" A Preliminary Model Relating Dissociation, Paranormal Belief Systems and Self-Esteem," *Journal of the Society for Psychical Research* 78, no 5 (2014): 1.

80. Elizabeth Roxburgh and Chris Roe, "A Survey of Dissociation, Boundary-Thinness, and Psychological Well-Being in Spiritualist Mental Mediumship," *Journal of Parapsychology* 75, no. 1 (2011): 279.

81. Ibid., 282.

82. Harvey Irwin, *An Introduction to Parapsychology*. (London: McFarland, 2007).

83. A. Delorme, et al., "Electrocortical Activity Associated with Subjective Communication with the Deceased," *Frontiers of Psychology* 4 (2013): 834.

84. Brainworks, "What are Brainwaves?" *Brainworks Train Your Mind*, March 2013, www.brainworksneurotherapy.com/what-are-brainwaves (accessed May 12, 2016).

85. Arnauld Delorme, "Electrocortical Activity Associated with Subjective Communication with the Deceased," *Front. Psychol*, 20, (2013): 45.

86. Julio Fernando Peres, et al., "Neuroimaging during Trance State: A contribution to the Study of Dissociation," *PLOS ONE* 7, (2012): 14.

87. Ibid., 2.

88. Adam Rock and Julie Beischel, "Quantitative Analysis of Research Mediums' Conscious Experiences during a Discarnate Reading versus a Control Task: A Pilot Study," Australian Journal of *Parapsychology* 8 (2008): 157.

89. Richard Wiseman, "Belief in the Paranormal and Suggestion in the Seance Room," 42.

Chapter Seven: Connecting the Dots

1. Stuart Hameroff, "Quantum Coherence in Microtubules: A Neural Basis for Emergent Consciousness," *Journal of Consciousness Studies* 1, (1994): 98.

2. Henry P. Stapp, "Bell's Theorem and World Process," *Nuovo Cimento* 29, (1975): 270.

3. Robert Lanza, "*Robert Lanza*," March 2015, www.robertlanza.com/ (accessed August 18, 2016).

4. Janey Tracey, "Physicists Claim that Consciousness Lives in Quantum State after Death," *Outerplaces*, June `7, 2014, www.outerplaces.com/science/item/4518-physicists-claim-that-consciousness-lives-in-quantum-state-after-death?qs=2&utm_expid=68243097-1.LutSYZjjRsmSMx2YZefKRA.2&utm_referrer=https%3A%2F%2Fwww.google.com%2F (accessed July 10, 2016).

5. Gary Schwartz, *The Afterlife Experiments: Breakthrough Scientific Evidence of Life after Death* (New York: Atria Books, 2002), 29.

6. Ian Stevenson, C. Tart and M. Grosso, "The Possible Nature of Post Past Life Memory Case Studies: A Discussion," *Journal of the American Society for Psychical Research* 74, no. 5 (1980): 413.

7. Goodreads, "Quotes about Afterlife," *Goodreads*, June 12, 2014, www.goodreads.com/quotes/tag/afterlife (accessed August 3, 2016).

8. Famous Quotes on Reincarnation, "Famous Quotes on Reincarnation," *Reversespins*, April , 2015, www.reversespins.com/famousquotes.html (accessed August 14, 2016).

9. Ibid., 1

10. Famous Quotes on Reincarnation, 2

11. Famous Quotes on Reincarnation, 3

12. Goodreads, "I Cannot Conceive of a God who Rewards and Punishes," *Goodreads*, June 23, 2013, www.goodreads.com/quotes/894329-i-cannot-conceive-of-a-god-who-rewards-and-punishes (accessed August 3, 2016).

13. Ian Sample, "Stephen Hawking: There is No Heaven," May 15, 2011, www.theguardian.com/science/2011/may/15/stephen-hawking-interview-there-is-no-heaven (accessed August 4, 2016).

14. Carl Sagan, *Billions and Billions: Thoughts on Life and Death at the Brink of the Millennium* (New York: Ballantine Books, 1998), 152.

15. Goodreads, "Quotes about Afterlife," 1.

16. Dean Radin, *Entangled Minds* (New York: Paraview, 2006), 148.

17. Ibid., 167.

18. Stephen Braude, *Distant Mental Influence: Its Contributions to Science, Healing, and Human Interactions* (Newburyport: Hampton Roads Publishing, 2003), 87.

19. Stevenson, "The Possible Nature of Post Past Life Memory Case Studies: A Discussion," 417.

20. Michael Sudduth, "Super-Psi and the Survivalist Interpretation of Mediumship," *Journal of Scientific Exploration* 23, no. 7 (2009): 167.

21. David Rousseau, "Near-Death Experiences and the Mind-Body Relationship: A Systems Theoretical Perspective," *Journal of Near-Death Studies* 29, no. 4 (2011): 399.

22. Alan Gauld, "Mediumship and Survival: A Century of Investigations: Alan Gauld," *Esalen*, 1982, www.esalen.org/ctr-archive/mediumship.html (accessed August 12, 2016).

23. Ibid. 2.

24. Frederic W. H. Myers, *Fragments of Inner Life* (London: Society for Psychical Research, 1961), 152.

25. Menas Kafatos, Rudolph E. Tanzi and Deepak Chopra, "How Consciousness Becomes the Physical Universe," *Journal of Cosmology* 14, no. 3 (2011): 23.

26. Fred Alan Wolf, *The Spiritual Universe: One Physicists Vision of Spirit, Soul, Matter, and Self* (Portsmouth: Moment Point Press, 1998), 54.

27. Richard Miller, Burnt Webb and Darden Dickson, "A Holographic Concept of Reality," *Psychoenergetic Systems Journal* 1, (1975): 55.

28. Ken Wilbur, ed., *Quantum Questions: Mystical Writings of the World's Great*

Physicists (Boston, MA: Shambhala, 1984), 164.

29. Quantum Enigma, "Quantum Enigma," June 2014, http://quantum enigma. com/nutshell/notable-quotes-on-quantum physics/? (accessed July 23, 2016).

30. Edgar D. Mitchell and Robert Staretz, "The Quantum Hologram and the Nature of Consciousness," *Journal of Cosmology* 14, no. 3 (2011): 84.

31. Henry Stapp, "*Bell's Theorem and World Process*," 275.

32. Spiritual Cosmos, "Spiritual Cosmos," *Spiritual Cosmos,* February 2014, http:// spiritualcosmos.com/index.php?option=com_content&view=article&id=68:sc ientists-who-support-the-idea-of-a-spiritual-cosmos&catid=25:theories&Item id=53 (accessed August 23, 2016).

33 Goodreads, "Richard Feynman," *Goodreads*, 2015, www.goodreads.com/author/ quotes/1429989.Richard_Feynman (accessed July 12, 2016).

34. Ibid., 2.

35. Mitchell, *The Quantum Hologram*, 87.

36. Janey Tracey, "Physicists Claim that Consciousness Lives in Quantum State after Death," *Outerplaces*, 3.

37. Ibid., 4.

38. Alan Gauld, "Mediumship and Survival: A Century of Investigations: Alan Gauld," 6.

39. Claude Swanson, *The Synchronized Universe: New Science of the Paranormal* (New York: Poseidia Press, 2003).

40. Ibid., 178.

41. Swanson, *The Synchronized Universe: New Science of the Paranormal*, 179.

42. Swanson, *The Synchronized Universe: New Science of the Paranormal*, 180.

43. Rudy Schild and Darryl Leiter, "Black hole or MECO? Decided by a Thin Luminous Ring Structure Deep within Quasar," *Journal of Cosmology* 6 (2010): 1400.

44. Ibid., 1403.

45. Paul Bernstein, Rudolph Schild, Metod Saniga, Petr Pracna, Luboš Neslušan and Kala Perkins, "Non-Locality, Cognition, and Cosmic Structures," *Journal of Cosmology* 14, (2011): 214.

45a. Stephen W. Hawking, Malcolm J. Perry, and Andrew Strominger, "Soft Hair on Black Holes," January 5, 2016, https://arxiv.org/pdf/1601.00921v1.pdf (accessed June 10, 2017).

46. Pim Van Lommel, *Consciousness Beyond Life: The Science of the Near-Death Experience* (New York: HarperOne, 2010), 47.

47. Henry P. Stapp, *The Mindful Universe: Quantum Mechanics and the Participating Observer* (Heidelberg: Springer-Verlag, 2007), 76.

48. Stuart Hameroff, "Quantum Coherence in Microtubules," *Journal of Consciousness Studies* 1, (1994): 98.

49. Ibid., 101.

50. Johnjoe Mcfadden and Jim Al-Khalili, *Life on the Edge: The Coming of Age of Quantum*. (Kindle Edition: Biology Crown Publishing, 2015), 253.

51. Danah Zohar, *The Quantum Self* (New York: William Morrow, 1991), 153.

52. P. Rosch, ed., Bioelectromagnetic Medicine (New York: Dekker, 2004), 165.

53. Swanson, *The Synchronized Universe*, 241.
54. Simon Berkovich, "On the Information Processing Capabilities of the Brain: Shifting the Paradigm," *Nanobiology* 2, no. 3 (1993): 99.
55. Ibid., 103.
56. Hems Romijn, "About the Origin of Consciousness. A new, Multidisciplinary Perspective on the Relationship between Brain and Mind," *Proc Kon Ned Akad v Wetensch* 100, no 8. (1997): 181.
57. Ibid., 203.
58. Janey Tracey, "Consciousness," *Outerplaces,* June 17, 2014, www.outerplaces. com/science/item/4518-physicists-claim-that-consciousness-lives-in-quantum-state-after-death (accessed July 10, 2016).
59. Ibid., 3.
60. Matt Ridlel, Genome. *The Autobiography of a Species in 23 Chapters* (New York: Harper Collins Publishers, 2000), 67.
61. Simon Berkovich, "A Note on Science and NDE," *NDERF,* June 14, 2012, www.nderf.org/NDERF/Research/Berkovich.htm (accessed July 24, 2016).
62. Erwin Schrödinger, *What is Life?* (Cambridge: Cambridge University Press, 1944), 187.
63. Stuart Hameroff, "Quantum computing in DNA," *University of Arizona*, June 2014, www.consciousness.arizona.edu/hameroff/New/ Quantum_computing_in_DNA/index.htm (accessed July 24, 2016).
64. Pim Van Lommel, "About the Continuity of Our Consciousness," *Adv Exp Med Biology* 550, no. 3 (2004): 115.
65. Ibid., 117.
66. Aaron Kase, "Science Is Proving Some Memories Are Passed Down from Our Ancestors," *Reset Me,* February 20, 2015, http://reset.me/story/science-proving-memories-passed-ancestors/ (accessed July 18, 2016).
67. Ibid., 2.
68. Aaron Kase, "Science Is Proving Some Memories Are Passed Down from Our Ancestors," 3.
69. Swanson, *The Synchronized Universe*, 243.
70. Mitchell, *The Quantum Hologram*, 92.
71. The Psychic Children, "Russian DNA Research," *Psychic Children*, May 2014, www.psychicchildren.co.uk/4-3-RussianDNAResearch.html (accessed July 8, 2016).
72. Eric Dubay, "Our Holographic Brains," *The Atlantean Conspiracy*, February 9, 2013, www.atlanteanconspiracy.com/2013/02/our-holographic-brains.html (accessed August 2, 2016).
73. Ibid., 2.
74. Swanson, *The Synchronized Universe*, 256.
75. Michael Nahm and Bruce Greyson, "Terminal Lucidity in Patients with Chronic Schizophrenia and Dementia: A Survey of the Literature," *The Journal of Nervous and Mental Disease* 3, no. 4 (2009): 942.

76. Delphine Baudoin, "Curious Dissociation between Cerebral Imaging and Clinical Findings," *The Lancet* 347, no 5 (2006): 965.

77. Lisa Melton, "How Brainpower Can Help You Cheat Old Age," *New Scientist* 7, (2005): 2530.

78. Hugh Everett, "Relative State Formulation of Quantum Mechanics," *Reviews of Modern Physics* 29, (1957): 454.

79. Ibid., 455.

80. Robert Lanza, "Biocentrism: Robert Lanza's Theory of Everything," 2017, www.robertlanza.com/biocentrism-how-life-and-consciousness-are-the-keys-to-understanding-the-true-nature-of-the-universe/ (accessed July 20, 2016).

81. John Bockris, *The New Paradigm: A Confrontation Between Physics and the Paranormal Phenomena* (New Energy Foundation, 2013), 38.

82. Ibid., 27.

83. Stephan Hawking, *The Grand Design*. (New York: Bantam, 2012), 39.

84. Stephen Hawking, "Space and Time Warps," June 2016, www.hawking.org.uk/space-and-time-warps.html (accessed August 23, 2016).

84a. Goodreads, "Nikola Tesla," Goodreads. April 14, 2015, "www.goodreads.com/quotes/139502-the-day-science-begins-to-study-non-physical-phenomena (accessed June 11, 2017).

Chapter Eight: Conclusion

1. Goodreads, "Carl Sagan Quotes," *Goodreads,* January 2016, www.goodreads.com/author/quotes/10538.Carl_Sagan (accessed August 23, 2016).

Bibliography

Agrillo, C. "Near-Death Experience: Out-of-Body and Out-of-Brain?" *Rev. Gen. Psychol*, 15 (2011): 1–15.

Alan, Fred. *The Spiritual Universe: One Physicists Vision of Spirit, Soul, Matter, and Self*. Portsmouth, NH: Moment Point Press, 1998.

Alcock, James. "Electronic Voice Phenomena: Voices of the Dead?" *Csicop.org* 7, (2004): 23–27.

Alcock, James. *Science and Supernature: A Critical Appraisal of Parapsychology*. Buffalo: Prometheus Books, 1990.

Alexander, Eben. *Proof of Heaven: A Neurosurgeon's Journey into the Afterlife*. New York: Simon and Schuster, 2012.

Alvarado, Carlos. "Out-of-Body Experiences." In *Varieties of Anomalous Experience: Examining the Scientific Evidence*, edited by E. Cardeña, S. J. Lynn, and S. Krippner, 156–162. Washington: Charles C. Thomas, 2000.

Alvarado, Carlos, and A. Martinez-Taboas. "The Super-Psi Hypothesis: A Review." *Theta,* 11 (1983): 57.

Arcangel, D. *Afterlife Encounters: Ordinary People, Extraordinary Experiences*. Charlottesville: Hampton Roads, 2005.

Ariès, Philippe. *The Hour of Our Death*. Melbourne: Penguin, 1983.

Arnette, J. "On the Mind/Body Problem: The Theory of Essence." *Journal of Near-Death Studies* 11, (1992): 5–16.

Assante, Julia. *The Last Frontier*. Novato: New World Library, 2012.

Atwater, P. M. H. *Beyond the Light*. New York: Birch Lane, 1994.

Baars, Bernard. "The Conscious Access Hypothesis: Origins and Recent Evidence." *Trends in Cognitive Sciences*, 12, no. 6 (2002): no. 6: 47-52.

Barbato, M., et al., "Parapsychological Phenomena Near the Time of Death." *Journal of Palliative Care* 15, no. 3 (1999): 30-43.

Barrett, William. *Death Bed Visions*. London: Methuen, 1926.

Bartolomei, Fabrice, J. Emmanuel, and Barbeau Rhinal. "Hippocampal Interactions During déjà vu." *Clinical Neurophysiology* 123, no. 3 (2012): 489–494.

Baruss, Imants. "Failure to Replicate Electronic Voice Phenomenon." *Journal of Scientific Exploration* 15, no. 2 (2001): 355–367.

Batthyany, Alan. "Complex Visual Imagery and Cognition during Near-Death Experiences." *Journal of Near-Death Studies* 34, no. 3 (2015): 232–239.

Baudoin, Delphine. "Curious Dissociation between Cerebral Imaging and Clinical Findings." *The Lancet* 347, no 5 (2006): 965–978.

Beischel, Julie. "Anomalous Information Reception by Research Mediums under Blinded Conditions II: Replication and Extension." *Explore* (2015). 1–15.

Beischel, Julie. "Assisted After-Death Communication: A Self-Prescribed Treatment for Grief." *Journal of Near-Death Studies* 32, no 3 (2014): 161–175.

Beischel, Julie, and Gary Schwartz. "Anomalous Information Reception by Research Mediums Demonstrated Using a Novel Triple-Blind Protocol." *Explore* 3 (2007): 23.

Bem, Daryl. "The Afterlife Experiments: Breakthrough Scientific Evidence of Life After Death." *The Journal of Parapsychology* 69, no. 2 (2005): 173–181.

Bender, Hans. "Mediumistic Psychoses." *Parapsychology* 4, no 3 (1966): 574–582.

Berkovich, Simon. "On the Information Processing Capabilities of the Brain: Shifting the Paradigm." *Nanobiology* 2, no. 6 (1993): 99–113.

Berman, Bob, and Robert Lanza. *Biocentrism: How Life and Consciousness Are the Keys to Understanding the True Nature of the Universe*. New York: BenBella Books, 2010.

Bernard, J. B. "The Conscious Access Hypothesis: Origins and Recent Evidence." *Trends in Cognitive Sciences* 6, no. 5 (2002): 47.

Bernstein, Paul, et al., "Non-Locality, Cognition, and Cosmic Structures." *Journal of Cosmology* 14, no. 7 (2011): 214–220.

Bhattacharya, P. K. "Is There Science Behind the Near-Death Experience: Does Human Consciousness Survive after Death?" *Ann Trop Med Public Health* 2, no. 3 (2013): 151–167.

Bierman, Dick. "Exploring Correlations between Local Emotional and Global Emotional Events and the Behavior of a Random Number Generator." *Journal of Scientific Exploration*, no. 10 (1996): 363.

Blackmore, Susan. *Beyond the Body: An Investigation of the Out-of-Body Experience*. London: Heinemann, 1982.

Blackmore, Susan. *Dying to Live*. Amherst: Prometheus Books, 1993.

Blackmore, Susan. "Near-Death Experiences: In or Out of the Body?" *Skeptical Inquirer* 16, no. 3 (1991): 34–42.

Blanke, O. C. Mohr, and C. Michel. "Linking Out-of-Body Experience and Self Processing to Mental Own-Body Imagery at the Temporoparietal Junction." *Journal of Neuroscience* 25, no. 3 (2005): 550–557.

Blanke, et al., "Stimulating Illusory Own-Body Perceptions." *Nature* 419, no. 4 (2002): 269–278.

Bockris, John. *The New Paradigm: A Confrontation Between Physics and the Paranormal Phenomena*. New Energy Foundation, 2013.

Bohm, David. *Quantum Theory*. Englewood Cliffs: Prentice-Hall, 1951.

Bohm, David. *Wholeness and the Implicate Order*. Routledge: London, 1980.

Bókkon, I. B. Mallick, and J. Tuszynski. "Near Death Experiences: A Multidisciplinary Hypothesis." *Front. Hum. Neuroscience* 4, no. 5 (2013): 235–245.

Bozzano, Ernest. *Phénomenes Psychiques au Moment de la Mort*. Paris, France: JMG, 1998.

Brandon, Carla. *One Last Hug Before I Go: The Mystery and Meaning of Deathbed Visions*. London: HCI, 2010.

Braude, Stephan. *Distant Mental Influence: Its Contributions to Science, Healing, and Human Interactions*. Newburyport: Hampton Roads Publishing, 2003.

Braude, Stephan. "Survival or Super-Psi?" *Journal of Scientific Exploration* 6, no. 4 (1992): 127–136.

Brody, E. "Review of Cases of the Reincarnation Type: Ten Cases in Sri Lanka." *Journal of Nervous and Mental Disease* 12, no. 5 (1979): 769–773.

Byrd, R. "Positive Therapeutic Effect of Intercessory Prayer in a Coronary Care Population." *Southern Medical Journal*, no. 81 (1998): 826–834.

Byrd, R. "Positive Therapeutic Effects of Intercessory Prayer in a Coronary Care Population II." *Southern Medical Journal*, 4, no. 6 (1988): 835–847.

Carr, B. "Worlds Apart?" *Proceedings of the Society for Psychical Research* 59, no. 4 (2008): 1–15.

Carr, D. and S. Sharp. "Do Afterlife Beliefs Affect Psychological Adjustment to Late-Life Spousal Loss?" *Journal of Gerontology Psychol Sci* 69, no. 1 (2014): 103–112

Carter, Chis. *Science and the Afterlife Experience*. Rochester: Inner Traditions, 2012.

Chalmers, David. "The Puzzle of Conscious Experience." *Scientific America*, no. 92 (2002): 21–34.

Chalmers, David. "The Hard Problems of Consciousness," In *Consciousness*, edited by Max Velmans and Susan Schneider, 117–134. London: Blackwell, 2007.

Cheyne, James, S. Rueffer, and I. Newby-Clark. "Hypnagogic and Hypnopompic Hallucinations during Sleep Paralysis: Neurological and Cultural Construction of the Night-Mare." 8, *Conscious Cognition* 8 (1999): 319–328.

Clark, K. "Near Death Experiencers." In *The Near-Death Experience*, edited by Bruce Greyson and C. P. Flynn, 34–54. Springfield: Charles C. Thomas, 1984.

Cook, C., Bruce Greyson, and Ian Stevenson. "Do Any Near-Death Experiences Provide Evidence for the Survival of Human Personality after Death?" *Journal of Scientific Exploration* 12, no. 4 (1998): 377–389.

Crick, Francis. *The Astonishing Hypothesis: The Scientific Search for the Soul*. London: Simon and Schuster, 1994.

Dannenbaum, Stuart, and R. Kinnier. "Imaginal Relationships with the Dead: Applications for Psychotherapy." *Journal of Humanistic Psychology* 49, no. 4 (2009): 100–113.

Darnell, Senesio. *Voces sin Rostro*. Barcelona: Fausi, 1979.

Datson, S., and S. Marwitt. "Personality Constructs and Perceived Presence of Deceased Loved Ones." *Death Studies* 21, no. 1 (1997): 131–145.

Davies, Paul, and John Gribbin. *The Matter Myth: Discoveries That Challenge Our Understanding of Physical Reality*. New York: Simon and Schuster, 2007.

de O Maraldi, E. "Medium or author? A Preliminary Model Relating Dissociation, Paranormal Belief Systems and Self-Esteem." *Journal of the Society for Psychical Research* 78, no. 6 (2014): 1–14.

Dell'Olio, A. J. "Do Near-Death Experiences Provide a Rational Basis for Belief in Life after Death?" *Sophia* 49, no. 6 (2010): 113–123.

Delorme, Arnaud, et al., "Electrocortical Activity Associated with Subjective Communication with the Deceased." *Frontiers of Psychology* 4, no. 4 (2013): 834–845.

Dossey, Larry. *Healing Beyond the Body*. New York: Time Warner, 2002.

Dossey, Larry, et al. "Consciousness—What Is It?" *Journal of Cosmology* 14, no. 4 (2011): 84–97.

Droulez, T. "Conscience, Espace, Réalité. Implications d'une Critique du Réalisme Perceptuel Direct." *Cahiers Philosophiques de Strasbourg* 4, no. 1 (2010): 28–34.

Duncan, L., and W. Roll. *Psychic Connections*. New York: Bantam Doubleday, 1995.

Dunne, Brenda. "Gender Differences in Human/Machine Anomalies." *Journal of Scientific Exploration* 12, no. 5 (1998): 3–14.

Dunning, Brian. "The Scole Experiment." *Skeptoid Media* 10, no. 4 (2015): 23–34.

Dywan, J., and K. Bowers. "The Use of Hypnosis to Enhance Recall." *Science* 222, no 2 (1983): 184–198.

Edelmann, J., and W. Bernet. "Setting Criteria for Ideal Reincarnation Research." *Journal of Consciousness Studies* 14, no. 2 (2007): 92–102.

Facco, E., and C. Agrillo. "Near-Death-Like Experiences Without Life-Threatening Conditions or Brain Disorders: A Hypothesis From a Case Report." *Front. Psychol* 2, no. 3 (2012):490–503.

Fenwick, Peter, and E. Fenwick. *The Art of Dying: A Journey to Elsewhere*. London: Continuum, 2008.

Fisher, Joe. *The Case for Reincarnation*. London: Granada, 1986.

Fontanna, David. *Is There an Afterlife*. Park Lane: O Books, 2005.

Gabbard, Glen, and S. Tremlow. *With the Eye of the Mind*. New York: Prager, 1984.

Gauld, Alan. "A Series of 'Drop-In' Communicators." *Proceedings of the Society for Psychical Research* 55, no. 5 (1971): 273–288.

Gauld, Alan. "Discarnate Survival." In *Handbook of Parapsychology*, edited by B. B. Wolman, 134–167. New York: Van Nostrand Reinhold, 1977.

Gauld, Alan. *Mediumship and Survival: A Century of Investigations*. London: Heinemann, 1982.

Gearhart, Larry, and Michael A. Persinger. "Geophysical Variables and Behavior: Onsets of Historical and Contemporary Poltergeist Episodes Occurred with Sudden Increases in Geomagnetic Activity." *Perceptual and Motor Skills* 62, no. 4 (1986): 440–453.

Goswami, Amit. *Physics of the Soul: The Quantum Book of Living, Dying, Reincarnation, and Immortality*. New York: Hampton Roads Publishing, 2001.

Goswami, Amit. *The Paranormal Perception of Color*. New York: Parapsychological Monographs, 16, 1993.

Goswami, Amit. *The Self-Aware Universe*. Los Angeles: Tarcher/Putnam, 1994.

Gow, K. M., and S. Robertson. "Do Fantasy Proneness and Personality Affect the Vividness and Certainty of Past-life Experience Reports II?" *Australian Journal of Clinical and Experimental Hypnosis,* 27, no. 6 (1999): 149–162.

Grad, B. "Some Biological Effects of the Laying-On of Hands: A Review of Experiments with Animals and Plants." *Journal of the American Society for Psychical Research*, no. 59 (1965): 95–102.

Granqvist, P., et al. "Sensed Presence and Mystical Experiences are Predicted by Suggestibility, Not by the Application of Transcranial Weak Complex Magnetic Fields. Randomized Controlled Trial." *Neuroscience Letters*, no. 29 (2005): 1–6.

Green, Celia, and Charles McCreery. *Apparition*s. London: Hamish Hamilton, 1975.

Grey, Margot. *Return from Death: An Exploration of the Near-Death Experience*. London: Arkana, 1985.

Greyson, Bruce. "A Typology of Near-Death Experiences." *Am J Psychiatry,* no. 142 (1985): 967–976.

Greyson, Bruce. "Biological Aspects of Near-Death Experiences." *Perspective in Biology and Medicine* 42, no. 3 (1998): 14–25.

Greyson, Bruce. "Dissociation in People Who have Near-Death Experiences: Out of their Bodies or Out of Their Minds?" *Lancet* 355, no. 3 (2000): 460–476.

Greyson, Bruce. "Incidence and Correlates of Near-Death Experiences in a Cardiac Care Unit." *Gen Hosp Psychiatry,* no. 25 (2003): 269–284.

Greyson, Bruce. "Near-Death Experiences, in Varieties of Anomalous Experiences: Examining the Scientific Evidence." In *American Psychological Association*, edited by Cardena, E. S. Lynn, and S. Krippner, 124–143. New York: Harper Collins, 2000.

Greyson, Bruce. "Near-Death Experiences and Personal Values." *American Journal of Psychiatry*, no. 140 (1983): 618–632.

Greyson, Bruce. "Near-Death Experiences: Clinical Implications." *Archives of Clinical Psychiatry*, no. 34 (2007): 145–156.

Greyson, Bruce. "Seeing Dead People Not Known to Have Died: Peak in Darien Experiences." *Anthropology and Humanism*, no. 35 (2010): 159–172.

Greyson, Bruce. "Telepathy in Mental Illness." *Journal of Nervous and Mental Disease*, no. 165 (1977): 184–198.

Greyson, Bruce. "The Incidence of Near-Death Experiences." *Med Psychiatry*, no. 23 (1998): 92–103.

Greyson, Bruce. "The Near-Death Experience as a Focus of Clinical Attention." *Journal of Nervous and Mental Disease*, no. 185 (1997): 327–339.

Greyson, Bruce, and Ian Stevenson. "The Phenomenology of Near-Death Experiences." *Am J Psychiatry* 137, no 4 (1980): 1193–1204.

Guggenheim, Bill, and Judy Guggenheim. *Hello from Heaven! A New Field of Research ~ After-Death Communication*. New York: Bantam Books, 1996.

Gurney, E., F. W. Myers, and F. Podmore. *Phantoms of the Living*. London: Trubner, 1886.

Hameroff, Stuart. "Quantum Coherence in Microtubules: A Neural Basis for Emergent Consciousness?" *Journal of Consciousness Studies*, no. 1 (1994): 98–112.

Haraldsson, Erlendur. "Birthmarks and Claims of Previous Life Memories I. The Case of Purnima Ekanayake." *Journal of the Society for Psychical Research* 64, no. 1 (2000): 16–24.

Haraldsson, Erlendur. "Children who Speak of Past-Life Experiences: Is There a Psychological Explanation?" *Psychological Psychotherapy*, no. 3 (2003): 55–68.

Haraldsson, Erlendur, et al., "National Survey of Psychical Experiences and Attitudes Towards the Paranormal in Iceland." In *Research in Parapsychology*, edited by J. D. Morris, W. G. Roll, and R. L. Morris. 90–124. Metuchen, New Jersey, Scarecrow Press, 1976.

Hart, Henry. "ESP Projection: Spontaneous Cases and the Experimental Method." *Journal of the American Society for Psychical Research*, 48, no. 3 (1954): 121–135.

Hart, Henry. "Six Theories about Apparitions." *Proceedings of the Society for Psychical Research*, 50, no. 5 (1956): 153–167.

Hawking, Stephen. *The Grand Design*. New York: Bantam, 2012.

Hendricks, Luke, William Bengston, and Jay Gunkelman. "The Healing Connection: EEG Harmonics, Entrainment, and Schumann's Resonances." *Journal of Scientific Exploration*, no. 24 (2010): 655–662.

Hernandez, Reinerio, Robert Davis, Rudolph Schild, Claude Swanson, Jon Klimo, and Giorgio Piacenza. "The Quantum Hologram Theory of Consciousness and the Multi-Dimensional Nature of Contact with Non-Human Intelligence," *Proceedings of the 2nd International Congress on Consciousness, Journal of Consciousness*, 19, no. 62 (2017).

Holden, Janice. "Response to 'Is it Rational to Extrapolate from the Presence of Consciousness During a Flat EEG to Survival of Consciousness After Death?'" *Journal of Near-Death Studies* 29, no 1. (2010): 362–378.

Holden, Janice. "Veridical Perception in Near-Death Experiences." In *The Handbook of Near-Death Experiences: Thirty Years of Investigation*, edited by Janice Holden, Bruce Greyson, and D. James, 23–78. Santa Barbara: Praeger/ABC-CLIO, 2009.

Holden, Janice, Bruce Greyson, and D. James. *The Handbook of Near-Death Experiences*. Santa Barbara: Praeger/ABC-CLIO, 2009.

Houran, J. "Toward a Psychology of Entity Encounter Experiences." *Journal of the American Society for Psychical Research* 64, no. 2 (2000): 141–158.

Hugh, Everett. "Relative State Formulation of Quantum Mechanics." *Reviews of Modern Physics* 29, no. 4 (1957): 454–463.

Hyman, Ray. "How Not to Test Mediums: Critiquing the Afterlife Experiments." *Skeptical Inquirer* 27, no. 1 (2003): 23–45.

Irwin, Harvey. *An Introduction to Parapsychology*. Jefferson: McFarlend and Company, 2003.

Irwin, Harvey. "Parapsychological Phenomena and the Absorption Domain." *Journal of the American Society for Psychical Research,* 79, no. 1 (1985): 1–14.

Jahn, Robert, et al., "Mind/Machine Interaction Consortium: PortREG Replication Experiments." *Journal of Scientific Exploration* 14, no. 4 (2000): 499–555.

Jahn, Robert, and Brian Dunne. "On the Quantum Mechanics of Consciousness, with Application to Anomalous Phenomena." *Foundations of Physics*, no. 16 (1986): 721–733.

Jourdan, Jean-Pierre. "Near Death Experiences and the 5th Dimensional Spatio-Temporal Perspective." *Journal of Cosmology* 14, no. 1 (2011): 23–33.

Jourdan, Jean-Pierre. "Near Death Experiences and Temporal Perspectives." *Journal of Cosmology* 14, no 3 (2011): 27–38.

Kafatos, Menas, and Robert Nadeau. *Over a Distance and In "No Time": Bell's Theorem*. New York: Oxford University Press, 1999.

Kafatos, Menas, Rudolph E. Tanzi, and Deepak Chopra. "How Consciousness Becomes the Physical Universe." *Journal of Cosmology* 14, no 2 (2011): 2–8.

Kampman, R. and R. Hirvenoja. "Dynamic Relation of the Secondary Personality Induced by Hypnosis to the Present Personality." In *Hypnosis at Its Bicentennial* edited by F. Frankel, and H. Zamansky, 143–167. New York: Plenum, 1978.

Keen, Montague. "The Scole Investigation: A Study in Critical Analysis of Paranormal Physical Phenomena." *Journal of Scientific Exploration,* 15, no. 2 (2001): 167–182.

Keil, Jurgen. "New Cases in Burma, Thailand, and Turkey: A Limited Field Study Replication of Some Aspects of Ian Stevenson's Research." *Journal of Scientific Explanation* 5, no. 1 (1991): 27–59.

Kellehear, Allan. *Experiences Near Death: Beyond Medicine and Religion*. New York: Oxford University Press, 1996.

Kelly, Edward, Emily W. Kelly, Adam Crabtree, Alan Gauld, M. Grasso, and Bruce Greyson. *Irreducible Mind: Toward a Psychology for the 21st Century*. Lanham: Rowman & Littlefield, 2007.

Kelly, Emily. "Near-Death Experiences with Reports of Meeting Deceased People." *Death Studies,* 25, no. 2 (2001): 229–239.

Kelly, Emily. "Some Directions for Mediumship Research." *Journal of Scientific Exploration* 24, no 1 (2010): 247–260.

Kelly, Emily, and Dianne Arcangel. "An Investigation of Mediums Who Claim to Give Information about Deceased Persons." *Journal Nervous Mental Disorders,* 199, no. 1 (2011): 11–17.

Kelly, Emily, Bruce Greyson, and Edward F. Kelly. "Unusual Experiences Near Death and Related Phenomena." In *Irreducible Mind: Toward a Psychology for the 21st Century*, edited by E. F. Kelly, E. W. Kelly, A. Crabtree, A. Gauld, M. Grosso, and B. Greyson, 167–189. Lanham: Rowman and Littlefield, 2007.

Kelly, Emily, Bruce Greyson, and Ian Stevenson. "Near Death Furnish Evidence of Life after Death?" *Omega* 50, no. 1 (2000): 523–537.

Kerr, Christopher. "End-of-Life Dreams and Visions: A Longitudinal Study of Hospice Patients' Experiences." *Journal of Palliative Medicine,* 17, no. 3 (2014): 43–52.

Kirsten, B. and G. Nicholas. "Supernatural Agency: Individual Difference Predictors and Situational Correlates." *The International Journal for the Psychology of Religion*, 23, no. 1 (2013): 1–16.

Klimo, Jon. *Channeling: Investigations on Receiving Information from Paranormal Sources.* Los Angeles: St. Martin's Press, 1987.

Klugman, Craig. "Dead Men Talking: Evidence of Post Death Contact and Continuing Bonds." *Journal of Death and Dying,* 53, no. 3 (2006) 249–262.

Knoblauch, Hubert, Ina Schmied, and Bernt Schnettler. "Different Kinds of Near-Death Experience: A Report on a Survey of NDEs in Germany." *Journal of Near-Death Studies*, no. 20 (2001): 15–30.

LaGrand, L. "The Nature and Therapeutic Implications of the Extraordinary Experiences of the Bereaved." *Journal of Near-Death Studies,* 24, no. 1 (2005): 3–20.

Lerma, John. *Into the Light: Real Life Stories about Angelic Visits, Visions of the Afterlife, and other Pre-Death Experiences.* Franklin Lakes: Career Press, 2007.

Libert, Benjamin. "Unconscious Cerebral Initiative and the Role of Conscious Will in Voluntary Action." *Behavioral and Brain Sciences*, no. 8 (1985): 529–534.

Long, Jeffrey. *Evidence of the Afterlife.* New York: HarperCollins, 2011.

Luczkiewicz, Debra., et al., "End-of-Life Dreams and Visions: A Qualitative Perspective From Hospice Patients." *American Journal of Hospice and Palliative Care*, 1, (2014): 1–12.

Maquet, P., et al., "Functional Neuroanatomy of Human Rapid Eye Movement Sleep and Dreaming." *Nature* 383, 2 (1996): 163–176.

Matlock, James. "Past Life Memory Case Studies." In *Advances in Parapsychological Research*, edited by S. Krippner, 32–56. Jefferson: McFarland, 1990.

McCready, W. C., and A. M. Greeley. *The Ultimate Values of the American Population.* Beverly Hills: Sage Publications, 1976.

McCreery, C., and C. Green. "A Follow-Up Study of People Reporting Apparitional Experiences." *Tenth International Conference, Society for Psychical Research*, Cambridge, UK, 1986.

McFadden, John, and Jim Al-Khalili. *Life on the Edge: The Coming of Age of Quantum.* Danver: Crown Publishing, 2015.

McGrath, John, Sukanta Saha, and Ali Al-Hamzawi. "Psychotic Experiences in the General Population: A Cross-National Analysis Based on 31,261 Respondents From 18 Countries." *JAMA Psychiatry* 72, no 2 (2015): 697–712.

Melton, Lisa. "How Brainpower Can Help You Cheat Old Age," *New Scientist*, 7, no. 1 (2005): 2530–2548.

Miller, Richard, B. Webb and D. Dickson. "A Holographic Concept of Reality." *Psychoenergetic Systems Journal,* 1, no. 1 (1975): 55–62.

Mills, Antonia. "Inferences from the Case of Ajendra Singh Chauhan: The Effect of Parental Questioning, of Meeting the 'Previous Life' Family, an Aborted Attempt to Quantify Probabilities, and the Impact on His Life as a Young Adult." *Journal of Scientific Exploration,* 18, no. 1 (2004): 609–620.

Mills, Antonia, and S. Lynn. "Past Life Experiences." In *Varieties of Anomalous Experience: Examining the Scientific Evidence*, edited by Etzel Cardeña, S. J. Lynn and S. Krippner, 189–207. Washington: American Psychological Association, 2000.

Mitchell, Edgar. "Nature's Mind: The Quantum Hologram." *International Journal of Computing Anticipatory Systems* 7, no 2 (2000): 295–305.

Mitchell, Edgar, and Robert Staretz. "The Quantum Hologram and the Nature of Consciousness." *Journal of Cosmology* 14, no 1 (2011): 143–157.

Moody, Raymond. *Life After Life: The Investigation of a Phenomenon-Survival of Bodily Death*. Covington: Mockingbird Books, 1975.

Moody, Raymond. *Reflections on Life after Life*. Covington Mockingbird Books, 1977.

Moody, Raymond, and Paul Perry. *Coming Back: A Psychiatrist Explores Past Life Journeys*. New York: Bantam Books, 1991.

Moody, Raymond, and P. Perry. *Glimpses of Eternity*. New York: Guideposts, 2010.

Morse, Melvin, and Paul Perry. *Parting Visions*. London: Piatkus Books, 1994.

Morse, Melvin, and Paul Perry. *Transformed by the Light: The Powerful Effect of Near-Death Experiences on People's Lives*. New York: Villard Books, 1992.

Morse, Melvin, D. Venecia, and J. Milstein. "Near-Death Experiences: A Neurophysiologic Explanatory Model." *Journal of Near-Death Studies,* 8, no. 3 (1989): 45–56.

Musgrave, Cassandra. "The Near-Death Experience: A Study of Spiritual Transformation." *Journal of Near-Death Studies*, 15, no. 3 (1997): 187–201.

Myers, F. W. "Case of the Will of James L. Chaffin." *Proceedings of the Society for Psychical Research,* 36, no. 1 (1927): 517–529.

Myers, F. W. *Fragments of Inner Life*. London: Society for Psychical Research, 1961.

Myers, F. W. *Human Personality and Its Survival of Bodily Death*. London: Longmans, 1903.

Myers, F. W. "On Recognized Apparitions Occurring More than a Year after Death." *Proceedings for the Society for Psychical Research* 6, no 1 (1889): 13.

Nadeau, Robert, and Menus, Kafatos. *Over a Distance and in "No Time": Bell's Theorem and the Aspect and Gisin Experiments*. New York: Oxford University Press, 1999.

Nahm, Michael, and Bruce Greyson. "Terminal Lucidity in Patients with Chronic Schizophrenia and Dementia: A Survey of the Literature." *The Journal of Nervous and Mental Disease,* 3, no. 4 (2009): 942–965.

Nees, Michael, and C. Phillips. "Auditory Pareidolia: Effects of Contextual Priming on Perceptions of Purportedly Paranormal and Ambiguous Auditory Stimuli." *Applied Cognitive Psychology*, 29, no. 1 (2014): 129–134.

Nelson, Roger, Robert Jahn, Brian Dunne, and Y. H. Dobynes. "Field REG: Consciousness Field Effects: Replication and Explorations." *Journal of Scientific Exploration*, no. 12 (1998): 425–430.

Nelson, Steven, et al. "Evidence Accumulation and Moment of Recognition: Dissociating Perceptual Recognition Processes Using fMRI." *Journal of Neuroscience,* 27, no 4 (2007): 44–57.

Newport, F., and M. Strausberg. "Americans' Belief in Psychic and Paranormal Phenomena is up Over Last Decade." *The Gallup Organization*, no. 1 (2001): 1–3.

Nickell, Joe. "Haunted Inns Tales of Spectral Guests." *Committee for Skeptical Inquiry*, no. 12 (2009): 1–5.

Nosek, C. "End-of-Life Dreams and Visions: A Qualitative Perspective from Hospice Patients." *Am Journal Hospital Palliative Care*, 2015, no 1: 235–243.

O'Keeffe, Ciaran, and Richard Wiseman. "Testing Alleged Mediumship: Methods and Results." *British Journal of Psychology*, 96, no. 1 (2005): 165–179.

Osis, K., and E. Haraldsson. *At the Hour of Death*. New York: Hastings House, 1986.

Parnia, Sam, et al., "AWARE—AWAreness during REsuscitation—A Prospective Study." *Resuscitation,* 85, no. 1 (2014): 1799–1811.

Parnia, S., et al., "A Qualitative and Quantitative Study of the Incidence, Features and Aetiology of Near Death Experiences in Cardiac Arrest Survivors." *Resuscitation* 48, no. 1 (2001): 149–158.

Parnia, Sam, and Peter Fenwick. "Near Death Experiences in Cardiac Arrest." *Resuscitation* 52, no. 2 (2002): 5–16.

Parnia, Sam, K. Spearpoint, and Peter Fenwick. "Near Death Experiences, Cognitive Function and Psychological Outcomes of Surviving Cardiac Arrest." *Resuscitation*, 74, no. 1 (2007): 215–226.

Penrose, Roger, and Karl Giberson. "The Man Who Fell to Earth." *Science and Spirit*, 23, no. 1 (2003): 189–192.

Peres, J., et al., "Neuroimaging during Trance State: A Contribution to the Study of Dissociation." *PLOS ONE* 7, no. 11 (2012).

Perry, C., et al., "Hypnotic Age Regression Techniques in the Elicitation of Memories: Applied Uses and Abuses." In *Hypnosis and Memory*, edited by H. M. Pettina, 178–190. New York: Guilford Press, 1988.

Persinger, Michael. "The Neuropsychiatry of Paranormal Experiences." *Journal of Neuropsychiatry and Clinical Neuroscience,* 13, no. 4 (2001): 515–524.

Persinger, Michael. "Vectorial Cerebral Hemisphericity as Differential Sources for the Sensed Presence, Mystical Experiences and Religious Conversations." *Perceptual and Motor Skills* 76, no. 2 (1993): 915–923.

Persinger, Michael, and K. Makarec. "The Feeling of a Presence and Verbal Meaningfulness in Context of Temporal Lobe Function: Factor Analysis Verification of the Muses?" *Brain and Cognition* 20, no 2 (1992): 217–231.

Playfair, Guy. *This House Is Haunted: An Investigation of the Enfield Poltergeist.* London: Souvenir Press, 1980.

Pope, J. "Near Death Experiences and Attitudes towards Life, Death, and Suicide." *Australian Parapsychological Review,* 19, no. 2 (1994): 23–26.

Potts, Michael. "The Evidential Value of Near-Death Experiences for Belief in Life after Death." *Journal of Near-Death Studies,* 20, no. 4 (2002): 233–258.

Pribram, Karl. *Brain and Perception: Holonomy and Structure in Figural Processing.* Hilldale: Lawrence Erlbaum Associates Publishers, 1991.

Radin, Dean. *Entangled Minds: Extrasensory Experiences in a Quantum Reality.* New York: Paraview Pocket Books, 2006.

Radin, Dean. "Event-Related EEG Correlations between Isolated Human Subjects." *Journal of Alternative and Complementary Medicine,* 10, no 2. (2004): 315–324.

Radin, Dean. "Testing Nonlocal Observation as a Source of Intuitive Knowledge." *Explore* 4, no. 1 (2007): 25–35.

Radin, Dean. *The Conscious Universe.* San Francisco: HarperCollins, 1997.

Radin, Dean. "Unconscious Perception of Future Emotions: An Experiment in Presentiment." *Journal Scientific Exploration,* 11, no. 1 (1997): 163–169.

Regal, Brian. *Pseudoscience: A Critical Encyclopedia.* New York: Greenwood 2009.

Rezaei, Saeed. "Nonlocal Intuition: Replication and Paired-Subjects Enhancement Effects." *Global Adv Health Med*, 4, no. 1 (2014): 23–34.

Rhine, Joseph. *The Reach of the Mind.* New York: William Sloane, 1947.

Rhine, L. E. "The Relationship of Agent and Percipient in Spontaneous Telepathy." *Journal of Parapsychology* 20, no 1. (1956): 1–32.

Ridley, Matt. *Genome. The Autobiography of a Species in 23 Chapters.* New York: Harper Collins Publishers, 2000.

Ring, Kenneth. *Heading toward Omega: In Search of Near-Death Experience.* New York: William Morrow, 1984.

Ring, Kenneth. *Lessons from the Light: What We Can Learn from the Near-Death Experience.* Reading: Perseus Books, 1998.

Ring, Kenneth. "Precognitive and Prophetic Visions in Near-Death Experiences." *Journal of Near-Death Studies* 2 (1984): 47–74.

Ring, Kenneth. "Solving the Riddle of Frightening Near-Death Experiences." *Journal of Near-Death Studies* 13, no. 1 (1994): 5–23.

Ring, Kenneth. *The Omega Project: Near Death Experiences, UFO Encounters and Mind at Large*. New York: William Morrow, 1992.

Ring, Kenneth, and S. Cooper. Mindsight: Near-Death and Out-of-Body Experiences in the Blind. *William James Center for Consciousness Studies*, 1999, 1: 1–5.

Ring, Kenneth, and Christopher J. Rosing. "The Omega Project: An Empirical Study of the NDE-Prone Personality." *Journal of Near-Death Studies* 8, no. 4 (1990): 211–239.

Ring, Kenneth, and E. Valarino. *Lessons from the Light*. Needham: Moment Point Press, 2000.

Roberts, Glen, and John Owen. "The Near-Death Experience." *British Journal of Psychiatry* 153, no. 1 (1988): 607–617.

Rocha, A., et al., "Investigating the Fit and Accuracy of Alleged Mediumistic Writing: A Case Study of Chico Xavier's Letters." Explore 10, no 5, (2014): 300–308.

Rock, Adam, and Julie Beischel. "Quantitative Analysis of Research Mediums' Conscious Experiences during a Discarnate Reading versus a Control Task: A Pilot Study." *Australian Journal of Parapsychology,* 8, no. 2 (2008): 157–179.

Roe, Chris. "Belief in the Paranormal and Attendance at Psychic Readings." *Journal of the American Society for Psychical Research,* 92, no. 1 (1998): 25–51.

Romijn, Hems. "About the Origin of Consciousness. A New Multidisciplinary Perspective on the Relationship between Brain and Mind." *Proc Kon Ned Akad v Wetensch* 100, no. 2 (1997): 181–193.

Rousseau, David. "Near-Death Experiences and the Mind-Body Relationship: A Systems-Theoretical Perspective." *Journal of Near-Death Studies,* 29, no. 3 (2011): 399–435.

Rousseau, David. "The Implications of Near-Death Experiences for Research into the Survival of Consciousness." *Journal of Scientific Exploration,* 26, no. 1 (2012): 43–80.

Roxburgh, E., and Chris Roe. "A Survey of Dissociation, Boundary-Thinness, and Psychological Well-Being in Spiritualist Mental Mediumship." *Journal of Parapsychology* 75 (2011): 279–299.

Roy, A., and T. Robertson. "Results of the Application of the Robertson-Roy Protocol to a Series of Experiments with Mediums and Participants." *Journal Society Psychical Research*, 68, no 2. (2004): 161–174.

Ruthsatz, Joanne, Kimberly Ruthsatz. "The Cognitive Bases of Exceptional Abilities in Child Prodigies by Domain: Similarities and Differences." *Intelligence* 44, no 1. (2014): 11–23.

Saavedra-Aguilar, J., and J. Gomez-Jeria. "A Neurobiological Model for Near-Death Experiences." *Journal of Near-Death Studies,* 7, no. 4 (1989): 205–222.

Sabom, Michael. *Light and Death: One Doctor's Fascinating Account of Near-Death Experiences*. Grand Rapids: Zondervan, 1998.

Sabom, Michael. *"The Near Death Experience." Journal of the American Medical Association.* 244, no. 1 (1980): 29–30.

Sagan, Carl. *Billions and Billions: Thoughts on Life and Death at the Brink of the Millennium.* New York: Ballantine Books, 1998.

Sagan, Carl. *The Demon-Haunted World: Science as a Candle in the Dark.* New York: Random House, 1995.

Sang, F., et al. "Depersonalisation/Derealisation Symptoms in Vestibular Disease." *Journal of Neurology and Neurosurgical Psychiatry* 77 (2006): 760–772.

Sartori, Penny. "A Prospective Study to Investigate the Incidence and Phenomenology of Near-Death Experiences in a Welsh Intensive Therapy Unit." *Unpublished doctoral dissertation.* University of Wales. 2005.

Sartori, Penny. *The Near-Death Experiences of Hospitalized Intensive Care Patients: A Five Year Clinical Study.* Lewiston: Edward Mellen Press, 2008.

Schild, Rudy, D. Leiter. "Black Hole or MECO?: Decided by a Thin Luminous Ring Structure Deep within Quasar." *Journal of Cosmology* 6, no 1. (2010): 1400–1415.

Schrödinger, Erwin. "Discussion of Probability Relations between Separated Systems." *Mathematical Proceedings of the Cambridge Philosophical Society,* no. 31 (1935): 555–569.

Schrödinger, Erwin. *What Is Life?* Cambridge: Cambridge University Press, 1944.

Schwartz, Gary. *The Afterlife Experiments: Breakthrough Scientific Evidence of Life After Death.* New York: Atria Books. 2002.

Schwartz, Gary, L. G. S. Russek, L. A. Nelson, and C. Barentsen. "Accuracy and Replicability of Anomalous After-Death Communication across Highly Skilled Mediums." *Journal of the Society for Psychical Research,* 65, no. 1 (2001):1–25.

Schwartz, Gary, et al., "Evidence of Anomalous Information Retrieval between Two Mediums: Replication in a Double Blind Design." *Journal Society Psychical Research* 67, no 1. (2003): 115–125.

Senkowski, E. *Instrumentelle Transkommunikation.* Frankfurt: F. G. Fischer, 1989.

Sheldrake, Roger. *Seven Experiments That Could Change the World.* New York: Riverhead Books, 1995.

Sidgwick, H. "Report on the Census of Hallucinations." *Proceedings of the Society for Psychical Research* 10, no 1 (1894): 25–36.

Smith, Alson. *The Psychic Source Book.* New York: Creative Age Press, 1951.

Smythies, John. "Space, Time and Consciousness." *Journal of Consciousness Studies,* 10, no. 1 (2003): 47–56.

Soal, S. "A Report on Some Communications Received through Mrs. Blanche Cooper." *Proceedings of the Society for Psychical Research,* 35, no. 1 (1925): 471–485.

Standish, Leanna, Clark Johnson, Todd Richards, and Lelia Kozak. "Evidence of Correlated Functional MRI Signals between Distant Human Brains." *Alternative Therapies. Health and Medicine,* 9, no. 2 (2003): 122–136.

Standish, L., et al. "Electroencephalographic Evidence of Correlated Event-Related Signals between the Brains of Spatially and Sensory Isolated Human Subjects." *Journal Alternative and Complementary Medicine,* 10, no. 2 (2004): 307–314.

Stapp, Henry. "Bell's Theorem and World Process." *Nuovo Cimento,* 29, no. 1 (1975): 270–286.

Stapp, Henry. *The Mindful Universe: Quantum Mechanics and the Participating Observer.* Heidelberg: Springer-Verlag, 2007.

Stephan, T., A. Deutschlander, and A. Nolte. "Functional MRI of Galvanic Vestibular Stimulation with Alternating Currents at Different Frequencies." *Neuroimage,* 26, no. 3 (2005): 721–732.

Stevenson, Ian. "American Children Who Claim to Remember Previous Lives." *Journal of Nervous and Mental Disease,* 71, no. 1 (1983a): 742–748.

Stevenson, Ian. "Are Poltergeists Living or Are They Dead?" *Journal of the American Society for Psychical Research,* 66, no. 1 (1972): 233–245.

Stevenson, Ian. "Birthmarks and Birth Defects Corresponding to Wounds on Deceased Persons." *Journal of Scientific Exploration,* 7, no. 4 (1993): 403–410.

Stevenson, Ian. *Cases of the Reincarnation Type. I: Ten Cases in India.* Charlottesville: University Press of Virginia, 1975b.

Stevenson, Ian. *Cases of the Reincarnation Type. II: Ten Cases in Sri Lanka.* Charlottesville: University Press of Virginia, 1977a.

Stevenson, Ian. *Cases of the Reincarnation Type. III: Twelve Cases in Lebanon and Turkey.* Charlottesville: University Press of Virginia, 1980.

Stevenson, Ian. *Cases of the Reincarnation Type. IV: Twelve Cases in Thailand and Burma.* Charlottesville: University Press of Virginia, 1983b.

Stevenson, Ian. *Reincarnation and Biology: A Contribution to the Etiology of Birthmarks and Birth Defects.* Westport: Praeger, 1997a.

Stevenson, Ian. "Reincarnation: Field Studies and Theoretical Issues." In *Handbook of Parapsychology:* edited by B. B. Wolman, 87–110. New York: Van Nostrand Rheinhold, 1977.

Stevenson, Ian. "The Contribution of Apparitions to the Evidence of Survival." *Journal of the American Society for Psychical Research*, no. 1 (1982): 341–352.

Stevenson, Ian. *Twenty Cases Suggestive of Reincarnation.* Charlottesville: University Press of Virginia, 1974.

Stevenson, Ian. "Twenty Cases Suggestive of Reincarnation." *Proceedings of the American Society for Psychical Research*, no. 26 (1966): 1–362.

Stevenson, Ian. *Unlearned Language: New Studies in Xenoglossy.* Charlottesville: University Press of Virginia, 1984.

Stevenson, Ian. *Where Reincarnation and Biology Intersect.* Westport, CT: Praeger, 1997.

Stevenson, Ian, and S. Pasricha. "A Preliminary Report on an Unusual Case of the Reincarnation Type with Xenoglossy." *Journal of the American Society for Psychical Research,* 74, no. 1 (1980): 331–342.

Stevenson, Ian, C. Tart, and M. Grosso. "The Possible Nature of Post Past Life Memory Case Studies: A Discussion." *Journal of the American Society for Psychical Research*, 74, no. 1 (1980): 413–432.

Stollznow, Karen. "Skepticism and Blogging." *Skeptical Inquirer* 33, no 1. (2009): 41–54.

Sudduth, Michael. "Super-Psi and the Survivalist Interpretation of Mediumship." *Journal of Scientific Exploration,* 23, no. 2 (2009): 167–193.

Sutherland, C. "Trailing Clouds of Glory: The Near-Death Experience of Western Children and Teens." In *The Handbook of Near-Death Experiences: Thirty Years of Investigation*, edited by J. Holden, B. Greyson, and D. James, 145–173. Westport: Praeger Publishers, 2009.

Sutherland, C. *Transformed by the Light: Life after Near-Death Experiences.* Sydney: Bantam Books, 1992.

Swanson, Claude. *The Synchronized Universe: New Science of the Paranormal.* New York: Poseidia Press, 2003.

Talbot, Michael. *The Holographic Universe.* New York, NY: HarperCollins, 1991.

Thonnard, Marie, et al. "Characteristics of Near-Death Experiences Memories as Compared to Real and Imagined Events Memories." *PLOS ONE* 8, no. 3 (2013): 1–5.

Tiller, William. "Subtle Energies and Their Roles." In *Bioelectromagnetic Phenomena*, edited by P. Rosch, 175–176. New York: Dekker, 2004.

Tittel, William, et al. "Violation of the Bell Inequalities by Photons More Than 10km Apart." *Physical Review Letters,* 81, no. 1 (1998): 3563–3578.

Toynbee, Arnold. "Man's Concern with Life after Death." In *Life after Death*, edited by Arnold Toynbee and Arthur Koestler, 92–117. London: Weidenfeld and Nicolson, 1996.

Tyrrell, G. N. *Apparitions*. New York: Collier, 1963.

Utts, Jessica. "Replication and Meta-Analysis in Parapsychology." *Statistical Science*, no. 16 (1991): 363–376.

Vandervert, L. "The Emergence of the Child Prodigy 10,000 years ago: An Evolutionary and Developmental Explanation." *The Journal of Mind and Behavior,* 30, no. 1 (2009): 15–25.

Van Lommel, Pim. "About the Continuity of Our Consciousness." *Adv Exp Med Biol,* 550, no. 3 (2004): 115–125.

Van Lommel, Pim. *Consciousness Beyond Life. The Science of the Near-Death Experience.* New York: Harper Collins, 2010.

Van Lommel, Pim. "Nonlocal Consciousness. A Concept Based on Scientific Research on Near-Death Experiences during Cardiac Arrest." *Journal of Consciousness Studies,* 20, no. 1–2, (2013): 7–48.

Van Lommel, Pim, R. Van Wees, V. Myers, and I. Elfferich. "Near-Death Experience in Survivors of Cardiac Arrest: A Prospective Study in the Netherlands." *Lancet* 358, no. 9298 (2001): 2039–2045.

Vriens, E., PFA, J. Bakker, G. de Vries, G. H. Wieneke, A. C. van Huffelen. "The Impact of Repeated Short Episodes of Circulatory Arrest on Cerebral Function." *Electroencephalography and Clinical Neurophysiology*, no. 98 (1996): 236–242.

Vulliamy, Colwyn. *Immortality*. London: Random House, 1997.

Weiss, Brian. *Many Lives, Many Masters*. New York: Warner, 1988.

West, D. J. "A Mass-Observation Questionnaire on Hallucinations." *Journal of the Society for Psychical Research, 34*, no. 2 (1948): 187–196.

Wigner, Eugene. "Remarks on the Mind-Body Problem." In *Quantum Theory and Measurement*, edited by John Wheeler, and Zurek Wojciech, 37–54. Princeton: Princeton University Press, 1983.

Wigner, Eugene. *Symmetries and Reflections*. Cambridge, MA: M.I.T Press, 1970.

Wilbur, Ken. *Quantum Questions: Mystical Writings of the World's Great Physicists*. Boston: Shambhala, 1984.

Wilson, S., and T. Barber. "The Fantasy-Prone Personality: Implications for Understanding Imagery, Hypnosis, and Parapsychological Phenomena." In *Imagery: Current Theory, Research, and Applications*: edited by A. Sheik, 102–134. New York: Wiley, 1983.

Wiseman, Richard. "Belief in the Paranormal and Suggestion in the Seance Room." *British Journal of Psychology,* 23, no. 1 (2003): 37–48.

Wiseman, Richard, and Ciarán O'Keeffe. "A Critique of Schwartz et al.'s After-Death Communication Studies." *Skeptical Inquirer,* 25, no. 6 (2001): 78–92.

Wiseman, Richard, and Ciarán O'Keeffe. "Testing Alleged Mediumship: Methods and Results," Paper presented at the annual meeting for the Parapsychological Association, New Orleans, November 3–5, 2004.

Wiseman, Richard, and C. Stevens. "An Investigation into Alleged Hauntings." *British Journal of Psychology,* 94, no. 1 (2003): 95–110.

Yuille, J., and J. Cutshall. "A Case Study of Eyewitness Memory of a Crime." *Journal of Applied Psychology,* 7, no. 2 (1986): 291–301.

Zohar, Danah. *The Quantum Self*. New York: William Morrow, 1991.

Internet Resources

Alcock, James. "Electronic Voice Phenomena: Voices of the Dead?" *The Committee for Skeptical Inquiry*, December 21, 2004. www.csicop.org/specialarticles/show/electronic_voice_phenomena_voices_of_the_dead (accessed September 2, 2016).

Alvarado, Carlos. "Compelling Evidence for the Afterlife." Afterlife, May 12, 2015. http://compellingevidencefortheafterlife.com/?p=273 (accessed March 8, 2016).

Alvarado, Carlos. "New Study of Electroencephalographic Detection of ESP." *Carlos Alvarado*, April 6, 2016. https://carlossalvarado.wordpress.com/2016/08/06/new-study-of-electroencephalographic-detection-of-esp/ (accessed March 8, 2016).

American Academy of Neurology. "People With Near Death Experiences Can Differ In Sleep-Wake Control." *ScienceDaily*, April 17, 2006. www.sciencedaily.com/ releases/2006/04/060417110256.htm (accessed June 23, 2016).

American Psychological Association. "Hypnosis." *APA*, June 12, 2015, www.apa. org/topics/hypnosis/ (accessed August 18, 2016).

Atwater, P. M. H. "Near-Death Experiences of Groups of People." Near Death, 2016. www.near-death.com/experiences/group.html (accessed May 10, 2016).

Based on Ian Stevenson Research. "Past Forward," *Past Forward*, January 12, 2014, www.healpastlives.com/future/rule/ruevplif.htm (accessed July 12, 2016).

Berkovich, Simon. "A Note on Science and NDE." *NDERF*, June 14, 2012, www.nderf.org/NDERF/Research/Berkovich.htm (accessed July 24, 2016).

Big Think Editors. "Max Planck: I Regard Consciousness as Fundamental." *The Observer*, January, 2016. http://bigthink.com/words-of-wisdom/max-planck-i-regard-consciousness-as-fundamental (accessed January 10, 2016).

Bischof, Marco. "Biophotons." *Bibliotecapleyades,* March 2005. www. bibliotecapleyades.net/ciencia/ciencia_fuerzasuniverso06.htm (accessed April 23, 2016).

Borjigin, Jimo, et al., "Surge of Neurophysiological Coherence and Connectivity in the Dying Brain." *Edited by Solomon Snyder*, July 9, 2013. www.pnas.org/ content/110/35/14432.abstract (accessed June 2, 2016).

Borreli, Lizelte. "Can An Organ Transplant Change A Recipient's Personality? Cell Memory Theory Affirms 'Yes'." *Medical Daily*, July 9, 2013, www.medicaldaily.com/can-organ-transplant-change-recipients-personality-cell-memory-theory-affirms-yes-247498 (accessed July 30, 2016).

Brainworks. "What Are Brainwaves?" *Brainworks Train Your Mind*, March 2013, www.brainworksneurotherapy.com/what-are-brainwaves (accessed May 12, 2016).

Brustein, Darrah. "This Entrepreneur's Near-Death Experience Revealed Her True Purpose." *Entrepreneur*, December 8, 2015. www.entrepreneur.com/ article/253350 (accessed May 19, 2016).

Butler, Tom. "Transcommunication." *Etheric Studies*, October 10, 2014, http:// ethericstudies.org/concepts/transcommunication.htm (accessed March 12, 2016).

CBS News Poll: Americans' Views on Death. *CBS News*, March 2015, www. cbsnews.com/news/cbs-news-poll-americans-views-on-death/ (accessed March 8, 2016).

Cell Press. "Neurorobotics Reveals Brain Mechanisms of Self-Consciousness." Cell Press, April 27, 2016. www.sciencedaily.com/releases/2011/04/110427131818. htm. (accessed March 19, 2016).

Clark, Chris. "A-Quantum Theory and Consciousness." Schumacher College, January 23, 2012. www.schumachercollege.org.uk/resources/audio-video-archive/chris-clarke%3A-quantum-theory-and-consciousness (accessed March 23, 2106).

Coleman, Tim. "The Afterlife Investigations: Has Science Proved the Afterlife?" *SPR*, June 2010, www.spr.ac.uk/publication/afterlife-investigations-has-science-proved-afterlife-dvd (accessed June 18, 2016).

Crick, Francis, and Christof Koch. "Consciousness and Neuroscience." *Cal Tech*, June, 1995. www.paradise.caltech.edu/cook/Workshop/Conscious/crick-koch-cc-97.html (accessed March 3, 2016).

Cunningham, Paul. "An Experimental Investigation of Past-Life Experiences by Dr. Paul F. Cunningham." *Paul Cunningham*, August 2009, www.rivier.edu/faculty/pcunningham/Research/Web%20Page%20Past-Life%20Experiences%204-29-11.pdf (accessed July 20, 2016).

Daily Grail. "Quantum Mind: Can Experienced Meditators Influence the Movement of Atomic Particles?" April 23, 2016. www.dailygrail.com/Mind-Mysteries/2016/6/Quantum-Mind-Can-Experienced-Meditators-Influence-the-Movement-Atomic (accessed April 3, 2016).

Davis, Bob. "Consciousness, the Brain, and Quantum Physics." *The Foundation for Research into Extraterrestrial Encounters*, February, 30, 2016. www.experiencer.org (accessed August 23, 2016).

Disinformation. "Nearly Half of Americans Believe in Ghosts." *Disinformation*, April 2012, http://disinfo.com/2013/02/nearly-half-of-americans-believe-in-ghosts/ (accessed Januaury, 14 2016).

Dubay, Eric. "Our Holographic Brains." *The Atlantean Conspiracy*, February 9, 2013, www.atlanteanconspiracy.com/2013/02/our-holographic-brains.html (accessed August 2, 2016).

Ecstacy. "Afterlife Encounters Survey Phase 3." *ECSTASY*, June 2012, http://ae.kfancher.com/survey2k7.html (accessed May 12, 2016).

Esalen. "Mediumship" *Esalen Institute*, July 2015. www.esalen.org/ctr-archive/mediumship.html (accessed May 30, 2016).

Eterna. "Mediumship." *Eterna*, July 2, 2015, http://eternea.org/Mediumship.aspx (accessed December 2, 2015).

Ethan, T. "Scientists Find Hints for the Immortality of the Soul." Skeptiko, August 3, 2014. www.skeptiko-forum.com/threads/scientists-find-hints-for-the-immortality-of-the-soul.1124/ (accessed March 23, 2016).

Famous Quotes on Reincarnation, "Famous Quotes on Reincarnation," *Reversespins*, April , 2015, www.reversespins.com/famousquotes.html (accessed August 14, 2016).

Femilab. "Fermi Lab Center." *Hogan*, January 20, 2016. http://astro.fnal.gov/people/hogan-nguyen/ (accessed May 12, 2016).

Gaines, Akemi. "Akashic Records." *Akashic Records of Souls*, 2014, www.akashicrecordsofsouls.com/ (accessed March 11, 2016).

Gauld, Alan. "Mediumship and Survival: A Century of Investigations: Alan Gauld." *Esalen*, 1982, www.esalen.org/ctr-archive/mediumship.html (accessed August 12, 2016).

Golonka, Sabrina, and Andrew Wilson. "Ecological Representations." *Ecological Representations*, June 15, 2016. http://biorxiv.org/content/ early/2016/06/15/058925 (accessed May 23, 2016).

Goodreads. "Carl Sagan Quotes." *Goodreads,* January 2016, www.goodreads.com/ author/quotes/10538.Carl_Sagan (accessed August 23, 2016).

Goodreads. "I Cannot Conceive of a God who Rewards and Punishes." *Goodreads*, June 23, 2013, www.goodreads.com/quotes/894329-i-cannot-conceive-of-a-god-who-rewards-and-punishes (accessed August 3, 2016).

Goodreads. "Quotes about Afterlife." *Goodreads*, June 12, 2014, www.goodreads. com/quotes/tag/afterlife (accessed August 3, 2016).

Goodreads. "Richard Feynman." *Goodreads*, 2015, www.goodreads.com/author/ quotes/1429989.Richard_Feynman (accessed July 12, 2016).

Greyson, Bruce. "NDE Scale." *IANDS*, July 2007. https://iands.org/research/ important-research-articles/698-greyson-nde-scale.html (accessed May 23, 2016).

Guggenheim, Bill, and Judy Guggenheim. *Bantam Books*, 1996, http://eternea.org/ ADC_Definition.aspx (accessed February 13, 2016).

Hameroff, Stuart. "Quantum computing in DNA." *University of Arizona*, June 2014, www.consciousness.arizona.edu/hameroff/New/ Quantum_computing_in_DNA/ index.htm (accessed July 24, 2016).

Hawking, Stephen. "Space and Time Warps." June 2016, www.hawking.org.uk/ space-and-time-warps.html (accessed August 23, 2016).

Hawking, Stephan, Malcolm J. Perry and Andrew Strominger. "Soft Hair on Black Holes," University of Cambridge, January 5, 2016, https://arxiv.org/ pdf/1601.00921v1.pdf (accessed June 10, 2017).

Henig, Robin. "Crossing Over: How Science Is Redefining Life and Death," *National Geographic,* April 2016. www.nationalgeographic.com/ magazine/2016/04/dying-death-brain-dead-body-consciousness-science/ (accessed June 12, 2017).

Herbert, Nick. "Nick Herbert Home Page." August 28, 2013. www2.cruzio. com/~quanta/ (accessed April 3, 2016).

Hoffman, Adam. "Lazarus Phenomenon." *Smithsonian*, March 31, 2016. www. smithsonianmag.com/science-nature/lazarus-phenomenon-explained-why-sometimes-deceased-are-not-dead-yet-180958613/?no-ist (accessed May 12, 2016).

IFLScience. "Consciousness, Science, and Life after Death. Researchers May Have Discovered The Consciousness On/Off Switch." June 10, 2016. www.iflscience. com/brain/researchers-may-have-discovered-consciousness-onoff-switch (accessed March 3, 2016).

Josephson, Brian. "String Theory, Universal Mind, and the Paranormal. Department of Physics." *Josephson, Brian,* December 2003. www.tcm.phy.cam.ac.uk/~bdj10 (accessed June 12, 2016).

Kase, Aaron. "Science Is Proving Some Memories Are Passed Down from Our Ancestors." *Reset Me*, February 20, 2015, http://reset.me/story/science-proving-memories-passed-ancestors/ (accessed July 18, 2016).

Krapton, Sarah. "Ghosts Created by Scientists." *The Telegraph*, 2014, www.telegraph.co.uk/news/science/science-news/11214511/Ghosts-created-by-scientists-in-disturbin g-lab-experiment.html (accessed January 18, 2016).

Lanza, Robert. "Biocentrism: Robert Lanza's Theory of Everything." 2017, www.robertlanza.com/biocentrism-how-life-and-consciousness-are-the-keys-to-understanding-the-true-nature-of-the-universe/ (accessed July 20, 2016).

Lanza, Robert. "*Robert Lanza*." *Robert Lanza*, March 2015, www.robertlanza.com/ (accessed August 18, 2016).

Leininger, Bruce. "Was a World War II Pilot Reincarnated in a Body of a Little Boy?" *Soul Survivor: The Reincarnation of a WW II Fighter Pilot*, November 22, 2010, www.wanttoknow.info/a-world-war-II-pilot-reincarnated-little-boy (accessed August 3, 2016).

Long, Jeffrey. "Dr. Jeff's Corner." *NDERF*, 1999. www.nderf.org/NDERF/Articles/jeff_corner.htm (accessed May 2, 2016).

Long, Jeffrey. "Stories of God's Love Common among Those who Almost Die." *The Washington Post*, June 29, 2016. www.washingtonpost.com/news/acts-of-faith/wp/2016/06/29/people-who-had-near-death-experiences-consistently-report-one-thing-gods-love/ (accessed July 8, 2016).

Maclsaac, Tara. "In Near-Death Experiences Blind People See for First Time." *The Epoch Times*, July 30, 2016. www.theepochtimes.com/n3/2128726-in-near-death-experiences-blind-people-see-for-first-time/?utm_expvariant=D001_01&utm_expid=21082672-11.b4WAd2xRR0ybC6ydhoAj9w.1 (accessed June 11, 2016).

Maclsaac, Tara. "Quantum Mechanics Has Reached Limit." *Epoch Times*, May 29, 2016. www.theepochtimes.com/n3/2078501-quantum-mechanics-has-reached-limit-says-stanford-scientist-who-offers-alternative/ (accessed March 18, 2016).

Menard, Louis. "What Comes Naturally: Does Evolution Explain Who We Are?" *The New Yorker*, November 25, 2002. www.newyorker.com/magazine/2002/11/25/what-comes-naturally-2 (accessed May 12, 2016).

Miller, Lisa. "Remembrances of Lives Past." *New York Times*, August 27, 2010, www.nytimes.com/2010/08/29/fashion/29PastLives.html?pagewanted=all&_r=2& (accessed June 20, 2016).

Nash, Kim. "Investigating Mediums: Interview with Dr. Julie Beischel," *Theresacheung*, Januuary 19, 2016, www.theresacheung.com/investigating-mediums-interview-with-dr-julie-beische/ (accessed January 14, 2016).

Near Death. "Evidence People Can Experience Someone Else in NDE." Near Death. July 2014. www.near-death.com/science/evidence/people-can-experience-someone-elses-nde.html. (accessed May 18, 2016).

Near-Death Experience Research Foundation. "Out of Body Research Experience." *NDERF*, June 2015. www.nderf.org (accessed May 20, 2016).

Nelson, Kevin. "Out-of-body Experiences May Be Caused By Arousal System Disturbances In Brain." *University of Kentucky*, March 6, 2007. www. sciencedaily.com/releases/2007/03/070305202657.htm. (accessed August 3, 2016).

New York Times. "What Is Consciousness." Anomalist, August 12, 2016. http:// mobile.nytimes.com/2016/07/05/science/what-is consciousness. html?r=2&referer=www.anomalist.com/ (accessed March 13, 2016).

Parnia, Sam. "Near Death Experiences During Cardiac Arrest." Goldsmith's London, February 2000. www.horizonresearch.org/video_case/near-death-experiences-during-cardiac-arrest/ (accessed May 12, 2016).

Paulson, Steve. "God Enough." *Salon*, November 19th, 2008. www.salon. com/2008/11/19/stuart_kauffman/ (accessed February 18, 2016).

Pratt, David. "John Eccles on Mind and Brain." *Theosophy,* June, 1995. www. theosophy-nw.org/theosnw/science/prat-bra.htm/ (accessed January 8, 2016).

Quantum Enigma. "Quantum Enigma." June 2014, http://quantum enigma.com/ nutshell/notable-quotes-on-quantum physics/? (accessed July 23, 2016).

Raivat, K. S. "The Case of Shanti Devi." *Venture Inward Magazine*, March 1997, www.carolbowman.com/dr-ian-stevenson/case-shanti-devi/ (accessed July 20, 2016).

Rogo, Scott. "Psychical Research and the Survival Controversy: Apparitions and the Case for Survival." *London Guild Publishing*, 1986, www.survivalafterdeath. info/articles/rogo/apparitions.htm (accessed February 12, 2016).

Rousseau, David. "Centre for Systems Philosophy." *Center for Systems Philosophy*, May 27, 2014. http://systemsphilosophy.org/david-rousseau.html (accessed June 2, 2016).

Sabom, Michael. "Dr. Michael Sabom's Near-Death Experience Research." *Near Death*, 2014. www.near-death.com/science/experts/michael-sabom.html (accessed May 18, 2016).

Sample, Ian. "Stephen Hawking: There Is No Heaven." May 15, 2011, www. theguardian.com/science/2011/may/15/stephen-hawking-interview-there-is-no-heaven (accessed August 4, 2016).

Sartori, Penny. "Empathic or Shared Death Experiences How Do We Explain Them." *Dr. Penny Sartori*, November 8, 2011, https://drpennysartori.wordpress.com /2011/11/08/empathic-or-shared-death-experiences-how-do-we-explain-them/ (accessed May 14, 2016).

Schaeffer, Karen. "Near Death Experience." *Near Death*, 2016. www.near-death. com/experiences/notable/karen-schaeffer.html (accessed May 24, 2016).

Science Daily. "Humans 'predisposed' to believe in gods and the afterlife." July 14, 2011. www.sciencedaily.com/releases/2011/07/110714103828.htm (accessed June 12, 2017).

Smart, Lisa. "Final Words Can Heal." Final Words, www.finalwordsproject.org/healing.html (accessed June 12, 2016).

Spiritual Cosmos. "Spiritual Cosmos." *Spiritual Cosmos,* February 2014, http://spiritualcosmos.com/index.php?option=com_content&view=article&id=68:scientists-who-support-the-idea-of-a-spiritual-cosmos&catid=25:theories&Itemid=53 (accessed August 23, 2016).

Sprague, Ryan. "The Most Haunted Theater on Broadway." *Paranormal Braintrust,* March 8, 2016, http://jimharold.com/haunted-theater-broadway-mr-belasco/ (accessed June 15, 2016).

Stapp, Henry. "Henry Stapp." August 30, 2012. www-physics.lbl.gov/~stapp/Compatibility.pdf (accessed March 12, 2016).

Sunfellow, David. "Parting Visions," January 6, 1995, *Parting Visions*, www.nhne.com/articles/sapartingvisions.html (accessed March 20 2016).

Survival After Death, "Is there Life Beyond Death?" *Survival After Death*, 2014, www.survivalafterdeath.info/articles/sargent/beyond.htm (accessed January 23, 2016).

Survival After Death. "Psychical Research and the Survival Controversy: Apparitions and the Case for Survival." Hornel Hart, 2015, www.survivalafterdeath.info/articles/rogo/apparitions.htm (accessed February 12, 2016).

The Austin Institute for the Study of Family and Culture. The Austin Institute, June 2015, www.austin-institute.org/ (accessed March 12, 2016).

The Center for Sleep and Consciousness. "*Neural Substrates for Consciousness.*" Center for Sleep and Consciousness, September 14, 2015. www.centerforsleepandconsciousness.med.wisc.edu/ (accessed March 10, 2016).

The Harris Poll. "The Religious and Other Beliefs of Americans." *Gallup News Service*, February 26, 2003, www.theharrispoll.com/ (accessed July, 12, 2016).

The Professor Forum. "The Professor Forum." *Invision Free*, August 11, 2007, http://z6.invisionfree.com/The_Professor_Forum/ar/t1226.htm (accessed February 13, 2016).

The Psychic Children. "Russian DNA Research." *Psychic Children*, May 2014, www.psychicchildren.co.uk/4-3-RussianDNAResearch.html (accessed July 8, 2016).

The Scole Experiment. "The Scole Experiment." SCOLE, 2006, www.thescoleexperiment.com/article_05.htm (accessed July 12, 2016).

The Windbridge Institute. "The Windbridge Institute." *Windbridge Institute*, 2015, www.windbridge.org/about-us/ (accessed January 3, 2016).

Theophanes. "Cellular Memories in Organ Transplant Recipients." *Theophanes*, January 25, 2013, http://hubpages.com/health/Cellular-Memories-in-Organ-Transplant-Recipients (accessed July 14, 2016).

Tiller, William. "How the Power of Intention Alters Matter." *Spirit of Matter*, February 23, 2014. www.spiritofmaat.com/archive/mar2/tiller.htm (accessed April 5, 2016).

Tiller, William. "William Tiller." *The Tiller Institute*, March 2016. www. tillerinstitute.com/ (accessed April 6, 2016).

Tracey, Janey. "Consciousness." *Outerplaces,* June 17, 2014, www.outerplaces.com/ science/item/4518-physicists-claim-that-consciousness-lives-in-quantum-state-after-death (accessed July 10, 2016).

Tracey, Janey. "New Theory Claims Quantum Weirdness Only Exists in Our Imaginations." Outerplaces, December 1, 2015. www.outerplaces.com/science/ item/10547-new-theory-claims-quantum-weirdness-only-exists-in-our-imaginations (accessed March 14, 2016).

Tracey, Janey. "Physicists Claim that Consciousness Lives in Quantum State After Death." Outerplaces, June 17, 2014. www.outerplaces.com/science/item/4518-physicists-claim-that-consciousness-lives-in-quantum-state-after-death (accessed March 22, 2016).

Tymn, Michael. "Mediumship: Direct Connection to a Level of the Afterlife, Telepathy or Fraud?" *International Survivalist Society*, 2002, www. survivalafterdeath.info/articles/other/tymn.htm (accessed December 8, 2015).

UCLA Newsroom. "UCLA Psychologists Report New Insights on the Human Brain and Consciousness." *UCLA*, October 17, 2013. http://newsroom.ucla.edu/ releases/ucla-psychologists-report-new-248299 (accessed March 3, 2016).

Van Lommel, Pim. "Continuity of Consciousness," IANDS, April 25, 2015, http:// iands.org/research/nde-research/important-research-articles/43-dr-pim-van-lommel-md-continuity-of-consciousness.html?showall=&start=3 (accessed June 12, 2017).

Vanier, L. "Global Consciousness the Mind Blowing Effects of Mass Meditation." Collective Evolution, July 12, 2016. www.collective-evolution.com/2015/10/07/ (accessed April 12, 2016).

Victor Zammit, "Victor Zammit," 2006, www.victorzammit.com/book/4thedition/ chapter19.html (accessed January 12, 2016).

Weatherly, David. "IONS to Study Channeling," *Two Crow Paranormal*, August 1, 2016, http://twocrowsparanormal.blogspot.com/2016/08/ions-to-study-channeling.html?m=1 (accessed August 8, 2016).

Wolf, Fred. "The Yoga of Time Travel and Dr. Quantum's World." *Fred Alan Wolf*, November 9, 2012. http://fredalanwolf.blogspot.com/ (accessed June 8, 2016).

Zammit, Victor. "Victor Zammit," Zammit, April 2001, www.victorzammit.com. (accessed June 12, 2016).